MINORITY LANGUAGES TODAY

TO THE MEMORY OF DAVID GREENE,
WHO DIED SUDDENLY

MINORITY LANGUAGES TODAY

A Selection from the Papers
read at the
First International Conference
on Minority Languages
held at Glasgow University
from 8 to 13 September

1980

edited by

EINAR HAUGEN

J. DERRICK McCLURE

DERICK THOMSON

EDINBURGH
University
Press

© E. Haugen, J. D. McClure, D. Thomson 1981

Paperback edition
with corrections and additions 1990

Edinburgh University Press
22 George Square, Edinburgh

Set in Linoterm Times Roman
by Speedspools, Edinburgh
and printed in Great Britain by
Page Bros, Norwich

British Library Cataloguing
   in Publication Data
Minority languages today.
1. Linguistic minorities—Congresses
I. Haugen, Einar   II. McClure, J. Derrick
III. Thomson, Derick
400   P119.315

ISBN 0 85224 642 0 pbk

Contents

v

Foreword

The organisers of the conference of which this book is an outcome found, like others before us (e.g. Price 1969, Oftedal 1969), that the term 'minority language' presented paradoxes and uncertainties of definition. Quite often a language which is a 'minority language' of a nation as a whole is very much a majority language of the population of a region or enclave of that nation, as, say, Gaelic is in Lewis or Welsh in Gwynedd or Frisian in Friesland or, some might claim, Lowland Scots in mainland Scotland. Then there are other languages which, though they are used regularly by a majority of the population of an entire nation, yet resemble minority languages in that they are not the only languages used by their speakers: for some purposes, often the highest status literary and official functions, they are replaced by some other language, as happens to Swiss German in Switzerland, Faroese in Faroe, Luxemburgish in Luxemburg. Again, the majority languages of one nation also often serve as minority languages in some other nation: the cases of Swedish, Danish and German in this situation are described in this book.

Some fuller definition of the proposed conference's intended theme was then evidently necessary. This was supplied in the circulars announcing the conference in a formulation by J. M. Y. Simpson. Minority languages were defined as 'those "at risk" because of a culturally dominant language (there may even be active opposition) and furthermore [they] are not usually the languages used in all areas of activity indulged in by their speakers.' Simpson has amplified his characterisation of a minority language in his paper printed below.

Our first concern was thus to be the present circumstances and future prospects of languages 'at risk' today – or threatened, pressured, beleaguered, being encroached on, in recession, declining, dying – in face of a culturally dominant language. But we naturally wished to compare the situations of the declining languages with the situations of those other tongues which similarly confront alternative or higher status languages within their own nations without, in their cases, showing any obvious sign of recession before them. Languages within the area which we had decided upon as our main concern which seemed in this way to be maintaining a stable diglossic relationship with their nations' 'high' languages were Faroese and Luxemburgish, and we therefore invited contributions from authorities on these tongues. As we were to learn from D. Strauss, the German spoken in East Belgium, in Denmark and in Italy, is likewise fairly stable. With hindsight, it is perhaps a pity we did not enlist a speaker to illuminate similarly for us the situation in Belgium.

The other limitations of theme and scope of the Glasgow conference followed naturally from its originating in Scotland. The conference circulars stated these to be 'the present-day problems of minority languages, particularly those of the British Isles, The Netherlands and Scandinavia, although it is hoped that some attention may be given to the situation of minority languages in neighbouring countries.' Though we elected not to spell this out, the prime target which the conference organisers had in view was *indigenous* minority languages of the area specified, those of long established native communities or nations, like the Irish, the Welsh, the Scottish Gaels, the Lowland Scots, the Frisians, the Sámi and the Swedish-speaking Finns. Among other indicators, the names of our invited speakers and of the languages they were to discuss, and perhaps also our highlighting of the theme of languages at risk, doubtless suggested this. But while we intended that the bulk of the papers should be in this general field, we hoped also to welcome one or two speakers who would deal with problems of the languages of more or less new immigrant communities, such as Italian, Chinese, Indonesian, Panjabi, Gujurati, West Indian Creoles and numerous others, or of those less recent immigrants, the Romany-speaking Gypsies. We hoped that one or two other speakers again might discuss indigenous minority languages of more distant countries. Indeed we attempted, unsuccessfully as it proved, to enlist speakers on Breton, Alsatian, and Basque, and other omissions in the immediate periphery of our chosen region will readily occur to our readers (Inuit in Greenland?, Occitan?, Corsican?). But one conference could not of course encompass everything. The conference did indeed include a number of contributions both on the situations of non-indigenous minority languages and of those indigenous to more southerly parts of Europe, one of which, Rosita Rindler Schjerve's account of language maintenance and language shift in present-day Sardinia, appears below. And there were two papers concentrating on the language problems of Canada.

One language long established in a country of which its users constitute a native minority and clearly under pressure in face of a majority dominant language is British Sign Language. This language differs from all the others considered at the conference in several obvious respects: most strikingly in its linguistic form, since it is non-oral, and in that the non-linguistic attribute common to its deaf users is neither ethnical nor, in the first instance, social. Yet in the attitudes of the wider community to it, and particularly in the discouraging or hostile responses it evokes from some educationists and others, it does display similarities or analogies with some other minority languages, as well as with non-standard dialects of majority languages. It too is educationally stigmatised or suppressed in the belief or on the pretext that it is 'deficient' or communicationally inadequate, or that its possession inhibits a pupil's acquisition of the culturally dominant language.

The paper on BSL was, for me and I expect for others, one of the conference's most stimulating experiences. A substantial part of it was delivered, through an instantaneous translator, in BSL itself, thus providing a highly convincing demonstration of the elegance, expressiveness and flexibility of this most interesting language. We are fortunate in having below in printed form this account of BSL's linguistic characteristics and its sociolinguistic and educational situation.

The list of possible topics given in the conference circulars, as well as such briefing as we gave to invited speakers, no doubt indicated that we expected the bulk of the papers to be about the societal (political, economic, socio-cultural, educational, etc.) situations of the languages discussed rather than on the linguistic phenomena resulting from these, that is, to be on the sociology of language rather than on sociolinguistics or on the linguistic manifestations of language contact. The great majority of the papers presented at the conference, and consequently of the selection printed below, did indeed largely so confine themselves; and as the theme of 'risk' no doubt dictated, the focus of many papers was on prospects for survival, not least the opening paper by Greene which was intended to 'key-note' the conference. Even so, a number of these papers also discuss, in necessarily general terms, since time was so limited, the penetration from the dominant language into the vocabulary and idiom of the minority language as one indicator of weakening resistance to the threat to the latter's existence. Several papers also go on to consider the need for language cultivation and/or purification as bulwarks or counter-attacks to this threat. Rather more specific attention to linguistic detail was offered by McClure and, in one part of his paper, by Keskitalo, both of whom in their different ways fruitfully apply more purely linguistic considerations to the central problem of survival or revival of their respective minority languages.

In his paper Greene indicates some of the general conditions for survival of a minority language. Haugen elaborates for us his famous model of language planning, reminds us of his concept of language ecology, and puts forward here for the first time the notion of the language market. Keskitalo sums up several critical factors for the viability of a minority language, which need not be confined to examination of the situation of Sámi alone. These and other authors identify circumstances, geographic, political, ideological, economic, demographic, social, cultural and educational, as well as, in some instances, linguistic, which are or have been favourable or unfavourable to the continued flourishing of the particular languages concerned. Some papers point to sociolinguistic, as well as linguistic, symptoms of a minority language's current state of health: for example, is it the first choice language in casual encounters with strangers?

Several authors build into their hopeful predictions or their forebodings the hedge that the final crucial factor is the apparently intangible one of the collective will of the community of speakers to sustain or revive (or, alternatively, discard) its language, a notion most emphatically expressed by Fennell, but explicit or implicit in several other papers. As Fennell also emphasises and as is illustrated in the histories of several of the languages described below, especially those of the successes in the struggle for survival or revival (see especially the papers by Feitsma, Haugen, Hoffmann, Poulsen), this collective will may be prompted or catalysed 'through the agency of a prophetic individual or group' arising from the community itself or coming to it from outside and identifying with it (the first rather than the second of these alternatives in the cases just instanced).

Perhaps few or none of the authors represented below would disallow the possibility of inspired, and thus presumably inherently unpredictable, intervention of this sort in favour of a more mechanistically deterministic view of events. Notwithstanding this, all of course accept and some (such as Greene, Fennell, Haugen, Hoffmann, Keskitalo, Strauss) emphasise and exemplify the overriding importance of political, economic and other external agencies, acting both in the past and in the present, in determining present linguistic choices and attitudes; is it not this, also, that ultimately underlies Haugen's notions of the ecology of language and the language market?

In such ways the book makes a significant contribution of concept, information and suggestion towards the construction of an as yet unrealised, and admittedly still distant, general theory or model or typology which will give fuller understanding of the complex conjunctions of variables affecting the destinies of minority languages and languages at risk. Of more immediate value, however, is the book's provision of a compendium of authoritative first-hand assessments – descriptive, diagnostic and prognostic – of the situations and prospects of all the principal minority languages of northwestern Europe and some other similarly situated languages in other parts of Europe. Thus the book has something to offer to specialists of many complexions, from linguists to students and practitioners of politics, who are from their different standpoints concerned with the cultural histories and the spiritual well-being of the nations whose languages are discussed in this book.

Students of Lowland Scots, especially those who have dreamed of reversing its long decline, have at times contemplated the apparently happier fortunes of other minority languages in somewhat similar situations across the North Sea. In particular, my own distinguished former chief, Sir William Craigie, was much given to contrasting what he believed to be the much greater language loyalty of the Frisians with the Scots' apparent acquiescence in the demise of their own Lowland tongue. Information on these languages of our neighbour nations was indeed to be found both in compendious works like Ellis and Mac a'Ghobhainn (1971) and, in due course, Stephens (1976) and in at least one intensive case-study of the language problems of a single nation (Haugen 1966); and incidental allusions and discussion of many relevant theoretic considerations are available especially in works written or assembled by J. A. Fishman, such as Fishman (1971), particularly Fishman's own essay there. Even so, I was doubtless not alone among my compatriots in welcoming James Chisholm's original suggestion of a symposium for mutual information and comparison of cases between scholars of Scots and Frisian, which he put to the Language Committee of the Association for Scottish Literary Studies in November 1975.

Ultimately this suggestion led to the formation of a committee charged with organising in Scotland a major academic conference on the minority languages of northern Europe. With the blessing of the Council of the Association for Scottish Literary Studies, the conference organising committee convened for the first of its twenty-one meetings in March 1978. J. M. Y. Simpson, later succeeded by J. D. McClure, was Chairman, I. K. Williamson Secretary and May G. Williamson Treasurer, and the other members were A. J. Aitken (subsequently President of the Conference), Carol H. L. Mills, D. S. Thomson, later succeeded by C. Ó Dochartaigh, and, later, D. Hewitt.

The organising committee's early decision to hold the conference in Glasgow, out of a number of alternative venues in Scotland which had been canvassed had, we thought, both material and spiritual justifications – spiritual, as the city contains a large Gaelic-speaking minority and as its University gives greater prominence to Gaelic and Lowland Scottish studies than almost any other. The realisation of the conference was greatly furthered by generous grants which we subsequently received towards organisational, travelling and other expenses and to aid the publication of this volume from the Universities of Glasgow, Aberdeen, Edinburgh, Stirling and Dundee, and from the British Academy, the British Council and the Scottish Arts Council.

The first decision of all taken by the organising committee was to define more precisely the theme and scope of the conference by means of its fuller second title, and to settle on the conference's leading title of 'First International Conference on Minority Languages'. 'First', because of course we did not expect to exhaust the discussion of the problems of the languages most central to the conference's scope, let alone the numerous others of communities residing elsewhere in the world, and we hoped that successor conferences might follow to continue the discussion in both these directions. There have of course been earlier conferences on similar topics, and we learned later of two other rather briefer conferences on European cultural and linguistic minorities to be held in, respectively, Mannheim, West Germany, later in the same year as our own (December 1980), and Ljouwert, The Netherlands, in April of the next year (1981). By happy coincidence, these other conferences complemented the Glasgow conference in various ways, with very little overlap. In October 1980, also, the Culture and Education Committee of the Council of Europe published its report on minority languages, with recommendations for action to the Assembly of the Council of Europe which echo much that was stated or implied at the Glasgow conference and is expressed in the papers printed below. The Glasgow conference in its final session voted to entrust the 'Second' of our own series to the Nordic Language Board (*Nordisk språkråd*) in the person of its Chairman, Professor Bertil Molde, a delegate at the conference. Alternative proposals to hold successor conferences in Catalonia or in Ireland were postponed, it may be hoped, only to a later occasion.

The original organising committee decided to follow the precedent of the Association for Scottish Literary Studies International Conference of 1975 on Medieval Scottish Language and Literature and invite a number of scholars generally held to be among the leading authorities on certain of the languages to be discussed to address the conference as a whole for one hour each. We heard eight 'plenary papers' of this kind, all of them printed below, and some thirty-five shorter papers were also given. And as an 'International' conference we brought together ninety-four participants from nineteen countries.

In the preparation of this volume Derrick McClure acted as co-ordinating editor, dealing with all papers submitted, Einar Haugen and Derick Thomson attending thereafter respectively to the contributions on Scandinavian and on Celtic.

A. J. Aitken, April 1981

References

Ellis, P. B. and Mac a'Ghobhainn, S. (1971) *The Problem of Language Revival*. Club Leabhar: Inverness.

Fishman, J. A. (ed.) (1971, 1972) *Advances in the Sociology of Language*, 2 vols. The Hague: Mouton.

Haugen, E. (1966) *Language Conflict and Language Planning: The Case of Modern Norwegian*. Cambridge, Mass.: Harvard.

Oftedal, M. (1969) What are minorities?, in *Lingual Minorities in Europe* (eds E. Holmestad and A. J. Lade). Oslo: Det Norske Samlaget.

Price, G. (1969) *The Present Position of Minority Languages in Western Europe: A Selective Bibliography*. Cardiff: University of Wales Press.

Stephens, M. (1976) *Linguistic Minorities in Western Europe*. Llandysul, Dyfed, Wales: Gomer Press.

†DAVID GREENE

1. The Atlantic Group: Neo-Celtic and Faroese

I will deal with the Atlantic group of minority languages defined geographically as lying west of the Greenwich meridian and north of parallel 47 N. All the minority languages in that sector are so placed that most or all of their speakers must also master a dominant language of culture, and use that language in many domains of their everyday life.

Wolfgang Dressler in his paper on the phonology of language death (Dressler 1972) begins by pointing out that research on language change has been one-sided: 'One asks how a new grammar emerges by means of new rules, but not how a new grammar emerges by simple rule loss . . . This can be studied, and under ideal conditions in disintegrating or dying languages'. Dressler's study is concerned with the partial breakdown of the system of initial mutations in a Breton dialect; and his results are, as he had envisaged, of considerable interest. It is in accordance with his approach to these matters that he concludes his article by protesting against the usual practice of selecting informants who are 'trustworthy' and 'reliable', by which is meant that they have full command of a still vigorous language system. Dressler thinks that the use of informants with inferior command of the language would 'enable linguists to obtain material which could be important for solving problems of linguistic theory, for the process of decomposition shows the structure of a system'.

As linguists we must agree with Dressler that the obsession with reliable informants has the necessary result of revealing only a small part of linguistic reality. Some linguists seem to think that, if you cannot find a monoglot, a language is hardly worth investigation. Just over thirty years ago, when my colleague Heinrich Wagner was beginning to plan his *Linguistic Atlas and Survey of Irish Dialects*, that great scholar T. F. O'Rahilly told him that it was a useless undertaking, since 'das echte Irische' was practically dead (Wagner 1972, 300). Wagner went ahead just the same, and produced four splendid volumes over the years 1958 to 1969; but he himself has recently been reproaching certain colleagues for reporting the Irish of young bilinguals.

1

The truth of the matter is, of course, that it is impossible to record the actual usage of any of the languages which I am discussing here without taking account of forms which many speakers would find of dubious acceptability or even incorrect; the shadow of the dominant language, whether it be Danish, English or French, lies over every utterance. Once that stage has been reached we always have to ask ourselves whether these languages are not ultimately doomed to go the same way as Manx, another language belonging to this Atlantic area, which disappeared only a few short years ago. O'Rahilly would, I think, have had few doubts on the subject: speaking of Manx he said 'From the beginning of its career as a written language English influence played havoc with its syntax, and it could be said without exaggeration that some of the Manx that has been printed is merely English disguised in a Manx vocabulary. Manx hardly deserved to live. When a language surrenders itself to foreign idiom, and when all its speakers become bilingual, the penalty is death' (O'Rahilly 1932, 121).

If O'Rahilly is right, then the only attitude which linguists can take to our minority languages is that of Dressler; the processes of disintegration and decay should be studied as carefully as possible. But he may not be right; and, in general, those who concern themselves with minority languages tend to a certain optimism: I notice that one of the most eminent of them, Joshua Fishman, has just published a volume of papers under the title *Never Say Die* (1980), and I feel that this is the spirit of most of us.

The most striking fact is, of course, that while Faroese can show a steadily increasing number of speakers, all the Neo-Celtic languages have been in consistent decline ever since statistical evidence has been available. The speed of that decline may be illustrated by the fact that in 1871 25.6 per cent of the population of the Isle of Man returned themselves as being Manx-speaking; contrast that with the 20 per cent of the population of Wales who returned themselves as Welsh-speaking in 1971! Of course, it must be said at once that the two cases are in no way comparable. Manx in 1871 was the language of the middle-aged and old in the more remote parts of the island; apart from its ritual use on Tynwald it had no official status. Its 13,600 speakers were somewhat more numerous than the entire population of the Faroe Islands at the time, which was only 11,220 – some of whom must have been Danish officials and traders; but, while Manx was dying, Faroese was beginning to move towards the status of a literary language, the necessary preliminary for its contemporary use as a language of administration.

One notable exception to the steady decline of the Neo-Celtic languages was the 10 per cent rise in the number of speakers of Scottish Gaelic recorded in the 1971 census, from 81,000 in 1961 to nearly 90,000. But these new speakers are found in areas outside the Highlands and Islands, where decline has continued in very much the same way as in other Neo-Celtic countries. Lewis is probably the real stronghold with over 80 per cent of its population Gaelic-speaking; it offers a rough comparison with the Faroes, though its population is less than the 41,000 of the latter. But Stornoway, the capital of Lewis, is not only much smaller in population than the 12,000 of Tórshavn, the capital of the Faroes; it is also radically different in its relation to its hinterland. In Tórshavn everything is done through Faroese, or so it seems; while in Stornoway everything is done through English. In fact, the Danish High Commissioner in Tórshavn uses Danish in his administration, which includes control of the law courts and of the police, so that Danish has an active presence there; but this is hardly perceptible to the visitor, who sees and hears only Faroese in the streets, in shops and in offices. In Stornoway, on the other hand, you can find Gaelic, but you have to look for it. This is by no means a new state of affairs: in 1879 a careful observer reported that Lewis could be regarded as almost entirely Gaelic-speaking, were it not for the town of Stornoway, where two-thirds of the inhabitants were said to have no Gaelic (Ravenstein 1879, 595). The situation is not quite as bad as that today, because of recent immigration from the Gaelic countryside; but Stornoway is in no sense a Gaelic-speaking town. If we could only settle those 8,000 new speakers of Gaelic there, and remove its English monoglots to more congenial surroundings, we might then have a town as Gaelic as Tórshavn is Faroese! But the sober reality is that Gaelic does not own a town of 12,000 inhabitants, nor does Irish, nor does Breton, though each of these languages has considerably more speakers than has Faroese. Even Welsh, with well over half a million speakers, and considerable cultural development, now happily to include a television channel of its own, has no town that size. The nearest approach would be Caernarfon, which is just under the 10,000 mark, but is predominantly Welsh-speaking – it even has an urban slang which marks out its speakers from those of the surrounding countryside. But it is not the capital of a linguistic community, and it lies in the shadow of its much larger neighbour Bangor, in which Welsh is now a declining minority language.

Everybody knows D. A. Binchy's description of early Irish society as 'tribal, rural, hierarchical and familiar (using this word in its oldest sense, to mean a society in which the family, not the individual, is the unit) – a complete contrast to the unitary, urbanised, egalitarian and individualist society of our time' (see Dillon 1954). Binchy was speaking of the Irish society of thirteen centuries ago, but his description of early Irish society would apply quite well (with some modification) to the Neo-Celtic societies which have survived down to the present day, and which find themselves confronted with the urbanised and individualist society of our time. Indeed, to speak of confrontation is empty rhetoric, since there is never any contrast; urbanisation does not proceed beyond the modest level of Caernarfon. My teacher Alf Sommerfelt, who had contributed much to sociolinguistics before that term was invented, said about the revival of Irish: 'On s'imagine alors la tâche immense que représente la réintroduction de l'irlandais, et l'on peut prédire que, si les irlandais ne parviennent pas a créer un véritable foyer de civilisation et de langue irlandaise, l'irlandais ne deviendra jamais une langage commune au sens propre du mot.' I would prefer to put it more bluntly, and to say that what was needed was an Irish-speaking urban centre, and I think that is what Sommerfelt meant too. We should remember that his assessment of the chances of Irish was not based on purely theoretical considerations. When he wrote those words some forty years ago he was able to look back on nearly a century of Norwegian language struggle, and to see that Nynorsk had failed to win a single town: had failed, in short, to establish itself as the language of the modern world, of 'neo-events', to use the current jargon. He knew also that Nynorsk, based on the dialects of a country still overwhelmingly rural at the time when it first received official recognition, had had far better chances than Irish – and still had not succeeded in making itself the dominant language of Norway by conquering the towns. The chances of Irish, native speakers of which made up only five per cent of the population at the time Sommerfelt was writing, were obviously much poorer, even if the government of that state was officially committed to the extension of Irish to the whole country.

Their respective language movements brought great cultural enrichment to both Ireland and Norway, recalling the urban populations to the traditions of the past, and producing a remarkable flowering of literature in linguistic forms hitherto considered unfit for such cultivation. Not unnaturally, creative writers tend to attach a quite exaggerated importance to the effect that a national literature has on the masses of the people; and, since academics are also manipulators of the written word, it is easy for them to fall into the same error. But Mistral did nothing to arrest the decay and disintegration of Provençal, nor is there any evidence that the presence of poets of international stature writing in Scottish Gaelic today has had any effect on the state of that language in the Western Isles, though it is most likely to be closely linked with the emergence of those 8,000 new speakers scattered through English-speaking Scotland. We can talk about speakers of minority languages being disadvantaged, but we are not thinking primarily about cultural matters. If we take Ireland as an example, the immensely rich oral culture preserved in Irish almost up to the present day would have been infinitely more satisfying to the Irish people than the drab and utilitarian English literacy presented to them through the primary-school system in the middle of the last century, when the flight from Irish assumed the dimensions of a rout. It was not from the cultural values of the Irish language that they were fleeing, but from the poverty and failure which they associated with that language: an association powerfully reinforced by the terrible famine years of the 1840s, which wiped out completely the poorest section of the population, almost all of them Irish monoglots. By 1851, while children under 10 years of age made up 22.2 per cent of the population of Ireland, that age group represented only 11 per cent of the Irish-speaking population. The first generation to have learned English at school was beginning to select that language for their children.

The simple fact that bilingualism constantly offers this choice to parents is often overlooked by those who recommend it as a solution for the problems of our minority languages. As long as a monoglot remains in that state, his language loyalty is not in doubt; he has nowhere else to go. Once some measure of bilingualism has been achieved, however, loyalties become much more problematical. Given that the second, and dominant, language has been acquired basically for the purpose of taking part in the economic activities of a wider society, the question of the utility of the vernacular can never be far away. As Ian Thomas has noted for Cardiganshire: 'In a context which includes other issues, conscious concern for the language tends to decline. Surveys show that only 7 per cent of respondents mentioned the Welsh language to be an important local issue, as compared with 18 per cent mentioning unemployment and 16 per cent rising prices' (Thomas 1979, 43). It was Einar Haugen who first taught us to consider the ecology of language; and in many cases we observe that language activists find themselves in pretty much the same situation as the earnest ecologist who asks the people of some area of natural beauty not to permit development there, and is met with the reply: 'You can't eat the view'. It is a fact of our modern society that a large number of young people prefer a forty-hour working week in a factory, however boring, to the more open-ended commitment of agricultural life, however rewarding. If, as is invariably the case in the Neo-Celtic areas, the language of urban life is also the dominant one, bilingualism will shift to diglossia of such an uneven nature that the lapse into functional monolingualism takes place without any conscious decision being made.

Even for the more committed, the decision to remain with the minority language brings with it palpable disadvantages. In Ireland, for example, this extends to the standard of Irish taught in the schools, which is deliberately kept at a very low level so that the inadequacy of non-native speakers will not be too cruelly reflected in examination results; nobody seems worried by the fact that the native Irish speaker has thus a far more challenging and interesting course in English than in Irish. Those secondary schools which teach through Irish suffer from a crippling shortage of textbooks, and the situation is even worse in University College, Galway, which continues to offer a number of courses in Irish without adequate financial support. Once we come to the university level, the minority situation of the Neo-Celtic languages becomes abundantly clear, since none of them owns a town in which a university could be situated.

Again, even the most committed are aware that, while the dominant language offers an almost limitless range of registers, many of these are not available in the minority languages. When a linguist says that 'a basic maxim of linguistics is that anything can be expressed in any language' (Lenneberg 1953, 467), he is making the necessary point that there are no inherently inferior or superior languages. But there are certainly developed and undeveloped languages, and speakers of minority languages are often disadvantaged by the fact that their languages are not as highly developed as the languages of culture which are at their disposal. An Estonian linguist has recorded a remarkable *cri de cœur* from his compatriot Friedebert Tuglas, a distinguished writer in that language: 'Which of us has not suffered from the poverty and uncultured state of the Estonian language! Who has not struggled with it, like Jacob with the Lord! It is only necessary to translate from some cultured language a scientific article or a psychological short story to see how poor, uncultured and vulgar Estonian really is' (Tauli 1968, 176). Máirtín Ó Cadhain, the greatest prose-writer of modern Irish, often spoke of difficulties of this kind, and within the last two years Breandán Ó hEithir, a successful journalist and novelist, has made the point again. For Irish, as for the other Neo-Celtic languages, the urban society necessary to widen the range of the language does not exist, nor is there any prospect of its emergence.

In Ireland, at least, it was hoped that the teaching of Irish intensively in the schools would restore the language in urban areas as well. As we all know, this did not happen; but the results were not entirely negligible either. At the 1971 Census 28.3 per cent of the population of the Republic of Ireland, which we may take to be 3,000,000 for the purpose of this survey (it is in fact somewhat more), returned themselves as able to speak Irish. At the time of the Census a research team was already investigating the attitudes of the Irish people to the Irish language, so that this figure was a matter of some interest, since it was common knowledge that there were not 816,000 Irish speakers in the state. The team found out that the 28.3 per cent represented those who were strongly supportive of the language. The real figures for speakers of Irish were very different: 1.9 per cent of the population, say 57,000, were native speakers, and a further 7.4 per cent, say 220,000, 'at least fairly fluent non-native speakers' (Committee on Language Attitudes Research 1975, 129). The effective figures were, therefore, somewhat less than 300,000, and it was this reasonably respectable linguistic group which was able to maintain writers such as those mentioned above. But there were many weaknesses. First, the group of native speakers was pitifully small, representing a community threatened by imminent collapse. Secondly, the non-native speakers were an unrepresentative though influential section of Irish society, being overwhelmingly drawn from those who had received a good secondary education. Outside Irish-speaking districts, therefore, fluent Irish was a fairly reliable indicator of middle-class status, and the working class remained functionally ignorant of the language. Finally, nowhere had Irish conquered so much as a street as a result of these developments; the new bilinguals constituted a network, not a community, and only a small number of them might be expected to pass the language on to the next generation.

These results of the Irish experiment have been quoted to show that, while bilingual education can have quite significant results, it does not appear that it can affect the ultimate prospects of survival; and it seems difficult to get away from O'Rahilly's bleak statement about the permanent effects of bilingualism, as far as the Neo-Celtic languages are concerned. But Faroese is in a quite different position, since it is not a minority language within its own territory, where it is the only language that the Faroese use in speaking to one another. It exists in a diglossic position which has many points of resemblance to that of Schwyzertütsch in Switzerland or Lëtzeburgesch in Luxembourg, these vernaculars being as universally spoken within their respective areas as Faroese is in the Faroe Islands. But, while the speakers of Schwyzertütsch and Lëtzeburgesch are quite happy to use Standard German, in the former case, and both Standard German and Standard French in the latter, as their languages of culture, the Faroese would apparently like to dispense with Danish altogether. They could, of course, take that decision, but only in order to switch to another language of culture which, in their political and economic circumstances, would have to be English. This enforced diglossia derives from sheer lack of numbers; 40,000 speakers cannot build up a state providing the economic and social diversification which enables some at least of its citizens to remain monoglots without at the same time suffering economic and cultural disadvantages. We have not to look far from the Faroes to see what the probable minimum population of such a state will be: Iceland has just a quarter of a million speakers, and is almost certainly the smallest linguistic community in which a citizen can choose to remain a functional monoglot and yet play a full part in the economic life of his country, and participate in every aspect of the culture of the modern world.

The healthy state of Schwyzertütsch and Lëtzeburgesch is a guarantee that Faroese is in no danger of death, even if the possibility of its emergence from diglossia remains remote. For the Neo-Celtic areas some form of diglossia has often been seen as the solution to the language problem: in 1967 Joshua Fishman noted that: 'like many other countries today, Ireland seeks not merely individual bilingualism but rather societally patterned and functionally differentiated diglossia'. This statement was quoted with approval by Ó Murchú (1970, 32), who said that 'the value-position relevant to sociolinguistic planning involves the valid belief that it is essential to our authenticity and self-confidence as a nation that the Irish language be re-established in a central rather than a marginal position in the communicational matrix of our society. This, in effect, means setting as our immediate goal the attainment of an Irish–English diglossia in which Irish would have a significant part to play consistent with its function as the national language'. The sentiments are impeccable, but the fact remains that the whole field of economic life, whether at worker or at manager level, is in the hands of the English-speakers, so that the chances of winning that vital domain for Irish seem very poor. Furthermore, the reference to national authenticity and self-confidence brings us face to face with the basic fact about the Irish language movement, which is that it was not a case of disadvantaged speakers claiming more favourable treatment for themselves, but rather of urban intellectuals deciding that the Irish language was a necessary element in the process of the de-anglicisation of Ireland. In order to save the Irish language in the areas where it was still spoken at the time of the foundation of the state in 1921, it would have been necessary to make those poverty-stricken parts into models of the development of an independent Ireland, and also into a coherent society safe for monoglots. But this was, of course, the last idea to enter the minds of politicians dedicated to *laisser faire* economics; the Minister for Finance who declared, in the hungry twenties, that it was no part of the duty of the Government to provide employment was not likely to devote funds to the economic rehabilitation of those areas. As we have seen, the results of the revival movement elsewhere are better than might have been expected, but those 7.4 per cent of 'fairly fluent non-native speakers' are no substitute for the Irish-speaking communities lost; there were more native Irish speakers in Co. Donegal alone 100 years ago than there are in the whole of Ireland today.

But the nub of the matter is that the native speakers of the Neo-Celtic languages, whether in Wales or Ireland, Scotland or Brittany, failed to develop any corporate resistance to the erosion of their languages; they never thought of claiming the right to be monoglots, the right which a new generation of Israelis has established well within living memory. Even in Wales, where the language had been highly developed by the time that universal education was introduced, only a few fanatics ever dreamed of making it the language of instruction, and the Welsh people opted for a bilingualism in which no Englishman ever participated and in which the losses were invariably in one direction. In recent times that situation has changed for the better, but it remains doubtful whether the gains in the anglicised south make up for the constant erosion of the Welsh-speaking heartland; as the Irish experience has shown, a network is no substitute for a community. In Brittany the battle would appear to have been finally lost; the French policy of linguicide, maintained stubbornly by governments of every political complexion for two hundred years, is about to be crowned by success. Scotland offers, in some ways, a greater potential than that of the other three countries in that Gaelic has for so long been a minority language that the programme of making a last stand in the Western Isles need not be interpreted as defeatist. But the number of speakers is considerably less than the quarter million which has been seen to be necessary for linguistic independence, nor does it seem likely that the prospect of making Gaelic safe for monoglots is one that would have much political appeal. And yet the whole history of Neo-Celtic languages suggests that O'Rahilly was right, and that to choose bilingualism is to choose the road which led Cornish and Manx to decay and extinction.

References
Committee on Irish Language Attitudes Research (1975) *Main Report.*
    Dublin: Stationery Office.
Dillon, M. (ed.) (1954) *Early Irish Society,* p. 54. Dublin.
Dressler, W. (1972) On the Phonology of Language Death. 8th Regional
    Meeting, Chicago Linguistic Society.
Fishman, J. (1980) *Never Say Die.* Mouton.
Lenneberg, E. (1953) Cognition in Linguistics, in *Language 29,* 463-71.

Ó Murchú, M. (1970) *Language and Community.* Dublin:
    Stationery Office.
O'Rahilly, T. F. (1932) *Irish Dialects Past and Present* [Reprinted
    Dublin: Dublin Institute for Advanced Studies.]
Ravenstein, E. G. (1879) On the Celtic Languages in the British Isles;
    a Statistical Survey. *Proceedings of the Forty-fifth Anniversary
    Meeting of the Statistical Society.* London.
Sommerfelt, A. (1962) *Diachronic and Synchronic Aspects of Language,*
    p. 53. Mouton.
Tauli, V. (1968) *Introduction to a theory of language planning.* Uppsala:
    Almqvist & Wiksell.
Thomas, I. (1979) Language Policy and Economic Development in the
    Celtic Periphery, in *Anglo-Irish Studies* IV. Chalfont St Giles:
    Alpha Academic.
Wagner, H. (1972) Review of Wigger, *Nominalformen im Conamara-
    Irischen,* in *Zeitschrift für Celtische Philologie* XXXII.

A brief footnote, 1989

Without attempting to update the above paper in a systematic way, it is worth noting a few developments. The 1981 Census showed over 82,000 people able to speak, read or write Gaelic (1.7 per cent of the population of Scotland). Further financial support for Gaelic has come from Government sources, and is largely channelled into Gaelic education, e.g. Gaelic-medium schools in Glasgow, Inverness, Skye and Lewis, or Gaelic Nursery Schools, or educational materials. Highland Regional Council has become much more supportive of Gaelic initiatives. The average weekly broadcasting time in Gaelic has increased significantly for radio, but not much for TV, although STV have had a few extended Gaelic poetry programmes between midnight and dawn. Gaelic publishing has continued to flourish in a modest way, much children's publishing now being followed by some much-needed adolescent and popular fiction. A large team of contributors has provided a very useful compendium of information, *The Companion to Gaelic Scotland* (ed. D. S. Thomson, 1983. ISBN 0-631-12502-7).

2. Gaelic in Scotland:
Assessment and Prognosis

Gaelic in Scotland is open to a wide range of interpretations, and misinter-pretations, inside and outside Scotland. Some visitors and some natives have virtually never heard of the language; others confuse it with Scots; some think it is the universal and official language of Scotland; others think it should be buried if this has not already been attended to – so some factual introduction concerning the extent and place of Gaelic in Scotland is no doubt called for. This will be firmly set in the present. When we move to analysis and prognosis the time-scale will of course be more elastic, and fact will sometimes yield to speculation.

The 1971 census has to be used for figures of Gaelic speakers. There will be a census in 1981, but it will be some time before the next Gaelic report will be issued. The 1971 Gaelic figures did indeed raise some speculation, as they showed a rise of some 8,000, or 9.8 per cent in the number of speakers, to approximately 89,000. This rise was decisively against the trend of the last eighty years, and seemed clearly to reflect the upsurge of interest in learning Gaelic, especially in non-Highland Scotland. It presumably also reflected, marginally, some political bravado, and there is no doubt that the wish was father to the thought in the case of some of these new Gaels. But we need not doubt that interest in Gaelic had grown sharply in the decades since the second world war, and has begun to affect the level of Gaelic speech, and no doubt its ethos as we shall see. Both the Gaelic radio course in the 1950s and the Gaelic television course in 1979–80 attracted large audiences, and achieved sales in excess of 10,000 for the publications involved; and it may be that the 1981 census, and perhaps more the 1991 census, will continue to show some of the effects of this.

That 89,000 figure of Gaelic speakers represents 1.7 per cent of the Scottish population. The main areas of Gaelic strength in 1971 were Lewis Landward, North Uist, Harris, Barra and South Uist, with percentages ranging downwards from 89.5 to 77.2. Only one mainland parish, Loch-carron, topped 50 per cent (50.7 in fact), but there were significant Gaelic colonies in towns and cities (over 12,000 in Glasgow, 3,340 in Edinburgh, 2,245 in Inverness, etc.), and there were 25,000 Gaelic speakers (more than 25 per cent of the total) in Scotland excluding the Highlands, Nairn, Bute and Glasgow). The figure for Gaelic-only speakers (477) presumably represents, virtually *in toto*, children aged 3–5 *en route* to bilingualism, and its implications are grave.

We shall return to the significance of some of these figures later. Meantime we can attempt a factual, but not statistically precise, account of the position that Gaelic occupies in the country: in its public life, the media, the educational system, and so on. This is still intended as scene-setting, and attempts to exclude value judgements at this stage.

Gaelic in Public Life
Beginning with public life, including the Churches, we find that public worship is one of the main areas of strength of the Gaelic language, which is used in preaching, the general conduct of church services, extempore prayer, and to some extent in church business in the Gaelic area, though even there English is the normal language of record-keeping, and of debate at the level of Presbytery and beyond. In that we see an assumption of the educational system intruding on the stronger ecclesiastical citadel of Gaelic. But this position of relative strength is intruded on gradually in other ways; e.g. by summer, monthly or sometimes weekly services in English. This attrition takes place in both the main denominations (Free Church and Church of Scotland).

By contrast, Gaelic is very marginally used in any other forms of public gathering, e.g. sports fixtures, political meetings, local associations, local government meetings, parent–teacher meetings, etc. Insofar as I am able to judge, Gaelic is used only occasionally in the council and committee meetings of the Western Isles Council (Comhairle nan Eilean), though facilities for simultaneous translation have been installed in the Council's new building. Gaelic is used regularly in some aspects of local authority work, e.g. social work with the elderly, and also by mutual choice in other office and public-contact work in the Western Isles; but again its position as a language of paperwork seems severely restricted. Without an intensive and extended campaign to produce the appropriate registers and attitudes we can expect little improvement in this aspect.

Gaelic has no part in national government, and next to none in the official literature associated with national government: an occasional flourish of a Gaelic airmail letter form, a Gaelic sign on a Government building in the Highland area, or a Gaelic leaflet issued by a quasi-official body such as the Nature Conservancy or the Commission of the European Communities. In other public signs, e.g. street and road signs, each appearance of Gaelic seems hard won, and Highland Region has a notorious record of official opposition to any such developments. The Western Isles authority is of course sympathetic, and active to some degree, but not perhaps overzealous. Gaelic has very little place in the law. An interpreter could still be obtained for a Gaelic speaker, but there are no statutory requirements for judges to have the language. Nor does the Land Court now consider it necessary to have a Gaelic-speaking member. Gaelic has for over twenty-five years not been a subject in Civil Service examinations.

In commerce, there is a minimal amount of what might justly be termed eye-service to Gaelic (I avoid the more evocative term lip-service). The banks are ready to provide Gaelic cheque-books, and sometimes Gaelic bank-signs; they and other commercial groups advertise in Gaelic in the local press and in a periodical such as *Gairm*. A few firms use Gaelic labelling, at least for brand-names (Blàr Liath, Gruth, Glayva). Gaelic is used in local commercial transactions, but with varying levels of interference, sometimes gross. Again, much work needs to be done on developing and popularising the relevant registers, e.g. a code for the use of number, weights and measures, simple arithmetical calculations, etc., and not all of this should be by-passed by the introduction of cash-registers. But there is a base for advance here, in advertising, labelling etc., if the general political climate allowed such advance.

Gaelic in Education
The role of Gaelic in education is of great, if not crucial, importance. Looking back, one can distinguish different kinds of initiative in this field and reflect that at no time has the ideal combination of circumstances been achieved, nor is it still. In the seventeenth and eighteenth centuries, when Gaelic enjoyed a hegemony in the greater Highland area and its canon was largely unimpaired, the system of schools was extremely patchy, and the language had largely lost its native political power-houses, while it was still groping for alternative power-houses (e.g. in the universities, an achievement still far in the future). Already in the eighteenth century the schools system of the SPCK, with its limited Gaelic base, was suffering the distortion of evangelical dogmatism. This was continued in the nineteenth century, when the Gaelic Schools Societies greatly extended the schooling provision and reinforced the role of Gaelic in teaching; but, by limiting the objects of education (to evangelical ones largely) and restricting the curricular range severely, they may indeed have given Gaelic education a bad name, for the exodus from the Highlands, in search of work, was in full swing, and the backlash against an education that did not prepare people to cope with another sort of world was dangerously present. When Gaelic began to revive again within the educational system (post-1872, and especially towards the end of the nineteenth century), the memory of that backlash was strong. It was now a cardinal principle of education in the Highlands that it must fit the population for a working life where they could find it (normally in the English-speaking world). I think some recent educational theorists have forgotten the powerful logic of that position, but few Highland teachers, and especially headmasters, could afford to forget it. I doubt if they can yet.

Meantime also the effects of the two World Wars, with conscription, the increasing centralisation and bureaucratising of life in Scotland and the U.K., and the communications revolution, were exposing the Gaelic area mercilessly to non-Gaelic influence, with the effects we see on linguistic usage and sociolinguistic attitudes. It is in this situation, already far advanced, that we find a new initiative in bilingual education, including as its main ingredient a development of environmental education, being undertaken, especially in the Western Isles. The Gaelic linguistic background is at the least supportive level it has ever been, at least since Norse times. The pressure, however, to migrate from the area in search of work is less, though perhaps only temporarily; and the public climate for Gaelic is more favourable than it has been for a very long time. On the other hand, the larger political support that might be afforded by an independent Scotland is, temporarily perhaps, not in sight.

Thus we can see that the fortunate conjunction of favourable linguistic background, educational system, educational thinking, and economic and political conditions, has not yet occurred, either in the past or in the present. For all that, it may be thought that the position of Gaelic in education is the most promising we have considered as yet. As a subject in the curriculum, Gaelic achieved a thoroughly respectable status much earlier this century, and has been consolidated throughout the educational system, including the full range of examinations, University undergraduate and postgraduate studies. It has its periodicals, learned and literary, and its institutions of scholarship also. All this was built on an apparently shaky and inadequate foundation in the primary schools, but, it must also be remembered, on a strong foundation of community speech, inherited oral tradition, and so on. Now as these foundations are assailed, the enhanced status of Gaelic in the primary schools is necessary; and we can only hope that it will be sufficient to restore the balance, and continue (as one product) to supply the strong stream of Gaelic scholastic competence we enjoyed in the 20s, 30s and 40s. Meanwhile, Gaelic has other roles in primary education, as a medium for the learning of other subjects, or importantly as a central ingredient of environmental education. It has a longer history of such use than is sometimes conceded·by contemporary propagandists, but there is ample scope for development.

The role of Gaelic in schools has reached a predictable crisis at the present time. The Gaelic Bilingual Project was begun in the Western Isles in 1975, a start being made in the first three years of primary school. The 1980–81 session therefore saw the first intake into secondary school. In June 1980 the Western Isles Education Committee unanimously passed proposals to introduce the use of Gaelic-medium teaching for certain subjects into selected secondary schools, but giving a choice to pupils who wanted to continue with English-medium teaching. These proposals were overturned by a badly-attended meeting of the full Council in June and accepted by a further meeting in August. The timing of this discussion does not seem very responsible, since such secondary provision can hardly be made at the drop of a hat. The discussion and vote reveal the deep divisions that exist in the strongest Gaelic area, on the role of Gaelic in education. Despite that badly managed incident I expect to see interesting developments in the use of Gaelic as a medium, with some quite positive support from the Scottish Education Department.

The geographical spread of Gaelic within the Scottish school system remains profoundly disappointing, and the lack of such spread clearly has grave repercussions on the status of the language even in the Gaelic area. Gaelic is taught in the schools of the Outer Isles, Skye, Tiree, Wester Ross, Lochaber, and in a few schools in Sutherland. Outwith the 'natural' Highland areas, the other main pockets are Inverness, Badenoch, Oban, the Perthshire schools that feed pupils to Breadalbane Academy, Aberfeldy, and a small nexus of Glasgow schools (three senior secondaries and a few feeder primaries). This geographical pattern has some relation to the strong-points of Gaelic speech in Scotland, but does not adequately reflect either the 25 per cent of Gaelic speakers outwith the Gaelic area or the recent widespread interest in the language. A much wider coverage of the country by such a school option is very desirable, and this could of course stop far short of making Gaelic available in every school (an ideal that would be quite unattainable at present). Some attempt should be made to have Gaelic/Celtic Studies more widely available: at present a tiny number of schools attempt to have such an ingredient in their curriculum.

The Media, Music, Entertainment and Literature
There has been a good deal of debate in recent years on the place of Gaelic in the media, and the current situation is far from being satisfactory. There has been a useful extension of local Gaelic broadcasting, including a little daily broadcasting over the Isles Radio and Radio Highland stations; in September 1980 the basic national service on VHF consisted of 7¼ hours per week, mainly composed of interviews and music, with occasional features. There is not much in the way of serious musical programmes and scarcely any drama, and there is perhaps a fear of any elitist content – resulting in an unambitious and humdrum general level. There is a little good news reporting and some regular re-hashing of English news bulletins. There is scarcely any Gaelic television, apart from a language-learning series in 1979–80, an occasional current affairs half-hour and an occasional light entertainment series. Gaelic television time, on BBC and commercial channels, rarely exceeds half-an-hour per week, and often falls short of that.

The interests of listeners throughout Scotland who are unable to follow programmes totally in Gaelic (or even in the English-influenced Gaelic sometimes used in these programmes) are largely neglected. There is little in the way of programmes about Gaelic, its history, literature or music, presented through English. The somewhat mindless mixture of birthday greetings, songs, simple competitions, country-and-western, pop, melodeon, rock and news about discos that is one of the great staples of current Gaelic broadcasting will be repellent to many potential listeners, and few people with any musical taste will be able to stomach it for long. But another sizable and sympathetic audience is being almost totally neglected: for example, a non-Gaelic audience, either deeply attracted to Gaelic music, including some choral music, or a well-defined public interested in Gaelic poetry, Highland history, and Highland economic and ecological topics.

As to other than broadcast entertainment, this consists largely of musical entertainment, represented by formal concerts, less formal ceilidhs, discos and pub singing, with very occasional recitals (of song or song and poetry). There is a strong cleavage between fashions: nostalgic ceilidhs versus rock music; folksong versus classical song; old versus young; and there is probably more dogmatism about than is healthy for the future of Gaelic musical culture. Most of the new musical composition is derivative or pop, or both, and seems to show a subservience to international commercial musical culture which may be encouraging for teenagers and more distasteful for older people. This end of the musical scene would seem healthier if other parts were in better health.

The main initiative in entertainment in recent times has been the founding of a Gaelic repertory company, Fir Chlis, which is funded by the Scottish Arts Council, the Western Isles Council and other bodies. It is based in Harris, and tours with productions which are often an amalgam of dramatic and musical entertainment, as well as producing occasional straight plays, such as their production of a translation of O'Casey's *Shadow of a Gunman*. The members of the company also do television work when it is available. This company is a development, in a sense, of the modest drama revival of the 1950s and 1960s, which produced various festivals and a small number of interesting new plays, e.g. by Iain Crichton Smith, Paul Macinnes and Finlay MacLeod.

Gaelic is only modestly represented in the press, by occasional items in papers such as the *Scotsman*, weekly articles in the *Stornoway Gazette* and some other local papers, and items in periodicals such as *North 7, Crùisgean* and especially *Gairm*, which is the only all-Gaelic periodical, and is now at the end of its twenty-eighth year. Yet Gaelic literature flourishes, with a long stream of distinguished work in poetry and a shorter but very interesting stream in fiction, and a good scatter, though not a torrent, of other kinds of books: biography, autobiography, children's books, essays, current affairs discussions, and some technical exposition. There is a respect in which Gaelic strongly belies its minority status: it shows an ability to adapt itself, given the opportunity, to a very wide range of uses.

It is worth noting here that non-native speakers have begun to contribute significantly to Gaelic writing in recent decades. We should not, I think, include George Campbell Hay in this category, though it was in his teens that he learned Gaelic; but many more recent writers could be cited, as Fearghas MacFhionnlaigh (Toronto, Clydebank), Victor Price (N. Ireland),

Dennis King (California), Girvan MacKay (S. America, Ireland), etc. There is a tendency for the literary Gaelic learner to be much more of a purist, in his attitude to vocabulary, than the native writer, and hence perhaps a polarising tendency which pushes some native writers to the opposite extreme. It is not easy to keep these opposing forces in balance. The Gaelic learners usually provide the majority of the militants (though these are thin on the ground); and it was characteristic that it was such a group that forced the SNP to include a clause requiring Gaelic recognition in Scottish courts generally, rather than a more realistic clause referring to Gaelic area courts. A policy of recognition of Gaelic in all Scottish courts may look very fine on paper, but may be stultified completely by the practical impossibility of enforcing it. The current position with regard to implementation of the Language Bill in Canada (in Courts especially) gives food for thought.

Some useful work has been done in recent decades on the development of Gaelic registers. The Gaelic Panel of the Examination Board produced a list of recommended vocabulary for use in teaching language and literature in the 1960s which is currently being extended; a list of terms for use in Gaelic news bulletins has been growing over recent decades; *Gairm* has for over a quarter of a century been extending other registers (e.g. for literary criticism, current affairs, and aspects of technology); and some detailed work has been done on the technical vocabulary of biological and biochemical exposition. A vocabulary of musical terms was published in 1972 (in *Gairm*, No. 72). There was a somewhat ill-judged attempt to adapt English electoral jargon to Gaelic (*Stornoway Gazette*, 18 October 1976). But there is no equivalent of the series of lists of technical vocabulary compiled and published for both Irish and Welsh. I have recently completed a new English–Gaelic Dictionary, due for publication in autumn 1981.

Gaelic publishing has made a fairly impressive recovery and advance over the last thirty years. This recovery can be seen to be gathering strength particularly from the late 50s, and it was given a powerful boost in the late 60s by the formation of the Gaelic Books Council, now centrally concerned with the encouragement of new writing over a wide range, the grant-aiding of publishing, and the distribution of books (using a mobile bookselling service). There are once again a number of Gaelic publishers actively involved, and a number of Scottish publishers have shown willingness to add an occasional Gaelic title to their list. Despite these advances, the position of Gaelic publishing is still precarious, for the reading public is limited, and making books has become very expensive, while public adjustment to high book-prices is more conservative.

I have, on the whole, been dwelling more on the dark than on the light side in these remarks, I think with justification. But this prognosis, with its suggestions of disease, should not exclude some evaluation of very healthy areas in the patient's system. There are still people often leading ordinary lives for whom Gaelic is fully alive and healthy, a finely honed instrument for the portrayal of a particular kind of Christian experience; the vehicle for an ancient tradition of story-telling or song, or for the art of the raconteur; a subtle tongue of infinite possibilities for the making of poetry. It is too easy for the politician (or even the academic) to blur the truth in such matters, to get the perspective wrong. A knowledgeable eavesdropper from another country or century might gain the most favourable impression of Gaelic's health and potential if he put his ear to the right keyholes, but it would be easily shattered, especially if he carried a transistor around with him.

There is another point worth remembering and emphasising about Gaelic life, viewed either historically or contemporarily, and it is a point often obscured by both the enemies and the friends of Gaelic. Gaelic life had, and has, a range of strands, a series of levels, in it. It was not merely peasant in its social organisation (as many would have us believe), nor merely folkish in its culture; and it will not do to invert the roles of high and low culture, and pretend that folk-culture is the high culture and therefore has no connotations of peasantry. Gaelic culture had, and has, its professional and intellectual as well as its folk-traditional aspects, its Mac Mhaighstir Alasdair as well as its Duncan Bàn Macintyre, its composers of *ceòl-mòr* as well as of *puirt-a-beul*; and we neglect these at our peril. Neglecting them would not only distort our own history, but sell the pass to those who would pigeon-hole us, and consequently ignore us. It is unfortunate that often this betrayal of history is done for good motives, e.g. to promote egalitarian theories, though at other times it may proceed from what is only political myopia.

The Re-Building of Confidence

There are recurrent phases in the history of Gaelic Scotland, during which renewed emphasis is given to the strengthening of the Gaelic ethos or identity, presumably in response to what is judged to be an assault on it, or a weakening of it. I think we can see evidence of one such phase between the '15 and '45 Risings in the eighteenth century, and that we can possibly regard the series of Jacobite Risings as partly conditioned by such Gaelic recrudescence; but in the inter-Rising period Mac Mhaighstir Alasdair can be seen as a leader in the Gaelic revival, and the University-trained Gaels are beginning to emerge as leaders, as later exemplified by the Rev. Donald MacNicol, Rev. James McLagan, or Ewen MacLachlan. James MacPherson also felt the need to assert the Gaelic tradition in his own way, and led others to do so with more integrity. Another peak occurs in the 1790s and early 1800s; aspects of the work of the Gaelic Schools movement fit into this pattern also; the late nineteenth century movements associated with land reform, Home Rule, and the founding of An Comunn Gaidhealach all have an element of Gaelic nationalism in them, though it is never quite so positive and sustained as in the case of the parallel Irish movements. This has continued in the present century also.

One of the features of such movements is the creation of structures in the society that are designed to strengthen and perpetuate aspects of Gaelic culture. If we look at our own century we can distinguish many such structures: the build-up of a virtually complete range of educational options involving Gaelic as a subject or discipline; the spread of a system of competitive Gaelic festivals (the Local and National Mods); the range of Gaelic Societies; the foundation of the Scottish Gaelic Texts Society (in the mid-30s), the College of Piping (1940s), the School of Scottish Studies (1951), the Place-name Survey (c. 1955), the Gaelic Drama Association (c. 1956), the Historical Dictionary of Scottish Gaelic (1966), the Joint Committee on Gaelic Text-books (1968), the Gaelic Books Council (1968).

Naturally, some of these developments lose impetus in the course of time; some are more successful than others. The range, however, of such structures has an important bearing on the morale of a minority culture, and on its resilience: in the case of Gaelic it goes some way to explaining the relative confidence that the Gael has in his own language. Yet in considering such a range of structures we are to an important extent concerned with the work of natural leaders, or innovators, and must also consider whether the ideals that activate them come to be widely shared. Here, in the Gaelic context, I think the picture is less rosy. The Gaelic identity is less than secure. Besides the historical reasons for this, and the social or quasi-social reasons, along-side the wholesale intrusion of non-Gaelic influences on the whole of the Gaelic community, it seems to me that there are other, internal, factors that fragment the Gaelic identity. It tends to become parochialised, so that Skye or Lewis or Uist becomes the unit or the touchstone and some very wasteful rivalry develops. Sometimes it shows evidence of class distortion: Gaelic must be equated with folk-culture, and so by a rough approximation with a so-called working class. It seems to me more healthy to look on Gaelic as a feature of our national life, and one potentially to be shared by all manner of men and occupations.

Such considerations can have a profound effect on matters that seem at first sight unrelated. They have a strong bearing on word coinage and language adaptation. So we find the grossest localisms sometimes intruded into textbooks ostensibly designed for the Western Isles Region (*dha duine*, for example), and find a strong pressure to tolerate a high degree of English interference in the Gaelic that is not only accepted but taught in schools there. It is in part the theory of the lowest common denominator, but it is depressing to find it strongly advocated in an educational context. But such attitudes also have an unpleasant narrowness and parochialism in them, and need to be countered by broader and more ambitious attitudes. To put the matter in an extreme form, if Gaelic is to end as a patois, or as a creolised speech, perhaps it is as well that it should end quickly. To say that, of course, betrays some historical pride and a frankly elitist attitude – there are times when one is goaded into such an attitude.

It seems to me that the more ambitious strategy is the preferable one: that we must look well beyond the immediate reactions to any language policy. Though it may seem impossible *now* to switch to a full Gaelic code for even local commercial transactions in, say, rural Lewis, *without such a code* there seems little prospect of long-term health for the language. It is equally important to have recognised, automatic equivalents for some of the central, everyday concepts of contemporary society: words for 'speedometer' (e.g. *astar-chleoc*) and 'speed-limit' (*astar-chrìoch*), for 'switchboard' (*suids-chlàr*), 'syringe' (*steallaire*), 'surtax' (*for-chàin*) and 'Brussels-sprouts' (*buinneagan Bruisealach*). And sometimes it is just as important to realise that we already have equivalents in the language though we have forgotten how to use them (as *aillse* for 'cancer' or *sìol* for 'sperm'). Similar thinking applies to a large range of language use, and there is sufficient world-wide experience of bilingual and multi-lingual situations to determine, at least within broad limits, what the minima are: how many sectors of usage have to be cultivated before linguistic health can be assured.

Though such criteria were established, there still remains the major problem of *implementing* policies, or *developing* them to a degree where it becomes possible to *think* of implementing them. There is a fairly serious shortage of trained Gaelic manpower for such tasks as the development of language registers, the production of the literature that would help to give these registers currency, the production of a wide enough range of writing of everyday kinds, and so on. We can scarcely produce, at present, enough manpower to satisfy current educational and academic needs, though these are the areas most favourably supplied.

Then we have to distinguish between the powers and potentials of different agencies. Much of what has been achieved in Gaelic development this century has been achieved by individuals and groups of like-minded people, and these avenues are still open. Moving to more complex organisations, it may still be possible to influence bodies such as the Churches, political parties, educational bodies. A good example of this is the comprehensive Gaelic policy by the SNP in 1978, described by James Shaw Grant as 'the most comprehensive, and coherent, policy for Gaelic ever framed' (*Stornoway Gazette* 20 January 1979). This policy provides for the use of Gaelic in a range of Government bills, regulations and official literature and documents and in certain public notices; for an extension of Gaelic or Gaelic Studies as an available school subject; the creation of Gaelic Colleges; a greater place in the Courts; development of cultural initiatives and of Gaelic's use in communications; language development work at various levels (specific registers, Translation Unit, Gaelic Academy); and the policy adds suggestions as to the progression of such work, regarding it as a ten-year programme (the fullest publication of the policy is in *Gairm* 104 (1978), in Gaelic).

The fact that the Western Isles Region is committed to a bilingual policy provides an invaluable power-base, and a wide range of development could take place there. Already there is evidence of this in fresh initiative in Gaelic publishing and some developmental work on Gaelic business vocabulary. It is within the Region's competence to develop the use of Gaelic much further in the educational system, in local Government and in its social and recreational work.

There is the possibility of some extension of these relatively favourable public conditions to Skye and Lochalsh or parts of Argyll, but one cannot rate the chances very highly.

Entirely missing, of course, is the top tier, that of national government; and it is doubtful if in our kind of society the unfavourable trend in Gaelic usage can be effectively reversed without large-scale involvement by national government. The indications are that only a Scottish Nationalist government could be expected to adopt such policies (and no other political party has committed itself significantly in this area).

It can be seen, therefore, that there is a range of actions, leading to minor improvements, that can be undertaken under the existing regime, by individuals, organisations and local authorities; but that a full-scale tackling of the problem, or to put it positively a full realisation of Gaelic potential, is not likely to be achieved without political revolution of a particular kind. Nor would its achievement be assured even under these conditions.

Gaelic has continually to learn to live with such realities, and also with the factiousness that creeps into language revival because of its quasi-political nature. There are many tensions which are introduced into the situation, both from political and from other sources: a few of these have been referred to, and there are others such as the conflict between books and oral work in education; between learners and native speakers; between the Gaidhealtachd and Scotland. But tensions can be either stimulating or destructive, and stimulation is preferable. The truth is that there is limitless work to be done in every sphere, and that there is no harm in much of it going on simultaneously. We must welcome and accommodate every kind of positive contribution.

3. Industrialisation and Minority-Language Loyalty: the Example of Lewis

When the island of Lewis in the Outer Hebrides acquired an oil-industry fabrication and service base, there were immediate fears that the demands of heavy industry would seriously undermine the social and cultural fabric of Gaelic-speaking Lewis. In a study financed by the North Sea Oil Panel (U.K.) I examined the economic and cultural effects of this industry on the area (Prattis 1980b). In this essay I will discuss the significance of language loyalty to the maintenance of Gaelic culture in Lewis. This requires a brief background description of Lewis and an outline of the general theoretical framework that was used in the research project. These steps are a prerequisite to presenting specific data about language use and a discussion of the effects of oil industrialisation on language loyalty.

Lewis Way of Life
Despite physical and cultural isolation the people of Lewis cannot be regarded as an autonomous or self-sufficient society. Lewis is functionally integrated with the larger, economically complex industrial system of which it is an interdependent part (Prattis 1979). Because of this interdependence, present-day Lewis culture can perhaps be regarded as a mosaic that embodies both traditional and modern traits in many sectors of social life. Work and many labour-force characteristics in particular sectors of the Lewis economy often owe more to traditional structures than to the demands of modern production or labour systems. Sex roles are still highly differentiated, and family firms and fishing vessels recruit their labour from socially related groups – usually their kin. Furthermore, one must realise that temporary work away from Lewis (in the armed services, the merchant navy, hotels or industrial sites) is not a total commitment to modern production systems but an absence for economic reasons – in order to maintain a family unit within Lewis. This tendency of many members of the population to compartmentalise activities into traditional and modern spheres does not mean that the people are semi-traditional, only that certain traditional

21

activities still have adaptive functions within the modern context of industrialisation on Lewis.

With economic marginality and continuing disadvantage in Lewis the
persistence of traditional modes of transaction and value systems, as well as
being valued in their own right, are also in many instances a vital support
structure for people as they adapt to the uncertainties and disadvantages of
the market economy and the requirements of industrialisation (Prattis 1977,
1980a). The vulnerability of the local people in attempting to cope with a
situation that is beyond their control, and the culture conflict and stress that
are involved, are alleviated if there are social structures and values that
provide an alternative source of gratification and support in conditions of
crisis and uncertainty.

In Lewis the distinctive way of life is more than a rural contrast to urban
society. There is a set of well-defined norms and cultural values relating to
land, sea, church, language, kin and community that differentiates the Lewis
people from mainland culture. To this profile it must be added, however,
that a consequence of economic marginality in the past has been that
patterns of mutual aid and reciprocity, as well as being part of extended
kin-networks, were often an economic necessity. I therefore sought to
examine the characteristics of the Lewis way of life which maintain a sense of
cultural distinctiveness. The task then was to assess whether the patterns of
association and social participation introduced by the oil-related development cut across or lessened the effectiveness of community solidarity and
shared consciousness. In other words, does the workforce directly employed
by the oil industry, Lewis Offshore, use significantly different patterns of

social participation and sets of values from those used by other population segments within Lewis? This consideration was basic to the whole design of the questionnaire and selection of population samples.

Theoretical Framework

The question of loyalty to the minority language in the face of large-scale industrialisation is part of a theoretical discussion about identity and culture and about the conditions minimally necessary to retain such identity and culture. This means that the particular question of language loyalty has to be put in a wider perspective. Before proceeding to a description of the case study, therefore, I would like to make some general theoretical remarks. The two perspectives within which language loyalty may usefully be placed are:

(1) The question of identity maintenance, and the part that minority-language use plays in this. One has to realise that language use is just one indicator amongst others that seek to maintain a distinct identity.

(2) The question of language loyalty itself and the conditions that are minimally necessary for adherence to a minority language.

Let me elaborate on these two considerations.

Ethnic Identity and Cultural Continuity

Ethnic identity provides one basis for individuals to organise their relationships. Alternative organisational modes are based on ties of occupation, religion, class, sex, age and ideology. These alternative modes of association often overlap with ethnicity but do not always do so. Each set of ties takes on a different degree of importance as social, economic and historical conditions change. The important thing to establish in the Lewis case study is whether the social and economic changes initiated by oil-related developments have, in fact, altered conditions to the extent that a shared cultural identity is no longer as relevant as it was for the population in its day-to-day activities. It is important to distinguish clearly between the areas of social and economic activity where Gaelic identity has salience and the areas where it does not.

The idea of community solidarity is also important. One of the basic functions of ethnic identity is to bind individuals to a group. The group's foundation is a sense of common manners, rituals, values, and a common speech community; and the extent to which members of the group share in this sets boundaries for group interaction and shared consciousness.

The notion of boundary maintenance is crucial (Barth 1969), and requires an examination of the mechanisms and institutions that symbolise the boundary between the Lewis population and other populations from which it is held to be distinct. When experience, institutions and activities continually reinforce ideas about difference then cultural identity can be retained and reinforced. However, if experience falsifies the categories, or demonstrates the lack of relevance of the categories for interaction and day-to-day

23

life, then cultural identity will not persist. The issue to be examined, then, is the effect of participation in oil-related developments on the distinctive attitudes to kin, church, language, community, land and sea that provide a profile of Gaelic culture: in other words, to see whether working in industry produces a shift in those mechanisms and values that have traditionally defined Gaelic culture as something worth retaining.

For the purpose of this study, Gaelic culture in Lewis was defined as clustering round a number of key elements, which were examined to see whether changes in attitudes or behaviour had been brought about by oil-related developments. The major elements examined in the wider study were: (1) Language use. (2) Presbyterianism. (3) Community solidarities: crofting; mutual aid and reciprocity; extended kinship networks and visiting patterns; fank; peat-cutting. (4) Oral and ceilidh tradition. (5) Attitudes.

In this essay, I will confine my discussion of results to the data on language use. I do feel, however, that it is necessary to provide the overall framework from which these results are extracted.

Conditions of Language Loyalty
The second perspective on language use concerns the conditions for the maintenance of minority-language loyalty. There are three major conditions:

(1) Institutional support for the language: (a) the legal definitions that accompany government initiatives with respect to language use; (b) the structural definitions that derive from voluntary associations and business and administrative bodies using the language.

(2) Isolation; this refers to the distance from interference by the dominant language group and can be gauged in terms of geography and communication.

(3) Recruitment; this refers to maintaining the linguistic pool by (a) births into minority-language families and schools and/or (b) repatriation of expatriate language-users.

These factors will now be examined in terms of the Lewis case study, although it should be apparent that I am trying to construct a general theoretical framework.

Oil Industry
There have been two distinct phases of the oil industry in Lewis: 1974–8, and 1978–present. 1974 marks the date that Lewis Offshore Ltd, a British subsidiary of the Norwegian Aker group, received planning consent to establish an offshore Fabrication and Service yard at Arnish Point, just outside Stornoway. 1978, when the yard was closed down, brings the story of Lewis Offshore to a temporary halt. The re-opening of the yard later in 1978 was accompanied by a different policy of labour recruitment. Instead of relying almost exclusively on local and expatriate labour the firm relied more on sub-contracted labour brought in from outside, despite having received

development grants from the u.k. and eec on the promise of using and training local labour (Prattis 1980b). (Although the political economy of the oil industry and its establishment in Stornoway is important, the remit of this essay does not permit me to do justice to this particular aspect.)

My data is on the first phase, 1974–8, and the main tool of data-collection was a survey. I designed a questionnaire to gather information on demographic characteristics, socio-economic variables, attitudes, and the cultural profile. To gain the necessary comparative controls the same information was gathered from samples of working males drawn from six distinct populations on Lewis. The samples were selected to avoid extremes of age, unemployment and income. The six populations surveyed were divided into the following categories: (1) Oil workers, local residents. Sample size 109. (2) Oil workers, repatriated. Sample size 75. (3) Lewis villages not directly affected by oil-related employment. Sample size 100. (4) Lewis villages directly affected by oil-related employment. Only working males from non-oil-employee households were interviewed. Sample size 105. (5) Stornoway residents. Only working males from non-oil-employee households were interviewed. Sample size 100. (6) Management from Lewis Offshore Ltd. Sample size 25.

The two oil-worker samples (1 and 2) were drawn from Stornoway and the industrial catchment villages. Practically all of Lewis Offshore's young trainees and apprentices were surveyed at Lews Castle College and the Inacleate Training School, and made up 45 per cent of Sample 1. I was particularly concerned to have this sample skewed to the under-19 age-group to assist in comparisons with other samples not heavily weighted towards the young Lewis worker. Randomness in the other areas was achieved by using employee networks in each of the catchment village areas and Stornoway. Furthermore, random selections were made from the firm's list of hourly-paid personnel. Over half of the local-resident category of Lewis Offshore's employees were covered, and almost all the repatriated workers were surveyed.

Sample 3 was drawn from fishing villages outside the oil catchment area that had a significant proportion of their adult males in full-time productive employment. There were only two village areas in the Long Isle that met this condition – the islands of Bernera and Scalpay, where 90 per cent of the working males were surveyed. Sample 4, of working males from non-oil-employee households from Lewis villages directly affected by oil, covered Point, Back, Ness, Barvas and Shawbost.

Sample 5 was made up of working males who were Stornoway residents and who were *not* employed in the oil industry. The housing pattern of the town of Stornoway is one in which private owner-occupied and local authority housing are fairly evenly distributed, although several areas can be distinguished with respect to age of property. For the purpose of the survey, the town was divided into six sectors, which Stornoway residents themselves might well be able to identify: Manor Park, South Beach, MacAuley Road,

Barony Square, Matheson Road and Bayhead.

Sample 6 covered Lewis Offshore management, where the total size of the population was slightly over 40. Some of the incoming management personnel were reluctant to complete a questionnaire, which kept the sample size down to 25. This did, however, constitute over half of the total population. Of the 25 surveyed 9 were Lewis-born, the rest incomers.

Survey Results: Language Use

Lewis has the largest and most homogeneous Gaelic-speaking community in Scotland, and Gaelic speech has symbolic importance in defining group life and cultural distinctiveness within Lewis. The question of language maintenance can be examined in terms of whether its speakers wish to define themselves linguistically as a distinct cultural entity (McKinnon 1977). This is because language transmits the values and cultural knowledge that demarcate a distinct boundary. Table 1 is interesting in this regard, as it shows significant variation in Gaelic-speaking across the six population samples. As might have been expected 80 per cent of the management sample did not speak Gaelic, and neither did 36 per cent of the Stornoway sample. This latter figure is not unexpected as Stornoway is a very distinct area of Lewis. It is the primary locale of government, administration, entertainment and employment, and traditionally many Stornowegians neither spoke Gaelic nor wished to do so. (The survey results provide the data in this and the remaining tables.)

Table 1. Gaelic speakers by population samples (as percentages)

Sample	1 Resident workers N=109	2 Expatriate workers N=75	3 Non-affected villages N=100	4 Affected villages N=105	5 Stornoway N=100	6 Management at Arnish N=25
No	20.2	10.7	3.0	8.5	36.0	80.0
Yes	66.1	80.0	95.0	90.5	50.0	16.0
A little	13.7	9.3	2.0	1.0	14.0	4.0

In the following discussion I will present only a selected set of tables. The full range of data for language use can be found in Prattis (1980b). The town-country differences within Lewis reveal that the proportion of Gaelic speakers increases with distance from the town (sample 4, 90.5 per cent; sample 3, 95 per cent Gaelic speakers). The repatriated oil-worker sample, with 80 per cent Gaelic speakers, shows an overwhelming commitment to the Gaelic-speech community. The sample of resident workers, of whom approximately half were drawn from the under-19 age-group, shows less of this commitment than the repatriated sample (66.1 per cent). I would stress, however, that I do not see this as a function of oil-industry employment, but simply as an indication that young Lewis people coming onto the job market are less committed to Gaelic usage than older members of the working

population, a language shift that was occurring independently of oil industrialisation.

Naming practices in Lewis – the use of Gaelic nicknames (Iain Nogaidh)
and patronymics (Murchadh 'ic Nèill 'ic Dhòmhnaill) – are traditionally an
important linguistic reinforcer of community solidarity. In communities
where there are a small number of surnames, naming practices of this kind
were essential to distinguish one Angus Morrison from a dozen other Angus
Morrisons. The use of Gaelic naming systems has the function of identifying
individuals but within a unique cultural style, and patronymics are therefore
an indicator of speech-community boundaries. Table 2 shows that patronymics are becoming less relevant in everyday usage. Stornoway's lack of
commitment to the Gaelic-speech community is evidenced in a figure of 21
per cent for patronymic use compared to 49 per cent and 53 per cent in rural
Lewis (samples 3 and 4). The repatriated sample has a comparable level of
patronymic usage (42.7 per cent) but the resident-worker sample, skewed as
it is to the younger oil-workers, again shows up the tendency for young
working people to place less importance on Gaelic usage in their day-to-day
lives than older workers (33.9 per cent sample 1: cf. 42.7 per cent sample 2).

Table 2. Use of patronymics by population samples (as percentages)

Sample	1 Resident workers N=109	2 Expatriate workers N=75	3 Non-affected villages N=100	4 Affected villages N=105	5 Stornoway N=100	6 Management at Arnish N=25
No	66.1	57.3	51.0	45.7	78.0	92.0
Yes	33.9	42.7	49.0	53.0	21.0	8.0

The fact that the Stornoway sample and a significant number of young
oil-workers have less of a commitment to Gaelic than other samples may
simply reflect a greater degree of acceptance of the dominant mass culture
and the effective power structure of economic and political decision making
(McKinnon 1977). This is seen particularly strongly in Tables 3, 4 and 5. In
Table 3 only 55 per cent of sample 1, which is skewed toward oil-workers
under 19, speak Gaelic with friends and neighbours, compared to 74.7 per
cent of the repatriated sample and 93 per cent and 87.6 per cent for rural
Lewis villages.

Table 3. Gaelic spoken with friends and neighbours
(as percentages)

Sample	1	2	3	4	5	6
No	7.3	4.0	3.0	1.0	4.0	4.0
Yes	55.0	74.7	93.0	87.6	43.0	16.0
Occasionally	16.5	13.3	2.0	4.8	16.0	4.0
Not applicable	20.2	8.0	2.0	6.7	36.0	76.0

Sample 3, which is drawn from fishing villages outside the oil catchment-area, exhibits the tendency for Gaelic usage to be reinforced with distance from Stornoway: 93 per cent of this sample use Gaelic at work, compared to 54.3 per cent for villages within the oil-catchment commuting area and 26 per cent for the Stornoway sample (Table 4). Sample 2 (repatriated workers) and sample 4 (from villages within the catchment area) are closely comparable in this regard: 49.3 per cent as compared with 54.3 per cent, while Gaelic is used less (39.4 per cent, Table 4) at work by sample 1.

Table 4. Gaelic spoken at work (as percentages)

Sample	1	2	3	4	5	6
No	11.9	6.7	2.0	9.5	12.0	4.0
Yes	39.4	49.3	93.0	54.3	26.0	—
Occasionally	28.4	36.0	3.0	21.9	22.0	20.0
Not applicable	20.2	8.0	2.0	12.4	38.0	76.0

There is, however, cause for optimism in these figures, in that the oil-worker samples do in fact use Gaelic in the industrial work situation (sample 1, 39.4 per cent; sample 2, 49.3 per cent). Given that the majority of foremen employed at Lewis Offshore are Gaelic speakers, these figures indicate that supervisory and general work-roles in the fabrication yard contained a surprising level of Gaelic use.

Mechanisms of linguistic transmission are again strongest in the rural fishing villages. The highest proportion of Gaelic spoken at home is found in this sample (93 per cent, Table 5), as is Gaelic spoken with old people and young people (Table 6).

Table 5. Gaelic spoken at home by population samples (as percentages)

Sample	1 Resident workers N=109	2 Expatriate workers N=75	3 Non-affected villages N=100	4 affected villages N=105	5 Stornoway N=100	6 Management at Arnish N=25
No	8.3	6.7	3.0	1.0	11.0	4.0
Yes	60.6	68.0	93.0	87.6	40.0	16.0
Occasionally	11.0	17.3	2.0	4.8	12.0	4.0
Not applicable	20.1	8.0	2.0	6.7	36.0	76.0

Comparisons between Gaelic spoken with old people and Gaelic spoken with young people (Table 6) reveals that in sample 3 (rural fishing villages) there is only an 8 per cent difference. In sample 2 (repatriated oil-workers) the disparity in language use to old and young people is 20 per cent; in sample 1, 36.6 per cent; sample 4, 32.4 per cent; sample 5, 38 per cent. This implies quite clearly that linguistic transmission between generations is strongest in the rural fishing villages and weakest in Stornoway, a set of statistics that is hardly surprising.

What is significant, however, is that the repatriated sample has less of a decline in spoken Gaelic *vis-à-vis* young and old than the resident oil-worker and oil-catchment-area villages (20 per cent, compared with 36.6 per cent and 32.4 per cent respectively).

Table 6. Differences in the proportion of Gaelic spoken to old people compared to Gaelic spoken to young people (as percentages)

Sample	1	2	3	4	5	6
Gaelic with old people	67.0	80.0	96.0	90.5	50.0	20.0
Gaelic with young people	40.4	60.0	88.0	58.1	12.0	4.0
Decrease in Gaelic use	−36.6	−20.0	−8.0	−32.4	−38.0	−16.0

These figures strongly indicate that there is more language loyalty exhibited by repatriated oil-workers at Arnish than by any other Lewis population outside the remoter fishing villages.

Taking Tables 1–6 together with data contained in the wider study (Prattis 1980b), one can generally say that Gaelic speakers across all samples use the language much more frequently at home, in church and amongst friends and neighbours. With the exception of sample 3, Gaelic is used less frequently at work than amongst friends and neighbours: and with the same exception, Gaelic is used less frequently in dealing with bosses, government officials and councillors (Prattis 1980b). Furthermore there are significant increases in Gaelic usage when government officials are replaced by councillors as a category – perhaps an encouraging statistic for Comhairle nan Eilean's bilingualism policy.

Conversations with members of each population sample elicited frequent references to the importance of Gaelic use for community identity; yet the voluntary, family and community mechanisms that would reinforce this linguistic boundary have been eroded to a significant extent in every population sample with the exception of the remoter fishing villages (sample 3).

Again this is part of a general process of cultural erosion and should not be attributed to the Arnish development. In recognition of this situation, Comhairle nan Eilean has instituted a vigorous bilingual policy, and introduced bilingual education into a number of primary schools. Public awareness concerning the Gaelic language has been translated into direct action by the local authority, so that in educational and local political spheres a great deal of significance is attached to Gaelic usage, where previously there was very little. Whether this is sufficient to reverse the general shift to English usage remains to be seen. It must be emphasised, however, that the Arnish development in the phase that I studied (1974–8) was not instrumental in any language shift from Gaelic to English. Although at most a fifth of the Arnish management (sample 6) speak Gaelic, the fact that it brought back some expatriate workers with an overwhelming commitment to the Gaelic speech community may be regarded as a positive contribution to the maintenance of the cultural boundary.

Conclusion

It is clear that the Gaelic language is decaying in Lewis, but the surprising thing is that oil industrialisation at Arnish between 1974 and 1978 did not accelerate this decay, as I certainly expected it to do. If we refer back to the general framework we can perhaps see why.

In terms of (1) Institutional Support, the 1974 inception of Comhairle nan Eilean has resulted in official bilingualism, Gaelic-medium instruction in selected schools, the establishment of a Gaelic publishing company, and Radio nan Eilean, among other things. In other words policies and institutions have been established to provide structural and legal definitions that can be used to reinforce the sense of boundary feedback. With respect to (2) Isolation: although Lewis is effectively integrated into the wider economic and political system of which it is a part, the stretch of water separating it from the Scottish mainland does insulate it from some of the effects of the mass Anglophile culture.

However, although these factors are significant, the most important consideration is quite clearly that of (3) Recruitment. By recruiting a labour force drawn from an expatriate pool, the oil development at Arnish brought back to Lewis a population overwhelmingly committed to the Gaelic speech community. Furthermore, this labour force contained foremen, skilled and semi-skilled workers and a number of management personnel, constituting overall a stable and committed population base (Prattis 1980b).

One sees that the repatriated sample, by their speaking Gaelic, and their participation in other elements of the cultural profile (Prattis 1980b), provided further positive feedback for the maintenance of the ethnic boundary. The question of whether this is enough to combat the general picture of language erosion is something on which one can only speculate. One must, to be realistic, acknowledge that the second phase of the oil industry (1978–present) may well have undermined the situation I have described, owing to the fact that in the present phase the firm has relied on sub-contracted labour brought in from outside. The major conclusion from the analysis was that recruitment factors were the most significant criteria in maintaining language loyalty; therefore significant changes in recruitment patterns would necessarily affect levels of language loyalty.

I do prefer, however, to remain an optimist; and in this regard I leave the last word with Malcolm Smith, a Stornoway Trustee: 'If a development will come to this island which will keep 500 men here for one decade, men who might otherwise be scattered all over the world looking for a living, if they can be kept here living at their own homes, talking their own language, participating in the life of the community, then more will have been done to keep the Gaelic language alive and to sustain our way of life than could be done by all the Gaelic societies in all the city halls of this country in 500 years' (*Stornoway Gazette* 9 February 1974).

Acknowledgement
I would like to thank my colleague, John de Vries at Carleton, for a helpful critique of an earlier draft.

References
Barth, F. (1969) *Ethnic Groups and Boundaries.* Boston:
    Little, Brown and Co.
McKinnon, K. (1977) *Language, Education and Cultural Processes in a
    Gaelic-speaking Community.* London: Routledge and Kegan Paul.
Prattis, J. I. (1977) *Economic Structures in the Highlands of Scotland.*
    Glasgow: Fraser of Allander Institute.
—— (1979) The Survival of Communities, in *Current Anthropology,*
    June 1979.
—— (1980a) Modernization and Modes of Production in the North
    Atlantic, in *American Journal of Economics and Sociology,*
    Vol. 39, 4, October 1980.
—— (1980b) *Impact of Oil Industrialization on the Island of Lewis,
    1974-1978.* Report to North Sea Oil Panel, s.s.r.c.,
    Glasgow University.
Stornoway Gazette (1974) 9 February edition.

4. Can a Shrinking
Linguistic Minority be Saved?
Lessons from the Irish Experience

In this study a 'linguistic minority' means a settled community, or a group of settled communities, within a state, which speaks a language other than the dominant language.

In Western Europe today there are many *shrinking* linguistic minorities. Each of them has its friends and well-wishers, people who would like to stop it shrinking because they value the language in question and the distinctive culture which, to a greater or lesser extent, is bound up with it. Many of these would-be saviours believe that appropriate state action could stop the disappearance of the community which concerns them. In particular, where the shrinking language minority forms a minority within a stateless nation – for example, the Gaelic-speaking minority in Scotland, the Welsh- and Basque-speaking minorities in Wales and Euzkadi respectively – its would-be saviours often believe that if their nation had a state of its own, that state could and would stop the erosion.

Is it possible to save a shrinking linguistic minority? More particularly, is it possible for a state to do this? I shall try to answer that dual question. As a way of arriving at an answer, I examine the attempt to save the Irish-speaking minority in Ireland over the past sixty years. This is a pertinent example both because it has been the biggest and most comprehensive attempt yet made in Europe to save a shrinking language minority, and because it was undertaken by a state representing the nation to which the minority belongs.

Irish or Gaelic (as it is also called) was the language of the original Irish nation – the people who called themselves the *Gaeil*. It was the common language of all of Ireland until the sixteenth century. Between then and the early twentieth century, under English domination, a gradual language change occurred. In the course of a social process operating from east to west across the country, people changed their language from Irish to English. Then, at the end of the nineteenth century, a movement for the revival of Irish began. It was based chiefly in Dublin, the administrative capital,

32

situated at the centre of the east coast, and in other English-speaking cities and towns. One of the aims of this movement, which inspired the political revolution of 1916–21, was the preservation of the shrinking Irish-speaking communities which were situated chiefly towards the west coast. The territories which these communities occupied – the places where Irish was the usual language – were referred to, collectively, as the Gaeltacht. We had adopted this name from its Scottish counterpart in the nineteenth century. When the Irish state was established in 1922, with Dublin as its capital, its two principal cultural aims were to revive Irish in English-speaking Ireland and to 'save the Gaeltacht'.

The surviving Gaeltacht communities were almost entirely rural. Most of them were situated on land of very poor quality, and, both for this reason and because of their high population density, most of them were very poor and suffered from a heavy drain of emigration to America and Britain. The government appointed a Commission to examine what should be done to prevent the further erosion of the Gaeltacht. This Commission – Coimisiún na Gaeltachta, 1926 – reported that it was necessary to do three things: (1) to counteract the feeling which was widespread in the Gaeltacht that Irish was a badge of inferiority and poverty; (2) to remove the pressures in favour of English which were exerted by the schools and the administrative system; and (3) to improve the standard of living and the economic conditions of the Gaeltacht. These recommendations were substantially adopted by the government of the time, and by subsequent governments, as guidelines for Gaeltacht policy.

The Attempt to Save the Gaeltacht
Both for the purpose of saving the Gaeltacht, and in order to revive Irish in English-speaking Ireland, a succession of Governments from the 1920s to the 1970s obtained the approval of parliament and people for a series of far-reaching measures. The Constitution declared that Irish was the first national language. Irish was made an obligatory examination subject in all schools, and it was required for entry into the public service. Since before independence, it was a necessary subject for admittance to four out of the five university colleges. Teacher-training colleges were established to train teachers who could teach all subjects through Irish, and Irish was made the language of teaching in all Gaeltacht schools. Extra payment was given to policemen and teachers working in the Gaeltacht. For every child of a Gaeltacht family who was certified by the school inspectors to be Irish-speaking, a grant, first of £2, later of £10, was paid to the parents, and qualification for these grants by the children of a family was made the qualifying criterion for various other benefits: for example, special house-building grants, scholarships to third-level education reserved for Gaeltacht children, and recognition of the family in question as a suitable family to lodge students attending summer language colleges in the Gaeltacht.

In 1956 a special Department of the Gaeltacht, headed by a Minister, was set up alongside the other government Departments. Its function was not to replace the ordinary agencies of central and local government in the Gaeltacht: the other Departments, other agencies of central government, and local county government, continued to operate in the Gaeltacht as theretofore. The function of the new Department was simply to coordinate the special measures directed towards the Gaeltacht. In 1958, Gaeltarra Eireann, a state company for the economic development of the Gaeltacht, was set up, and in 1968 it moved its headquarters from Dublin to the Gaeltacht. At first it confined its activity to organising and marketing certain textile and toy industries which were already established in the Gaeltacht. Gradually, however, during the 1960s and 1970s, it became an agency for the attraction of all kinds of industrial enterprise, native and foreign, to the Gaeltacht; for the development of the Gaeltacht's natural resources; and for the encouragement of Gaeltacht entrepreneurs in all fields.

Since 1926, when a national radio service was inaugurated, there had been radio programmes in Irish. When a television service was established, it followed suit. Then, in 1971, in response to a Gaeltacht political movement in which I participated and which I shall be mentioning again, the government authorised the national broadcasting service to set up a special Gaeltacht radio station with studios in the three principal Gaeltacht districts in Kerry, Connemara and Donegal. It should also be mentioned that, from the 1920s onwards, and partly in response to government urging and popular demand, the Catholic Church took measures to supply Irish-speaking clergy to the Gaeltacht. Since the replacement of Latin by the vernacular in the 1960s, all religious services in the Gaeltacht have been conducted in Irish.

As a result of these measures, Irish came to be used, to a greater or lesser degree, in all spheres of Gaeltacht life, including some from which it had previously been excluded; and it became the normal language in most spheres. By the 1970s, emigration from the Gaeltacht to foreign countries had virtually ceased. Bad living conditions were virtually eliminated, and poverty was replaced by prosperity, especially during the past fifteen years. But during all of this period, language change from Irish to English has continued along the fringes of the Gaeltacht. The Gaeltacht has continued to shrink territorially and, as a direct consequence of this, in population.

In 1926 the Gaeltacht Commission had defined 'Irish-speaking Districts' and 'Partly Irish-speaking Districts'. The former were groups of District Electoral Divisions (the smallest administrative units) in which, according to an enumeration made in 1925, 80 per cent or more of the population were Irish-speakers. In the Census of 1926 these Districts were found to contain 130,000 Irish-speakers. The 'Partly Irish-speaking Districts' were groups of DEDs in which from 25 to 79 per cent of the population were Irish-speakers, and these areas were credited by the same Census with 117,000 speakers of the language. Together, then, both kinds of Districts – also called *Fíor-Ghaeltacht* (True Gaeltacht) and *Breac-Ghaeltacht* (Speckled Gaeltacht) – had 247,000 enumerated Irish-speakers in 1926.

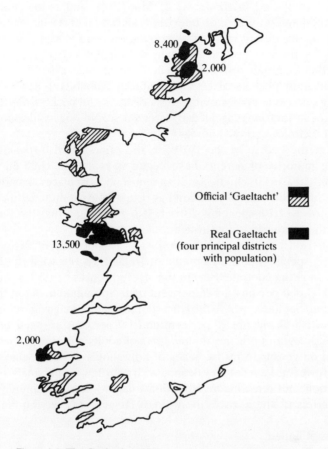

8,400

2,000

Official 'Gaeltacht'

Real Gaeltacht
(four principal districts
with population)

13,500

2,000

Figure 4.1. The Gaeltacht, 1976

Until 1956, when the Department of the Gaeltacht was established, this was as near as the state came to defining the Gaeltacht which it was trying to save. In that year the extent of the Gaeltacht was redefined, without sub-division into categories, as groups of D E Ds and part-D E Ds with 50 to 100 per cent Irish-speakers. The territories thus designated were considerably smaller in total extent than those which comprised the official 'Irish-speaking Districts' of 1926. They contained a population of 86,000 of whom 64,000 were Irish-speakers. But it was known at the time that even this reduced official Gaeltacht included, especially in Mayo, but also in other parts, considerable tracts of country which were in fact English-speaking. The reasons why they were included had to do with political considerations of a local nature which I shall not go into.

The census of 1971 showed the population of the official Gaeltacht as 71,000. In 1975 and 1976 I undertook a survey of the actual Gaeltacht, made population estimates for the various districts, and produced rough maps. My definitive map (published in *Amárach*, 21 May 1976, and subsequently discussed on radio and presented on television) showed that the larger part of the official Gaeltacht and most of its population were in fact English-speaking, and that the real Gaeltacht contained a population of only 29,000 people, located in four main districts – two in Donegal, one each in Galway and Kerry – and eight 'pockets' of less than a thousand inhabitants each (see figure 4.1). My criterion in determining these districts and pockets was the use of Irish as the normal language of daily intercourse. No-one has disputed the substantial accuracy of these findings.

Moreover, in the course of the 1970s, in the principal Irish-speaking territories, the majority of parents have begun to rear their children in English. A family rearing its children in Irish is now, in most places, a matter for comment. Since this kind of situation has been the usual prelude to the disappearance of an Irish-speaking district, it is fair to say that the final dissolution of the Gaeltacht is now in sight.

During the period I have been discussing – that is, since the 1920s – the number of Irish-speakers in the Republic of Ireland, as recorded by the census, has been rising continuously. In the last full census of 1971, it had reached over 800,000 persons, or 26 per cent of the population. As in the case of Wales and Scotland, where the corresponding percentage figures for Welsh and Scottish Gaelic are 20 per cent and 1.7 per cent, respectively, these figures represent in practice the numbers of adults and children who were recorded on census forms by heads of households as being 'able to speak Irish'. However, I am not now dealing with such figures, nor analysing their composition, but directing my attention solely to those communities and districts in Ireland where Irish is the ordinary language of everyday life.

Why the Attempt Failed

Why has the Irish state's sixty-year attempt to save the Gaeltacht failed? The attempt was based on a false assumption which was made not merely by the Irish government, but also by the language movement and the Irish people generally. This assumption was to the effect that the state bureaucracy, the semi-state companies, and particularly Gaeltarra Eireann, could stop the Gaeltacht shrinking. Acting on this assumption, the government gave that task to these agencies. But the assumption that these agencies could perform that task was quite mistaken. This becomes clear if we ask ourselves a simple question.

If there is a territory in which a particular language is usually spoken, and it is contracting continually through language change on the fringes, who can stop this contraction? Clearly, only the people of that territory – by deciding to do so and by taking appropriate measures. So another way of explaining why the state failed to save the Gaeltacht is by saying that the government failed to perceive this fact, and failed therefore to take action accordingly. It made no serious attempt to persuade the people of the Gaeltacht to decide to end the erosion – it never even asked a representative assembly of them whether they would try to end it – nor did it establish a representative regional institution which would have enabled them to 'take appropriate measures'.

Instead, as we have seen, it tried through its various agencies to do the job on their behalf, and without any commitment or activity on their part to end the linguistic erosion. A clear absurdity, when one looks at it; but such is the modern belief in the God-like omnipotence of the state that its faithful often believe it can do impossible things – work miracles.

During most of the period I have been discussing, the Gaeltacht itself voiced no opinion on the matter of its own survival. Collectively, the Gaeltacht people accepted and welcomed the things being done for and to them by the state. At the same time, on the fringes of the Gaeltacht, a succession of families, groups of individuals, and townlands, continued to participate in the social process of language change which had been moving across Ireland for four centuries. It was not until 1969–70, first in South Connemara, and then generally throughout the Gaeltacht, that a small body of Gaeltacht people spoke out on the matter of the Gaeltacht's survival. This was the political movement which I referred to earlier. Its principal organis-ational expression was Gluaiseacht Chearta Sibhialta na Gaeltachta (The Gaeltacht Civil Rights Movement) in South Connemara, where I was then living. Among the demands we put to the government, the chief one was for a democratically-elected regional authority to administer the Gaeltacht's affairs. We said that Dublin's attempt to save the Gaeltacht had failed, and that we – meaning the Gaeltacht people – were prepared to undertake responsibility for the task, and believed that we could succeed. We also called on the Irish language organisations to remove their headquarters from Dublin to the Gaeltacht and to base their revival effort there – it was patently clear that, based in Dublin, this effort was not succeeding either. The government did not accede to the demand for Gaeltacht self-govern-ment, nor did the language organisations move their headquarters to the Gaeltacht. In the course of the 1970s, and partly under the overshadowing influence of the events in Northern Ireland, the Gaeltacht political move-ment withered away.

I said above that the only people who can stop a shrinking language group from continuing to shrink are the group themselves – by deciding to do so and by taking appropriate measures. It follows that their collective will to stop the contraction is the basic factor in their salvation. Reasoning from this conclusion, it might seem correct to say that it was the lack of this will in the Gaeltacht which was the basic reason why the Irish state's attempt to save the Gaeltacht failed, and not, as I have asserted, the false assumption that the state's administrative and developmental apparatus could save it. But to reason in this manner would be to overlook the fact that the people of the Gaeltacht, or any other shrinking language minority, are, by definition, a people without the will to stop the contraction of their language community, and indeed, a people who are vaguely consenting to, and vaguely willing, their own disappearance as a linguistic entity. In other words, the lack of a will to stop shrinking is an intrinsic characteristic of a shrinking language minority. Consequently, any attempt to 'save' such a community must begin by arousing in them the will to save themselves.

The Role of the Language Movement

As we have seen, the Irish government made no serious attempt to arouse that will in the people of the Gaeltacht. But what of the language movement? Since it was this movement which infused the Irish state, and a succession of governments, with the will to save the Gaeltacht, why did it not infuse the Gaeltacht people with the will to save themselves? The answer is partly that the language movement arose outside the Gaeltacht, was centred chiefly in Dublin, and saw its role principally as one of reviving Irish in English-speaking Ireland. More fundamentally, however, it was because the language movement shared the government's assumption that the state apparatus could save the Gaeltacht. For both reasons, but chiefly for the second, the language movement has been characterised by a practical – if not an emotional – indifference to the Gaeltacht.

For the language enthusiasts, by and large, the Gaeltacht was simply a place to learn Irish and to spend summer holidays. Only one language organisation, Gael-linn, has engaged in some enterprises there; but even these – with one exception, a school in Mayo – were of a purely economic nature. Early in this century, Patrick Pearse, for one, maintained that the language movement should concentrate its effort in the Gaeltacht. Instead, and increasingly over the years, it concentrated its effort in Dublin and other English-speaking cities and towns, and left the saving of the Gaeltacht to the state.

If it had heeded Pearse's exhortation, if it had established its main base in the Gaeltacht, preached its gospel there and founded newspapers there, it would probably have succeeded in transforming the people of the Gaeltacht into something they have never become, namely, militant enthusiasts for their language, like the Flemings in Belgium. Then, with the state supplying material inducements, the first requirement for the saving of the Gaeltacht would have been achieved: its people would have decided to stop its erosion and to maintain Irish as the vernacular within certain defined boundaries. Faced with this popular decision, and with a language movement which was simultaneously a movement of the native Irish-speakers, the government could not have pursued the illusory Gaeltacht policy which it has pursued. Many years ago, when the Gaeltacht was much more extensive than it is now, its boundaries would have been accurately defined. A representative Gaeltacht body, on the lines of the Flemish Cultural Council, would have been empowered to take appropriate measures to maintain Irish as the vernacular within those boundaries.

Then, because the Gaeltacht comprised some of the poorest and least developed parts of Ireland, those 'appropriate measures' would have been seen to include infrastructural and economic development, and the representative Gaeltacht body would have become, in effect, a regional government and administration.

However, these things did not come about. The language movement maintained its practical indifference to the Gaeltacht; the state did not call on it to involve itself; and the state, for its part, never attempted to persuade the Gaeltacht people to assume responsibility for the Gaeltacht. Consequently, they continued, townland by townland, to abandon Irish, and to be mere spectators and material beneficiaries of the state's futile attempt to stop the erosion of their cultural communities.

Needless to say, it is easier to perceive now, with hindsight, what should have been done – easier than it would have been twenty, forty or fifty years ago. Attempts to stop the erosion of shrinking language minorities are a very new thing, and nowhere yet, to my knowledge, has such an attempt succeeded. Ireland was the first country in which a state and its resources were committed to the task. In the circumstances, it was probably inevitable that we would not know how to use these assets, and the language movement, in a successful combination.

The Prerequisites for Success

However, the attempt by the Irish state to save the dwindling Irish-speaking minority, and the failure of this attempt, offer valuable experience and lessons to all who would embark on such an enterprise. The Irish example serves to clarify certain things which were not clear beforehand. A shrinking language minority cannot be saved by the actions of well-wishers who do not belong to the minority in question. In particular, its shrinking cannot be halted by the action, however benevolent and intelligent, of a modern centralised state. It can be saved only by itself; and then only if its members acquire the will to stop it shrinking, acquire the institutions and financial means to take appropriate measures, and take them.

The basic prerequisite is that they acquire the will to stop their disappearance as a linguistic community, and they can acquire this through the agency of a prophetic individual or group who either arises among themselves or comes to them from outside, lives with them, and identifies with them. Having acquired the will to save themselves, they will almost inevitably – human nature being what it is – acquire the institutional and financial means to take appropriate measures, unless they are forcibly prevented from so doing. Consequently, we can say, in summary, that a shrinking linguistic minority can be saved from extinction only by itself; and on condition that it acquires the will to save itself, and is not prevented from taking appropriate measures but assisted in doing so.

5. Welsh:
Linguistic Conservation
and Shifting Bilingualism

More people speak it today than ever in its history; it is more widely read in proportion to its speakers than, possibly, any other language. One quarterly and two bimonthly magazines are published in it, some fifteen monthlies, as well as eighteen or twenty weekly papers. It has at last been given recognition by the British government; acts of parliament and other parliamentary papers are translated into it. The government pays for teaching it as a special subject in primary schools. . . . A century ago it was prophesied that it would be extinct within a hundred years. No-one today would dare utter a similar prophecy.

These words come from the concluding passage of an article on the Welsh language by Professor John Morris-Jones in the 1891 second edition of a Welsh encyclopaedia. In 1891 Morris-Jones could view with confidence the future of the language which he had recently been appointed to profess at the University College at Bangor. Ninety years later, despite increased governmental and educational recognition, Morris-Jones's successor at Bangor cannot share either his confidence or his optimism. Today it is the fate rather than the future of Welsh which concerns all of us who profess the language.

The year of John Morris-Jones's article also saw the first ever official census survey of the Welsh language (Southall 1895). Within the registration districts which it surveyed it reported 910,289 persons able to speak Welsh, or 54 per cent of the population who were then three years old or over. That 1891 figure of 54 per cent Welsh speakers, and therefore 46 per cent who spoke English only, compels us to pause a little. It indicates a decline in the position of the native language, even by that period, which would appear to question Morris-Jones's optimism. In national statistics there had been a retreat, and a rapid one – from the 71 per cent Welsh speakers estimated by Ravenstein (1879) in the early seventies to 54 per cent twenty years later. In the south-east of the country the large-scale immigration of workers from outside Wales into the industrial valleys of Gwent and eastern Morgannwg, especially since about 1860, had resulted in densely populated and heavily Anglicised communities becoming established in areas which had previously been primarily Welsh-speaking (J. P. Lewis 1960). It is also the case that over the remainder of the country the use of English had been on the increase in a growing number of small urban centres, as W. T. R. Pryce's (1978) analysis of the language of Anglican church services has documented. Recent statistical studies of Welsh–English linguistic distribution have rightly stressed the expanding extent of this nineteenth-century Anglicisation. Nonetheless Morris-Jones's confidence that Welsh had a central and secure place in the 'new Wales' which he and his Young Wales colleagues saw in the future was at the time understandable and justified.

Anglicisation of Welsh territory had been a factor for over eight hundred years, ever since the Anglo-Norman settlement of the fertile lowlands of Gwent and Morgannwg, of peninsular Gower and south Pembrokeshire. Along the eastern border there had been a westward shift in the language divide between areas where Welsh on the one hand and English on the other was for the majority of the population the medium of social and cultural interaction (D. T. Williams 1935, 1936; Pryce 1978; G. J. Lewis 1979); in Radnorshire a marked linguistic shift had taken place during the second half of the eighteenth century (Darlington 1895; Owen 1954). Yet this spatial shift along the periphery was not viewed as a serious danger. Apart from the change brought about by immigration into the south-east coalfield, Welsh Wales – *Y Gymru Gymraeg* – remained an extensive continuum, secure within an accepted boundary, and that in spite of three and a half centuries of antipathy on the part of government. State policy from the Tudor period onwards, both deliberately and indirectly, had encouraged the spread of English. It installed English in public affairs and in administration; it created an upper ruling class which grew increasingly Anglicised as it was increasingly attracted by the widening opportunities of an expanding social, economic and cultural London-based sphere. A pattern of diglossia without bilingualism was established, with the governing classes belonging to one linguistic community and the mass of the population to another. It was a situation not unlike that which prevailed in Ireland, and had it lasted the progressive sociopolitical drift in favour of English might well have undermined the position of the Welsh language and led to its virtual demise during the course of the last century. Before that happened, however, the evangelical Methodist revival of the eighteenth century transformed the situation. Welsh was enthroned in a public domain; it became an institutional language; literacy, and especially reading ability, in Welsh was successfully cultivated; a new Welsh-speaking cultural leadership developed; a standard spoken Welsh was established. The diglossic pattern was strengthened.

In 1891, over much the greater part of Wales, Welsh remained unquestionably dominant. Excepting Gwent and the Cardiff and Swansea registration districts, more than 70 per cent of the overall population spoke the

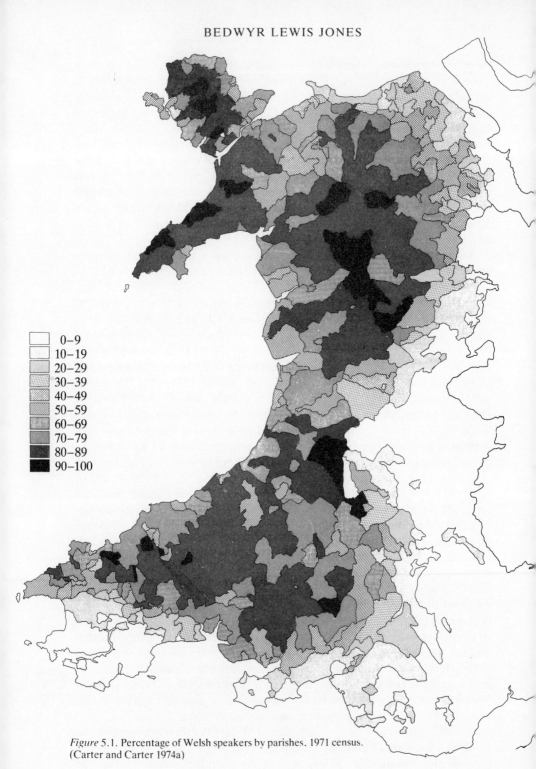

Figure 5.1. Percentage of Welsh speakers by parishes, 1971 census.
(Carter and Carter 1974a)

language (Southall 1895). Over extensive areas the intensity factor was substantially higher – 95 per cent or more in twelve of the fifty-two registration districts, between 90 and 95 per cent in a further seven districts. This surviving heartland included, besides most of rural agricultural Wales, two industrial or semi-industrial regions – the anthracite coal mining valleys of west Morgannwg and east Dyfed and the slate quarrying villages of Gwynedd, both of them the recipients of short-distance immigrants from Welsh rural areas. Throughout the area a mesh of Nonconformist chapels provided a unifying cultural structure which reached out to encompass dispersed Welsh-speaking networks in Anglicised Morgannwg and even on Merseyside. This Welsh cultural zone had its own indigenous communication systems. A viable press flourished. There were twenty Welsh-language weeklies. A denominational children's magazine distributed over 40,000 copies. The 1891 Welsh-medium encyclopaedia, from which I quoted at the outset, was the second edition of a successful ten-volume commercial venture. When Morris-Jones and his contemporaries viewed the state of the language from within this fastness, there seemed little reason to suspect an impending slump in its fortunes. Rather, with a change in educational practice and the effective teaching of Welsh to schoolchildren, instead of the previous policy of discouraging the language, there was every hope that the overall decline caused by industrial immigration could be halted, public antipathy towards Welsh altered, and the total number of speakers trebled. In 1885 Dan Isaac Davies, a schools inspector, published a pamphlet, *Tair Miliwn o Gymry Dwy-ieithog*, in which he foresaw three million Welsh speakers in the mid-nineteen-eighties.

Davies's vision, like Morris-Jones's optimism, proved to be illusory. The 1891 census is the only official linguistic survey to show Welsh in a majority position. By 1901, although the total number of speakers had increased, the percentage had dropped to under fifty. With each succeeding decade that percentage has plummeted; since 1911 the total has also decreased, from approximately a million to half that number.

1901	929,800	49.9 per cent
1911	977,400	43.5
1921	922,100	37.1
1931	909,100	36.8
1951	714,686	28.9
1961	656,002	26.0
1971	542,402	20.8

In the south-east, the area of high population density, the statistical drop has been heavy (Thomas 1956, E. G. Lewis 1979). English saturation in the wake of continuing large-scale immigration of workers from outside Wales in the early decades, emigration during the depression of the inter-war years from mining valleys such as the Rhondda where Welsh was widely spoken (C. W. Lewis 1974) and other factors have resulted within the old county of Morgannwg in a loss between 1911 and 1971 of a quarter of a million Welsh speakers, from almost 400,000 to under 150,000. It is a dramatic statistic; it materially affects the overall position of the language. And yet, as one interprets the census figures, there are, I would suggest, two other aspects which are more important.

In 1891 there was an extensive area within which Welsh was the dominant language with an intensity factor of 80 per cent or over. That spatial continuum has virtually disappeared. On a map based on the 1971 census only small, dispersed pockets of 90 per cent or more Welsh speakers are recorded: in a few parishes in central Anglesey, in restricted parts of Llŷn and Arfon, in limited areas in the central upland (Bowen and Carter 1974, Carter and Carter 1974a). The over 80 per cent area, although larger, is drastically reduced and patchy. It consists of four residual nuclei: central Anglesey, most of Llŷn and west Arfon, central Meirionnydd with an extension into Hiraethog in Clwyd and into north-west Powys, and central Dyfed, most of them areas of low or relatively low density and of continuing depopulation. The heartland has contracted; it has also fragmented. The break in the centre is, in part, a continuation of the westward linguistic shift along the border spearheaded through the Severn-Dyfi basin, but the extension of a corridor of Anglicisation into north Ceredigion and south-west Meirionnydd, as Carter and others have pointed out, is something different and recent. In Meirionnydd it is a creation of tourism and its secondary consequences: in-migration of retired people and second-home ownership. In Ceredigion it is the result of the suburban extension of Aberystwyth into neighbouring village communities. Again, the break between Llŷn and Meirionnydd, from Betws-y-coed through Beddgelert to Porthmadog, all tourist centres, is a post-1961 development. The effect, however one looks on it, has been devastating. The geographers Bowen and Carter (1974) compare the spatial change to one's view of a lake drying. The continuous expanse of water has vanished; what remains is a number of separate pools, patchy and uneven. The implications are obvious. The land area where Welsh is for its speakers the natural medium of almost all speech events has become small and limited.

Gwynedd, symbolically the stronghold of Welshness, is an example (James 1974). Here the total population since 1891 has remained relatively constant although rural depopulation, the eclipse of the slate industry, and more recently suburbanisation, tourism and the in-migration of retirement settlers has significantly altered its composition and demographic balance. In 1891 91 per cent of the 215,000 inhabitants were Welsh speakers. In 1921 that 90 per cent intensity remained in a hundred of its one hundred and fifty community divisions with a further thirty-six divisions in which more than three in every four spoke the language. As late as 1961 nine in every ten were Welsh-speaking in forty-five communities, three in four in sixty-five others. By 1971 the 90 per cent intensity prevailed in only thirteen divisions with seventy-eight communities in the 75–90 per cent category. In forty-nine community divisions, although Welsh was statistically in a majority position, there was a considerable and influential English presence; in eleven communities that English presence was predominant. This is at the local parish level. Allied to increased physical and social mobility it can only mean more and more situations where speech events – in the shop, on the street, in the playground – are in English. The habitual, natural use of Welsh is, of necessity, restricted.

It is the change or stability of habitual usage which, above all, concerns the student of language shift and language maintenance. Here there is for Welsh a dearth of researched information. The 1971 census, however, can be interpreted to reveal significant pointers. Bowen and Carter (1974) have shown that there is a close spatial correspondence between areas of between 40 and 70 per cent Welsh speakers – i.e. areas with a strong English presence – and areas where the percentage drop during the previous decade had been more than twice the national average. It was where a mixed language community existed that loss-rate was apparently highest. There is need for a great deal of detailed investigation at the local level, linking the drop in percentage with such factors as immigration, emigration, and a change in age distribution, but as a preliminary observation the implication is clear: – Welsh in these intermediate zones was not spoken by a sufficiently large proportion for it to be the accepted medium of everyday communication; a shift to English is facilitated. A further pointer is revealed by the difference between those who declared themselves able to speak Welsh and those able to read and write the language (Carter and Carter 1974b, Bowen and Carter 1975). Information concerning literacy in Welsh was requested for the first time in the 1971 census. Again conclusions are premature, but there are apparent signals. In Llŷn and in Penllyn, both areas with a dominant Welsh intensity factor, the difference between speakers and those able to write Welsh is minimal. In east Gwynedd and in central Clwyd where Welsh is in an intermediate position, with between 70 and 40 per cent intensity, there is a marked variance between speech and writing ability: a noticeable percentage of speakers are unable to write the language. Literacy is a stabilising influence on language. Inability to write could well suggest instability in those very areas where the incidence of English speech events is increasing; it could mark a stage in the decline of the language.

The erosion and break-up of an extensive core of pervading Welshness, especially in the post-Second-World-War period, is one aspect of the changing position of the language to which I wish to draw particular attention. The other aspect is the disappearance of monolinguals. In 1891 over 500,000 claimed or were reported to be 'Welsh only'. When the Census Report was published doubt was cast on the dependability of this figure (Southall 1895). Half a million, it was claimed, was an unduly inflated number. If 'Welsh only' is interpreted to mean non-ability to carry on a minimal conversation in English, one can accept that there was substance in the criticism. But if the term is taken to refer to people with a very limited command of English and hardly any opportunity to practise that modicum because they lived their

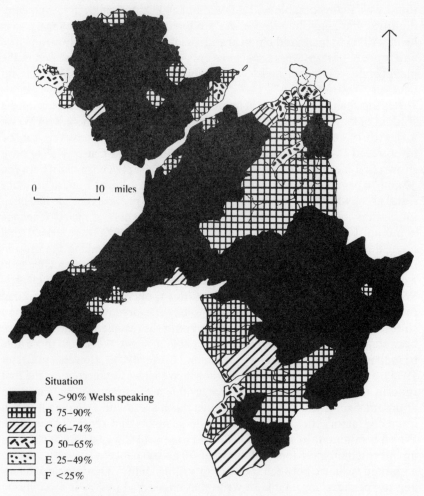

Situation
- A >90% Welsh speaking
- B 75–90%
- C 66–74%
- D 50–65%
- E 25–49%
- F <25%

Figure 5.2a. Language and communities in Gwynedd 1921. (C. James 1974)

lives totally, or almost totally, in their native language, then the reported statistic is by and large acceptable. In that case more than half the number of Welsh speakers were functionally monolingual. Over large tracts of the country – the whole of Anglesey, Ceredigion, Meirionnydd, for example – the figure was 70–75 per cent of the population. Even in 1931 100,000 – almost 11 per cent of all Welsh speakers, 20 per cent and more of the total population in large areas – still reported themselves in the 'Welsh only' category, and this after sixty years of a compulsory state educational provision which had as one of its main aims the teaching of English to Welsh-speaking pupils. Today, apart from very young children, monolinguals are a rare, if not an extinct, species. This aspect of linguistic change – the eclipse of monolingualism in the Welsh heartland – is just as much a consequence of

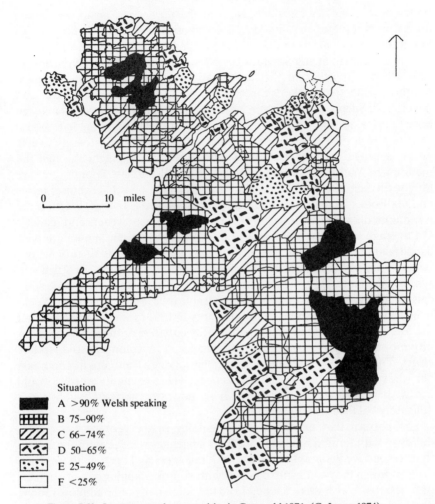

Situation

A >90% Welsh speaking
B 75–90%
C 66–74%
D 50–65%
E 25–49%
F <25%

Figure 5.2b. Language and communities in Gwynedd 1971. (C. James 1974)

out-of-school exposure to English as it is of formal classroom teaching. It is the increased habitual contact with English and the decrease in the total incidence of Welsh speech-events within communities which has in the twentieth century reduced Welsh to a real minority position.

Where does this find us in 1980? According to the last census some 540,000 claimed to speak the language; 450,000 reported an ability to read it. An arbitrary division would group the speakers in three roughly drawn segments. There is rural Gwynedd and parts of Clwyd in the north-west, and rural Dyfed extending into industrial Morgannwg in the south-west, both areas with some 200,000 speakers and, despite certain qualifications, an intensity factor of three or more in every four of the population. Thirdly there is the populous south-east with 100,000 speakers and an intensity of under one in ten. A fourth segment in the north-east, again with a low intensity, completes the division. Throughout these areas the language is taught in schools, at the primary and secondary level, with more energy and commitment than at any previous period: as a medium of instruction as well as a cultural inheritance in the case of native speakers, as a second language to others. Effective methods for teaching Welsh to non-speakers have been developed. Secondary schools in which Welsh is the official school language have been established in ten urban centres with a low or intermediate Welsh intensity factor; in these, and in other schools in more intensely Welsh areas, a range of subjects, both science and arts, is taught through the medium of Welsh. Sociology, History, Biblical Studies, Drama, etc. are taught through the medium of Welsh at University level. Technical terms and textbooks have been produced to support these activities. Welsh is the normal medium of literary activity for a viable body of writers and readers. On average some two hundred and fifty Welsh books per annum are published: some sixty or so items specifically for children, thirty titles of fiction, twenty volumes of poems. Translations of foreign literature – of Solzhenitsyn, Dürrenmatt, Böll, Camus, etc. – appear. There is a variety of periodicals, including a science quarterly comparable to *Scientific American*. Weekly newspapers have decreased, from twenty in 1891 to some half dozen, but the past decade has seen the founding of twenty-five or more new community monthly papers – *papurau bro* – produced by voluntary co-operative effort. There is a virtually full sound-radio service. There are fifteen hours per week of Welsh television programmes. There is vitality which I would not wish in any way to minimise. It is, however, linguistic vitality in a delicately balanced, shifting situation.

The pattern that existed at the beginning of the century was one of diglossia with limited bilingualism. Two languages were present, both with their respective geographical areas of dominance, and both, in those situations in which they came into contact, with non-overlapping sets of domains or functions. Welsh was excluded from the domain of public administration; its place in education was marginal; but at that period the average citizen's contact with government was minimal and the influence of education on those who left school at the end of the primary stage was restricted. In most other domains – home, neighbourhood, religion, entertainment, press, literature – Welsh was dominant over a wide territorial area. Where such a strong overlap of domains existed, assimilation of immigrants was possible.

Today that pattern is broken and fluid. Groups where English is dominant and exclusive in all domains are an increased presence everywhere. All Welsh speakers, on the other hand, are bilinguals; they have the capacity to engage in a prolonged conversation concerning the activities of daily life in English. They would be rated at the upper end of the scale of bilingual ability. It follows that in any interaction between Welsh and non-Welsh speakers the speech-event tends to be in English; it is often in English in certain role relationships between Welsh speakers. The Welsh component of the bilingual totality varies widely in fluency and in frequency of usage. It includes an increasing number of secondary bilinguals: persons who have acquired an ability in Welsh at school or in adult language classes. It ranges from individuals whose ability in the language is passive and dormant to groups within which Welsh is dominant in certain domains. In very few domains, however, and for only a small number, is that dominance exclusive. The old domain distribution has been disrupted. Welsh has been introduced into some domains from which it used to be excluded: public administration is an example. Within the classroom its place has been extended. But elsewhere, in the neighbourhood and in social interactions, its previous dominance is weakened. There are fewer employment contexts where it is dominant. Religion, an important linguistic support for Welsh in the past, holds the allegiance of fewer people. In every Welsh home television is a voluble and attractive alien presence. The natural domain supports of the language are being cut down by the homogenising aspects of modern mass culture, a culture which by its very nature induces conformity with the norms of a mass market at the expense of the traditional and the particular. Increased physical mobility and a widening range of social contacts work in the same direction. In all this the work of Fishman (1966, 1972) and others (Glazer 1966) on language maintenance amongst immigrants in America is disturbingly relevant. Welsh, although functioning as an ethnic language, occupies for a growing number of people a partial if not a marginal place in the overall picture.

I realise that every general observation which I have offered needs to be qualified in a number of directions. But the general drift which I am describing is, I fear, the reality; it is confirmed by the work of Clayton and others (1978). Co-ordinate or independent bilingualism is decreasing; compound or interdependent bilingualism is growing. Compound bilingualism is an accepted source of linguistic interference. That is present. Lexical borrowing from English into Welsh has a long-established tradition; it has extensively enriched Welsh colloquial vocabulary; it should not be resisted. Interference is another matter. It is the indiscriminate use of English words and phrases in Welsh utterances by speakers who are unaware at the time that they are using two distinct languages. This kind of improvisation switching is more frequent in speakers below the age of fifty with a low level of formal education in the language; it is also more common in informal speech situations within communities with a moderate Welsh intensity factor. It has the effect of undermining attitudes towards the language and encouraging a feeling of Welsh linguistic inadequacy. There is also interference in syntax. The use of prepositions to support the meaning of verbs, in expressions such as *rhoi esgidiau ar*, *rydw i'n mynd i*, goes beyond the acceptable extension of an existing pattern in Welsh. It is an imperfection, and a feature of the speech of young people brought up in an environment of low to moderate Welsh intensity. One must, of course, avoid the purist fallacy. The examples which I have quoted, however, are an indication that speech is being

49

mediated through another language. They are a mark of compound bilingualism and of linguistic instability.

The challenge is clear. It is to stabilise bilingualism. Two options seem to me open. One is to accept that present trends will continue. The areas of high Welsh frequency will attentuate and fragment still further. Those who acquire Welsh in the home-neighbouring domain will become fewer and fewer. Instead of the present half-million speakers, there will be a much reduced total who retain and pass on the language for self-conscious ethnic and nationalistic reasons. The total will include a growing proportion of secondary bilinguals. It will consist increasingly of professionals and the intelligentsia; the old Welsh-rural/English-urban contrast will become less obvious. Schools in which Welsh is the medium of instruction will be the main institutional support factor. A literature will be maintained with the support of state patronage and Arts Council grants. Welsh will, in fact, be the language of a number of fragmented and scattered networks of acquaintances and cultural activities; it will be a residual language. Its position will be that of an immigrant language, albeit in its native country.

The other option is to reverse existing trends: to maintain and strengthen those areas where Welsh is still strong in the home-neighbourhood domain, and to increase ability and usage in areas where intensity is low. It is to maintain the half-million or so speakers by increasing the societal distribution of the language. Here education is a crucial factor. In the north-east and in the south-east, areas with low Welsh intensities and high population density, and where a vigorous policy of second-language teaching has been pursued, the percentage of Welsh speakers amongst school children increased in the 1961–71 decade. But education, however effective, can only generate ability for a potential use of language. School and adult classes are an important *source* of bilinguals, but they do not *determine* the domain distribution of language. Any policy of using the educational system to bring about a language shift is, in the absence of complementary control over contexts of usage, severely restricted. To complement educational effort with public financial aid to voluntary organisations and cultural activities engaged in language support, as has been the policy in Wales hitherto, is again both essential and insufficient. In order to stabilise societal bilingualism something further is needed. Areas where Welsh has a strong hold in the home-neighbourhood domains need to be sociolinguistically consolidated by policies to bolster language loyalty and reduce to a minimum domains in which English presence is spreading. Welsh usage and the likelihood of Welsh speech events have to be propagated everywhere. These matters involve employment policies and plans for the siting and size of factories; they involve control over housing developments; they require the planned extension of the language in public administration and on television. They imply a political decision. It is a decision by Welsh men and women that the native language is essential to their authenticity as a distinct people and must therefore be re-established in a central rather than a marginal position. And it is a decision that will inevitably involve conflict.

I said at the outset that I cannot reiterate Morris-Jones's 1891 optimism for the prospects of what J.R.Tolkein described as 'the senior British language'. The present position of Welsh is one of rapid, ill-charted shift; its future is uncertain and, on the basis of any statistical projection, darkly foreboding. I speak as a participant in a language maintenance movement who, in the words of Romain Rolland, has to admit to pessimism of the intelligence but tenaciously retains an optimism of the will.

References

Bowen, E. G. and Carter, H. (1974) Preliminary observations on the distribution of the Welsh Language at the 1971 Census, *Geographical Journal* cxi, 432-40.
— (1975) The distribution of the Welsh Language in 1971: an analysis, *Geography* lx, 1-15.
Carter, H. and Carter, M. (1974a) Cyfrifiad 1971: Adroddiad ar yr Iaith Gymraeg yng Nghymru, *Barn* cxxxvii, 206-11.
— (1974b) Cyfrifiad yr Iaith Gymraeg 1971: Gwahaniaethau rhwng siarad ac ysgrifennu Cymraeg, *Barn* cxli, 398-402.
Clayton, P. (1978), Domain and register in the use of Welsh, in Williams, G. (ed.), *Social and Cultural Changes in Contemporary Wales*. London: Routledge & Kegan Paul.
Darlington, T. (1895) Radnorshire and the Welsh Language, *Wales* ii, 31-2.
Fishman, J. A. (1966) *Language Loyalty in the United States*. The Hague: Mouton.
— (1972) *Language in Sociocultural Change*. Stanford, California: Stanford University Press.
Glazer, N. (1966) The process and problems of language maintenance, in Fishman, J. A. (1966).
James, C. (1974) The state of the heartland: language and community in Gwynedd 1921-71, *Planet* xxiii, 3-15.
Lewis, C. W. (1974) The Welsh Language: its origin and later history in the Rhondda, in Hopkins, K. S. (ed.), *Rhondda Past and Future*. Ferndale: Rhondda Borough Council.
Lewis, E. G. (1979) A comparative study of language contact: the influence of demographic factors in Wales and the Soviet Union, in McCormock, C. and Wurm, S. A. (eds), *Language and Society: Anthropological Issues*. The Hague: Mouton.
Lewis, G. J. (1979) The geography of cultural transition: the Welsh Borderland 1750-1850, *The National Library of Wales Journal* xxi, 131-44.
Lewis, J. P. (1960) The Anglicisation of Glamorgan, *Morgannwg* iv, 28-49.
Morris-Jones, J. (1891) Cymraeg, in *Y Gwyddoniadur Cymreig*, 2nd ed., vol. 3, 48-79. Denbigh: T. Gee.
Owen, L. H. (1954) A history of the Welsh Language in Radnorshire since 1536. University of Liverpool unpublished M.A. thesis.
Pryce, W. T. R. (1978) Welsh and English in Wales, 1750-1971: a spatial analysis based on the linguistic affiliation of parochial communities, *Bulletin of the Board of Celtic Studies* xxviii, 1-36.
Ravenstein, E. G. (1879) On the Celtic Languages in the British Isles: a statistical survey, *Journal of the Royal Statistical Society* xlii, 579-636.
Southall, J. E. (1895) *The Welsh Language Census of 1891 with coloured Map*. Newport (Mon.): J. E. Southall.

BEDWYR LEWIS JONES

Thomas, J. G. (1956) The geographical distribution of the Welsh
Language, *The Geographical Journal* cxxii, 71-9.
Williams, D. T. (1935) Linguistic divides in south Wales, *Archaeologia
Cambrensis* xc, 239-66.
— (1936) Linguistic divides in north Wales, *Archaeologia Cambrensis*
xcl, 194-209.

JOHN E. AMBROSE and COLIN H. WILLIAMS

6. On the Spatial Definition of 'Minority':
Scale as an Influence on
the Geolinguistic Analysis of Welsh

Minority language groups in twentieth-century Europe have attracted the interest of students from a widening range of disciplines, each with something to contribute, by way of approaches and techniques, to the understanding of the increasingly urgent problems facing many linguistic minorities. These problems may be associated with the decrease in numbers of speakers, or with a reduction of quality and status in the languages themselves; with changing economic circumstances affecting individuals and communities, or with the political implications of language change. The research of geographers working in this field has been concentrated on the task of identifying and describing patterns of language change and the processes which underpin such change. Progress to date has recognized the complexity of the phenomenon under consideration, and has produced a promising, if limited, series of individual case studies (e.g. Ambrose 1980, Cartwright 1980, Lewis 1979). In general, though, most studies have been undertaken at one scale of analysis and have often recommended specific policy proposals based upon limited and scale-specific analyses of the situation (Betts 1976).

This chapter aims to supplement the information provided by previous studies undertaken in Wales by concentrating on the scale problem in geolinguistic analysis. After an introduction at the scale of the language area as a whole, the discussion will focus on progressively smaller localities within Wales, examining the effect which each increase in scale may have upon the understanding of the predicament of Welsh. Our purpose is not only to examine the Welsh language, but also to assess the part which geographical methods may play in the study of language decline more generally.

The National Scale
In the crudest numerical terms, one can summarise the decline of Welsh from a peak of 977,400 speakers in 1911 to 542,425 in 1971 and from 280,900 monoglot speakers in 1901 to 32,725 in 1971. The decline has, of course,

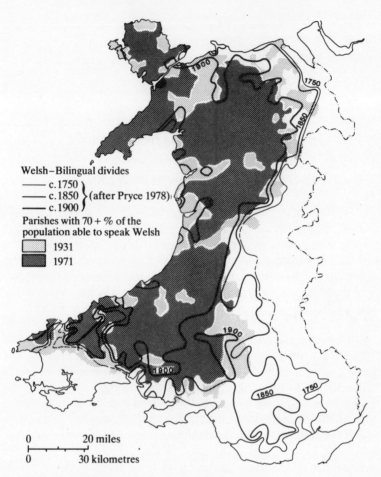

Figure 6.1. The territorial retreat of Welsh since 1750.

been much more than numerical. If the information were available it would almost certainly show, in addition, a decline in the frequency of use by speakers and, in many cases also, a reduced fluency and confidence in the use of Welsh as an everyday medium of conversation (Thomas and Williams 1978). By comparison with other European minorities, we are relatively fortunate in being able to document the decline in spoken Welsh in precise numerical terms; our apparently precise figures were obtained from the Census Report on the Welsh Language in Wales for 1971, and with the exception of 1941, a decennial count has been made of Welsh speakers since 1891. For earlier dates it is possible to substitute the information from sources such as the Anglican Church Visitation Returns (Pryce 1978a), Welsh-medium newspaper circulations, diaries and travellers' notebooks, so as to produce a map of territorial recession of the language at the national

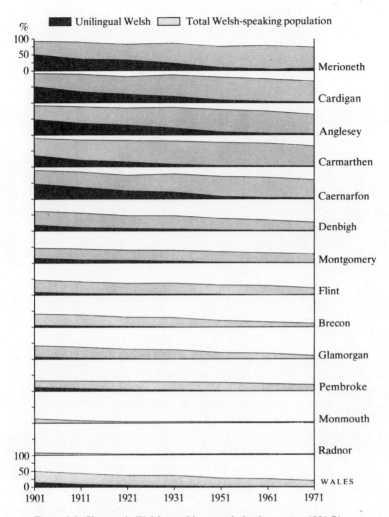

Figure 6.2. Changes in Welsh-speaking population by county, 1901-71.

scale (Figure 6.1.). Many of the features on this map will reappear later, but note the considerable area of the west, by 1971 almost divided into two by the Severn valley, where over 70 per cent of the population were able to speak the language. The indentations around the edge of this 'core' area (e.g. the Cardiganshire Bay coast, the North Wales coast, the Conway valley) offer some clue to the fact that the area has not yet ceased to shrink (Williams 1980a). Longstanding, strongly Anglicised areas may be identified in southern Pembrokeshire, the whole of the South Wales coalfield and along much of the national border. Yet even in the latter region the Welsh core area at one point closely approaches the English border and even extended across it into England itself until recent decades, according to the

Table 6.1. Welsh speakers by geographic county
(census figures in thousands)

	1901		1911		1921		1931		1951		1961		1971	
	Welsh only[1]	Total[2]	Welsh only	Total	Welsh only	Total	Welsh only	Total	Welsh only	Total	Welsh only	Total	Welsh only	Total
Anglesey	22.8	43.6	17.4	42.7	15.1	41.5	11.2	41.0	4.6	38.4	2.8	37.1	2.6	37.1
Breconshire	4.7	23.1	3.0	22.9	2.6	21.4	1.1	20.5	0.3	16.3	0.3	14.9	0.6	11.7
Caernarvonshire	56.0	105.3	42.1	101.2	32.7	93.7	24.9	91.9	10.6	85.1	5.8	79.9	5.1	73.1
Cardiganshire	29.1	53.6	19.5	51.1	15.2	47.6	10.6	46.3	3.8	40.6	2.4	38.5	2.0	35.8
Carmarthenshire	44.9	113.9	30.7	127.2	27.1	135.5	15.7	141.1	7.3	127.3	4.0	120.9	4.5	103.8
Denbighshire	22.4	75.6	13.6	76.9	12.4	70.6	8.1	73.1	3.7	62.5	2.2	57.9	3.2	49.6
Flintshire	5.7	37.3	2.9	36.5	2.3	32.8	1.0	34.1	0.4	29.1	0.4	27.2	1.4	24.4
Glamorgan	52.5	344.9	31.7	393.7	25.5	368.9	9.1	355.4	3.5	231.7	4.1	201.1	8.7	141.0
Merioneth	23.1	42.8	15.9	39.0	12.7	35.2	9.1	35.5	3.7	30.0	2.0	27.8	2.6	24.9
Monmouthshire	2.0	35.1	1.5	35.2	1.0	26.9	0.5	25.0	0.6	14.1	0.9	14.4	0.6	9.3
Montgomeryshire	8.0	24.3	5.4	22.4	4.3	20.4	3.2	18.8	1.4	15.3	0.6	13.6	0.5	11.6
Pembrokeshire	9.8	28.3	6.5	27.4	5.0	26.2	3.3	25.5	1.4	23.2	0.8	21.8	1.0	19.5
Radnorshire	0.1	1.4	0.0	1.1	0.1	1.4	0.0	1.0	0.0	0.9	0.6	0.8	0.0	0.7
Wales	280.9	929.8	190.3	977.4	156.0	922.1	97.9	909.3	41.2	714.7	26.2	656.0	32.7	542.4

[1] Persons aged 3 and over speaking Welsh only.
[2] All persons aged 3 and over speaking Welsh.

Source: Office of Population Censuses and Surveys

56

data here used. This is the border area upon which our later discussion will focus.

An alternative method of summarising language change is presented in Figure 6.2. Each county graph reveals the proportions of monoglot Welsh and bilingual Welsh–English speakers by counties and over time, 1901–71. In some counties there was a considerable monoglot reservoir until the 1920s and 1930s (cf. Table 6.1) indicating the operation of two distinct processes of language change, the one being the sequential abandonment of Welsh, the other the acquisition and spread of English producing a predominantly bilingual population in traditional Welsh-speaking communities. However, there is a notable disparity between the patterns for the various counties, some of which have maintained an overall high proportion of people able to speak Welsh but have without exception suffered a continuous decline in the monoglot element, and in others of which it is the total Welsh-speaking population which is suffering the relentless decline, while the monoglot reservoir is practically non-existent.

Figure 6.2 clearly expresses the several different states of survival of Welsh in the major regions of the Principality, inviting inspection of the pattern in more detail. Few geolinguists would be content to abandon the inspection at this level of generalisation, and Welsh geographers have been fortunate, since the early decades of this century, to have been able to make use of the parish and ward unit as a basis for census information presentation on Welsh speaking. Plotted in Figure 6.3, they give a much more satisfactory impression of the language's distribution at the national scale. Upon the availability of such data has been built a considerable literature discussing the fortunes and future of Welsh at a national and regional scale (D.T. Williams 1937, J.G.Thomas 1956, Jones and Griffiths 1963, Bowen and Carter 1974, Pryce 1978b, and C.H.Williams 1978a and 1980c).

The features mentioned in association with Figure 6.1 may now be seen to greater advantage. At this level of information it could be said that the map ceases to be simply a means of data presentation and starts to become a tool for analysis. This may be seen especially clearly if we add a time element to the parish map and, instead of merely portraying the percentage of parish populations able to speak Welsh, show the extent of the decline (or, more rarely, the increase) in the proportion of parish populations who can speak Welsh between one census and the next (Figure 6.4). Rates of change vary over the national territory, and for geolinguists the fact that there are coherent and recognisable patterns justifies the time-consuming task of plotting parish and ward information. Amongst the most interesting features to emerge has been a zone, generally surrounding the 'core area' of the language as previously defined, where the rate of decline has been more rapid than average (i.e. over five per cent between the 1961 and 1971 censuses). The decline is frequently much more: in seven cases it was more than twenty per cent over the ten-year period. This 'zone of collapse', as it might be termed, has been given some particular attention, and surveys of

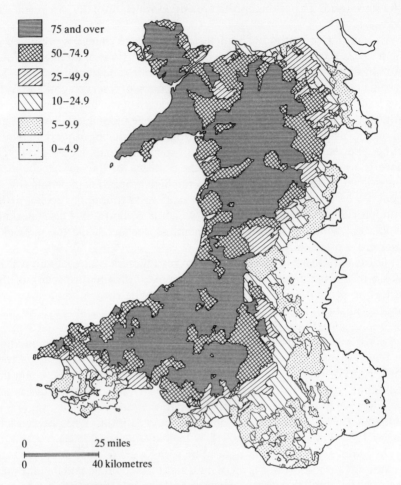

	75 and over
	50–74.9
	25–49.9
	10–24.9
	5–9.9
	0–4.9

0   25 miles

0   40 kilometres

Figure 6.3. Percentage of population aged three and over
able to speak Welsh, 1971.

attitudes to the Welsh language have indicated that in this zone there is a
degree of ambivalence concerning the importance of the survival of the
language (Thomas and Williams 1976 and 1977, Williams 1978b). At the
national scale the zone of collapse could be said to be a zone of uncertainty,
controversy and lack of unanimity concerning the language's future role;
and this is quite likely to exacerbate the rate of collapse.

The Regional Level
The first stage in the descent from the national scale examines a section of
the zone of collapse at a regional scale, taking some hundred parishes in the
Borderland country of Clwyd and Powys (until 1974 Denbigh, Flint and
Montgomery), and plotting their Welsh monoglot and bilingual populations

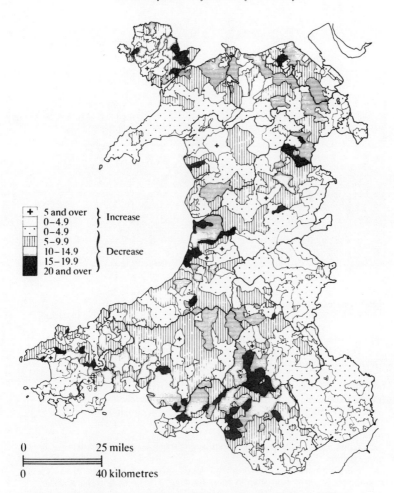

Figure 6.4. Change in percentage aged three and over able to speak Welsh.
by wards and parishes, 1961-71 (National decrease 5.2%).

as a proportion of their total populations. On the resultant graphs it is
possible to recognise a commonly occurring pattern of Welsh decline, with a
series of distinct phases, and to indicate, for the majority of parishes, at
which phase in this decline they stood in 1971 (Ambrose 1979). The phases
are outlined on Figure 6.5 and plotted cartographically on Figure 6.6. Levels
of Welsh-speaking ability may stay near a hundred per cent over a long and
uninterrupted period (though, as in the county graphs, the monoglot level is
continuously decreasing during this phase). Next, over a period of a few
decades in this border region, a rapid change of fortune seems to overtake
the language. There is a sudden crisis involving the whole numerical basis of
Welsh speaking within some parishes, while others nearby remain apparently unaffected, even though experiencing strongly similar economic, demo-

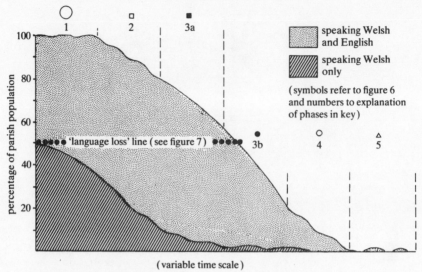

Key to phases of change:
1. With occasional exceptions, the whole parish population is able to speak Welsh. The 'monoglot reservoir' (speaking Welsh only) may occasionally approach half the population, but is declining rapidly.
2. The Welsh-speaking percentage fluctuates between 80 and 100. The monoglot reservoir has declined to 20 per cent or less.
3. The Welsh-speaking percentage is clearly in sharp decline, but more than half the parish population is still able to speak Welsh. The monoglot reservoir fluctuates between 1 and 10 per cent, or may be completely absent.
4. The Welsh-speaking percentage fluctuates between 1 and 20. The monoglot reservoir is usually less than 5 per cent, and may be completely absent.
5. Welsh speaking is sporadic or extinct and the monoglot reservoir non-existent.
? The parish in question does not fall clearly into any of the above categories. In some cases, parishes are in transition from one of these categories to another during the fifty-year period (1921–71) for which data were examined, and more than one of the symbols on the diagram appears on the map (figure 6).

Figure 6.5. Phases of change in Welsh speaking. Source: Reports on Welsh Speaking (Office of Population Censuses and Surveys) 1921-71.

graphic and other circumstances. As Figure 6.6. shows, the distribution of parishes in each phase is not a random one, but a series of narrow zones corresponding to the different phases may be seen. Such a pattern presents a problem, both for those seeking a coherent language-planning policy for the region and for the speakers themselves. The different circumstances occurring from one zone to another seem to demand distinctly different amounts of support for the language, whether this support be measured in terms of manpower or of financial expenditure. Further, when information from the 1981 Census is added to the graphs, it is likely to confirm what the examination of past figures has already indicated: that the successive zones are

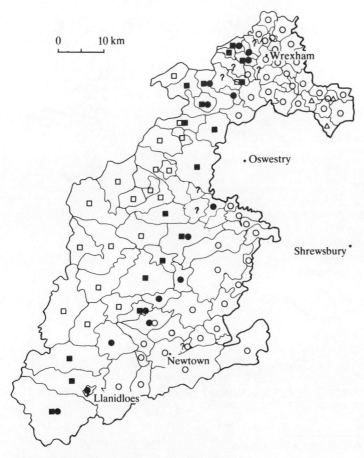

Figure 6.6. The 'zone of collapse' at a regional scale.
Symbols refer to phases of change shown in figure 6.5.

moving inward towards the core area of Welsh (Williams 1980c). Planning policies, as well as being variable from one part of the region to another, must be adaptable at short notice in order to accommodate the suddenly changing fortunes of the language in any locality.

As for individual bilingual Welsh speakers within the region, their predicament while the process of collapse is taking place may easily be imagined. All the usually clearly defined norms concerning the most appropriate choice of language for any given domain or relationship may be liable to sudden change over a short time and from one village to the next. In connection with the zone of collapse at the national scale, it has already been stated that an ambivalent feeling towards the survival of Welsh amongst those living in the zone is probably instrumental in hastening the language's disappearance. Now, at the regional level, it begins to become clear, as depicted in Figure 6.6, that most speakers, in pursuit of their daily or weekly

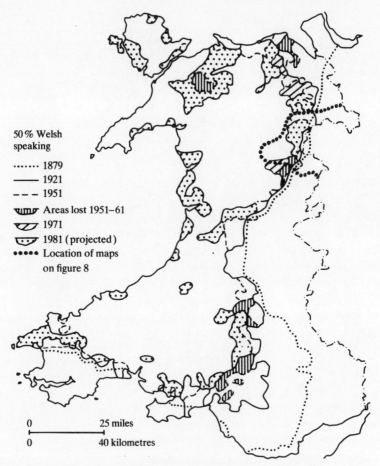

50% Welsh
speaking

······· 1879

——— 1921

– – – 1951

Areas lost 1951–61

1971

1981 (projected)

••••• Location of maps
on figure 8

0   25 miles

0   40 kilometres

Figure 6.7. Changes in the distribution of Welsh speaking, 1879-1981.

duties, must pass into areas where numerical conditions may be distinctly different from those immediately surrounding their home, and where quite different rules of usage may apply.

Figure 6.7 places the regional study area, for a moment, back into the context of the Welsh language area as a whole, and maps a feature which is closely associated with the phase of collapse: the decline of Welsh-speaking ability below fifty per cent of total parish populations (Williams 1980c). This may truly be said to mark the transition from a majority to a minority language locally. This point in the numerical change is taken to constitute the 'loss' of Welsh in the community in question, and further reference to the graph of change in Figure 6.5 shows that this is not too strong a term. The fifty per cent point corresponds with the central phase of collapse, and probably with the point at which confusion and demoralisation are at their peak. At this point many would-be speakers are likely to give up the language as a lost cause. The plotting of locations of parishes thus lost since 1951, along with those most likely to have suffered the same fate between 1971 and 1981 (Figure 6.7), shows one more aspect of the progress of the zone of collapse towards the centre of the language area.

The Limitations of Census Data at the Sub-Parish Scale

The figures from eight census reports on Welsh speaking have been the means of identifying those parts of the Welsh language area where the greatest numerical changes have taken place. The next step should be the detailed examination of the processes contributing to change, and for this purpose census data in their present form prove to be disappointingly ineffective. There are two main reasons for this. The first concerns the lack of data on the practice of Welsh speaking (as exemplified by its frequency of use by individuals when compared with English, or by the variety of circumstances in which it is used) as opposed to the mere ability to speak the language. Apart from the ability to read and write in Welsh, included for the first time in the census report on Welsh speaking in 1971 and discussed by Bowen and Carter (1975), no such data on Welsh use in practice are available from census sources. The numerical collapse in speaking ability recorded on earlier diagrams is almost certainly the final phase of a gradual weakening of the language's position, earlier stages of which may include a reduced frequency of use and a reduced fluency and confidence in the use of Welsh as an everyday medium of conversation. It could be proposed that the official statistics available represent only the *fait accompli* of change at the national and regional scale, without allowing the detailed examination of processes which might help to counteract such change; and that by the time numerical patterns reveal that the collapse has reached any particular area, effective counter-measures are already more difficult than they would have been had the problems been recognised earlier.

The second major deficiency in census data is particularly significant in the discussion of scale, since it is nearly impossible to obtain information on Welsh speaking in any more detail than that provided at the parish and ward level, because of confidentiality regulations at the Office of Population Censuses and Surveys (Robertson 1969, o.p.c.s. 1970-). Nearly impossible, because just one line of investigation remains: use of figures from a special tabulation at the scale of Enumeration District (e.d.), the unit used in the collection of census figures. The area marked in Figure 6.7, including a section of the zone of collapse, was chosen for a trial mapping of e.d. information, which appears in Figure 6.8. The upper map, using the more usual parish unit, is provided for comparison.

A casual inspection of Figure 6.8 might lead to the conclusion that a significant increase in detail has been achieved at e.d. level, but this is for the most part an illusion. There is certainly a proliferation of symbols on the lower map, particularly in urban areas such as Cefn (the area on the inset); but in respect of the linguistic processes at work, particularly those in the

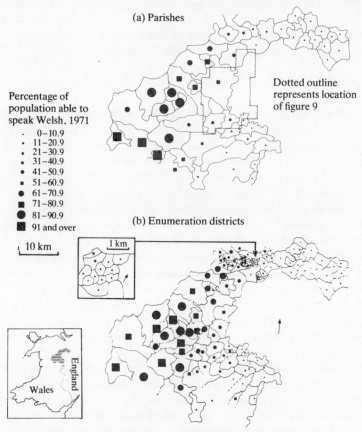

(a) Parishes

Dotted outline
represents location
of figure 9

Percentage of
population able to
speak Welsh, 1971

. 0–10.9
. 11–20.9
. 21–30.9
. 31–40.9
. 41–50.9
. 51–60.9
. 61–70.9
. 71–80.9
. 81–90.9
. 91 and over

10 km

(b) Enumeration districts

1 km

England

Wales

Figure 6.8. Census data: increase in detail provided by decreased mesh size.
(Broken lines indicate boundaries inadequately depicted or described on
census information, or for which incomplete information is available.)

zone of collapse, the exercise is disappointing. No additional conclusions
can be reached.

Numerical Language Ability at the Local Scale

It is at this point that most geographers part company with the pursuit of
detail, making a leap of scale – and also, frequently, of cultural context – to
sociolinguistic studies of the individual speaker, as for example in the
much-quoted work by Fishman (1965). It is frequently difficult to reconcile
information from such differing disciplines, and at such different scales; and
it was decided in this instance to attempt to produce maps of the distribution
of Welsh at an intermediate scale, for the area shown in dotted outline on the
upper part of Figure 6.8, and to show not only the numbers who can speak
Welsh, but also two aspects of its use in practice: the frequency and versatility of its use by speakers.

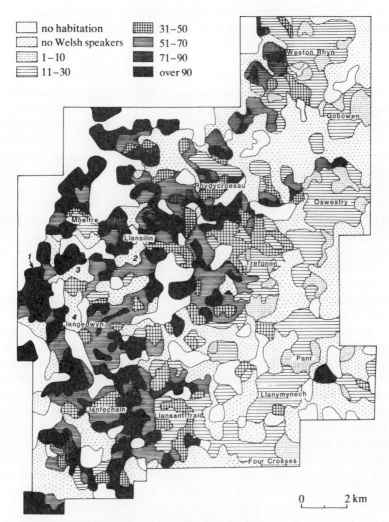

Figure 6.9. The local scale: percentage of households
with one or more persons able to speak Welsh, 1972.

Only when the results of the first part of this exercise are presented
(Figure 6.9) can the degree of generalisation in the language census be
appreciated. The map gives an impression of the complexity of the zone of
collapse as it must exist in other parts of Wales. While there is an overall
transition from west to east across the area, the most remarkable feature is
the great degree of fragmentation of the surface. If Figures 6.6 and 6.7 gave
the impression that the zone of collapse was a clearly-defined entity in
territorial terms, this enlargement tells a quite different tale, and one which
has rather different implications for the language-planning process. Some of
the many influences at work in the changing situation of Welsh may be

deduced from the map. In some places in the west (for example, at the point marked 1) may be seen remnants of the almost continuously Welsh surface, which, census data indicate, would have existed there even two decades ago. Now there are almost completely English pockets too. They correspond in some places with routeways (2 on the map), in others with hilltop small-holdings (3), and in still others with villages (4). The effect of these Anglicised pockets, interrupting, as they do, the more or less continuous Welsh-speaking surface, must be to reduce the confidence with which local people initiate Welsh conversation, and to interpose obstacles between groups of potential users of the language. Elsewhere on the map, as in the area stretching north-south between the villages of Gobowen and Four Crosses in the east, and in the market town of Oswestry, immigration of Welsh-speaking people produces a somewhat higher proportional Welsh ability than might be expected; and it is worth noting that since population densities are considerably higher in the east of the area than in the west, absolute numbers of speakers of the language are often as high as, or higher than, in other parts of the map (often over ten, and occasionally over fifty, per square kilometre).

The drawing of maps such as Figure 6.9 is one step; their analysis is quite another. A geographer's first reaction may well be to employ concepts of space, distance and density to seek answers to a number of questions. Is it the proportional or the absolute number of speakers which is more important? Is there a threshold number of speakers necessary to form a viable local speech group? Or does the continuance of the language relate perhaps to some crucial distance or density of speakers? There is, of course, no simple answer; were there one, the task of language planning would be considerably easier than it is. Many considerations, such as those of lifestyle,·ages, attitudes and perceptions of speakers, prevent generalisation. If it was imagined that the process of gradual enlargement of scale would solve those mysteries which existed at earlier levels of generalisation, that hope must be laid aside; it becomes clear that, far from being the final stage of geographical analysis, the large-scale map in Figure 6.9 is the beginning of a whole new phase of investigation, posing as many questions as it answers – questions which the existing data sources leave totally un-asked.

Local Patterns of Language in Practice
The difficulties in using numerical data on language ability, however detailed they may be, as a surrogate measure of language 'strength' or 'vitality', are reinforced when detailed patterns of Welsh use in practice are examined. If Figure 6.9 is compared with one showing the reported frequency with which speakers say they are able to use Welsh in their locality (Figure 6.10), this point is underlined. The darker the shading on Figure 6.10, the greater is the reported frequency of Welsh use in the area concerned.

As may be seen, there is a far from total correspondence between areas where Welsh speakers form a high proportion of the population and those

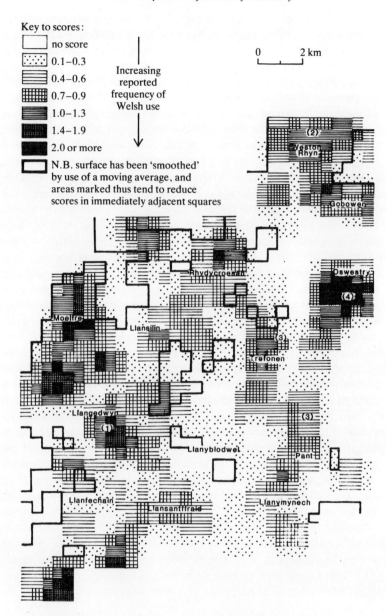

Key to scores:

☐ no score
▨ 0.1–0.3
▤ 0.4–0.6
▦ 0.7–0.9
▮ 1.0–1.3
▪ 1.4–1.9
■ 2.0 or more

N.B. surface has been 'smoothed' by use of a moving average, and areas marked thus tend to reduce scores in immediately adjacent squares

Increasing reported frequency of Welsh use

0   2 km

Figure 6.10. Average frequency scores for Welsh speaking. (A more detailed explanation of frequency scores may be found in Ambrose 1979.)

where the language appears to be used most frequently, though there are some places where the two coincide. At many points in the east where, according to the earlier map, fewer than thirty per cent – sometimes even fewer than ten per cent – of households have a Welsh speaker, there is an unexpectedly high frequency of use, apparently spontaneously generated in an area where the language might be assumed to be practically extinct. On the other hand, in a zone running down the centre of Figure 6.10, containing areas where over eighty per cent of households have a Welsh speaker, the potential for frequent use fails to be turned to account. Casual enquiry amongst speakers in the area elicits comments such as: 'It doesn't seem worth while using Welsh around here any more'. More systematic study of opinion on the strength and weakness of the language in various parts of the area reveals patterns far more complex than those which official statistics might lead the observer to expect (Ambrose 1979, chapter VII). All the evidence points to the part played in the local collapse by group uncertainty and lack of confidence in the future role of the language, corroborating the evidence at the regional and the national scale. A decreased faith in the role which should be allocated to the language seems to lead, in turn, to a decreased willingness – perhaps eventually even a decreased ability – to use it. Using census data, the whole area covered by this map was interpreted as suffering collapse, but the evidence at the local scale indicates a quite distinct set of sub-zonations within it. Under ideal circumstances each sub-area should receive quite a different language-planning approach; but realistically, even if Welsh ever becomes the subject of coherent planning proposals for language protection and development, it is difficult to imagine their ever reaching that level of sensitivity. As an attempt to produce evidence to corroborate the patterns for language frequency our enquiry took one further tentative step along the road of mapping Welsh use in practice: a series of maps was produced to show home locations of speakers who stated that they used Welsh in each of a series of daily situations (Figure 6.11). The idea was that if there were areas where, despite large proportions of potential Welsh speakers, the language was little used in practice, this lesser use might also be represented by a decreased variety of situations in which people would be willing to use it. The evidence in this case is far from conclusive, but it appears that each major activity of daily life produces its own geographical pattern of use. More importantly in this case if, as in the map at top right, a general map of the variety or versatility of Welsh use is constructed, a pattern is produced which tends to confirm that of speaking frequency as illustrated in Figure 6.10. The areas of greater and lesser variety of Welsh use are seen to coincide in few respects with the distribution which might have been predicted using the numerical pattern in Figure 6.9.

Scale and Interpretation; Concluding Remarks
It seems a salutary exercise, finally, to place the detailed study area back into the context of the Welsh language area as a whole (Figures 6.3 and 6.4), in an attempt to assess where this descent into detail has led. The attempt to draw and re-draw the patterns of language potential and practice at varying scales, producing as it does a series of contradictory patterns, may raise the understandable criticism that the evidence produced by geographers on the

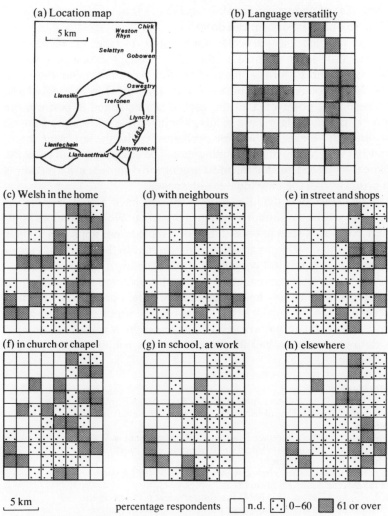

(a) Location map
(b) Language versatility
(c) Welsh in the home
(d) with neighbours
(e) in street and shops
(f) in church or chapel
(g) in school, at work
(h) elsewhere

5 km

percentage respondents ☐ n.d. ⋮ 0–60 ▨ 61 or over

Figure 6.11. Versatility of Welsh use. The shaded squares on (b)
represent areas where, on average, respondents used Welsh
in three or more of the above situations.

state of minority-language survival can be used in support of whatever case
the writer happens to find most convenient. The response is that the various
scales should be seen as complementary, rather than alternative, interpretations. There are considerable dangers in relying simply, for our impressions
of the state of survival of Welsh, upon one set of data generated once every
ten years. Even the evidence on whether Welsh is or is not a minority
language in any area has been seen to vary according to the scale at which
observation has been made; in any case the pure fact that the language is in a
numerical minority may not be particularly significant, since the evidence
has shown that the language is not necessarily 'safe' in places where over

69

eighty per cent of people can speak it, and that it is not necessarily 'lost' or 'dead' where only ten per cent can do so.

The scale problem has particular implications for language planners in their consideration, for example, of the zone of collapse. As seen in Figure 6.4, this may seem to form a 'linguistic buffer zone' protecting the more strongly Welsh core areas to the west. Examination at increasingly large scales has shown, however, that the zone is not equipped to perform the function effectively; it is an area in flux, where morale is low and where no two localities share exactly the same problems – quite the last place where the 'grand design' for language planning should be attempted – and yet at the same time the place in need of the most urgent and comprehensive measures for the protection of the individual Welsh speaker.

It can be concluded that the more ways we have at our disposal of assessing the position of minority languages such as Welsh, the more complex their position is seen to be and the more realistic our approach to their conservation and development is likely to become. In these days of expensive labour it is certainly not possible to produce detailed language maps for the whole of the language area, and most routine planning considerations in Wales will continue to rely heavily upon information provided by the language census. If, occasionally, these figures can be supplemented by information on the detailed patterns of language use by local speech groups, census data may perhaps be interpreted with new confidence and greater understanding.

References

Ambrose, J. E. (1979) *A Geographical Study of Language Borders in Wales and Brittany.* Unpublished ph.d. Thesis, University of Glasgow.

— (1980) Micro-scale Language Mapping: an Experiment in Wales and Brittany. *Discussion Papers in Geolinguistics 2.* North Staffordshire Polytechnic.

Betts, C. (1976) *Culture in Crisis: the Future of the Welsh Language.* Wirral, Merseyside: Ffynnon Press.

Bowen, E. G. and Carter, H. (1974) Preliminary observations on the distribution of the Welsh language at the 1971 Census, *Geogrl. J. 140*, 432-40.

Cartwright, D. (1980) Bilingual Districts: the Elusive Territorial Component in Canada's Official Languages Act. *Discussion Papers in Geolinguistics 1.* North Staffordshire Polytechnic.

Fishman, J. A. (1965) Who speaks what language to whom and when, *La Linguistique 2*, 67-88.

Jones, E. and Griffiths, I. L. (1963) A linguistic map of Wales, 1961, *Geogrl. J. 129*, 192-6.

Lewis, G. J. (1979) The geography of cultural transition: the Welsh Borderland 1750-1850, *The National Library of Wales Journal 21*, 131-44.

Office of Population Censuses and Surveys (o.p.c.s.) (1970-) *1971 Census Information Papers 1-5*, Titchfield, Fareham, Hants.

Pryce, W. T. R. (1978a) Welsh and English in Wales, 1750-1971: a spatial analysis based on the linguistic affiliation of parochial communities, *The Bulletin of the Board of Celtic Studies 28*, 1-36.

— (1978b) Wales as a culture region: patterns of change 1750-1971, *Transactions of the Honourable Society of Cymmrodorion* 1978, 229-61.

Robertson, I. M. L. (1969) The census and research: ideals and realities, *Trans. Inst. Br. Geogr. 48*, 173-87.

Thomas, C. J. and Williams, C. H. (1976) A behavioural approach to the study of linguistic decline and nationalist resurgence: a case study of the attitudes of sixth-formers in Wales (Part 1), *Cambria 3*, 102-24.

— (1977) A behavioural approach to the study of linguistic decline and nationalist resurgence: a case study of the attitudes of sixth-formers in Wales (Part 2), *Cambria 4*, 152-73.

— (1978) Language and nationalism in Wales: a case study, *Ethnic and Racial Studies 1*, 235-58.

Thomas, J. G. (1956) The geographical distribution of the Welsh language, *Geogrl. J. 122*, 71-9.

Williams, C. H. (1978a) *Language Decline and Nationalist Resurgence in Wales*. Unpublished ph.D. Thesis, University of Wales.

— (1978b) Cynllunio ar gyfer yr iaith yng Nghymru (Part 2), *Barn 180*, 2-5.

— (1978c) Some spatial considerations in Welsh language planning, *Cambria 5*, 173-81.

— (1980a) Ethnic separatism in Western Europe, *Tijdschr. Econ. Soc. Geogr. 71*, 142-58.

— (1980b) An ecological and behavioural analysis of ethnolinguistic change in Wales, in Giles, H. and Saint-Jaques, B. (eds), *Language and Ethnic Relations*. Oxford: Pergamon.

— (1980c) Language contact and language change: a study in historical geolinguistics, *Welsh History Review 10*, 207-38.

Williams, D. T. (1937) A linguistic map of Wales according to the 1931 Census, with some observations on its historical and geographical setting, *Geogrl. J. 89*, 146-51.

1989: There are clear signs that territorial considerations are entering the language planning and policy development process. In December 1988 the Welsh Office issued a circular to all County and District Authorities permitting them to take account of the needs of the language in their planning process. Specifically they advised that special attention could be given to the needs of Welsh in cases where (a) Welsh-speaking communities were likely to be threatened by undesirable developments; and (b) they were empowered to promote the use of Welsh as a distinctive characteristic of such communities. This legitimises the language as an issue for planning considerations, a feature which many planners, commentators and Cymdeithas yr Iaith Gymraeg have been pressing for a long time (Williams, C. H. 1978b).

Slowly and surely recognition is being given to the incorporation of Welsh into the agencies of both the central and local state. The vexed question now is to what extent having won the fight to legitimise Welsh we are faced with a more subtle reality, that the state agencies involved in the production and reproduction of Welsh are in reality agencies of social and cultural control. For as C. Williams (1987; 1988) and G. Williams (1987) warn the language may survive, but the culture, which is the real source of resistance, may atrophy and die.

Williams, C. H. (1987) Location and context in Welsh language reproduction: a geographic interpretation. *International Journal of the Sociology of Language 66*, 61-83.

Williams, C. H. (ed.) (1988) *Language in Geographic Context*. Clevedon: Multilingual Matters.

Williams, G. (ed.) (1987) The Sociology of Welsh, *International Journal of the Sociology of Language 66*, whole issue.

— (1975) The distribution of the Welsh language in 1971: an analysis, *Geography 60*, 1-15.

7. The Good Old Scots Tongue :
Does Scots have an Identity?

Though Scots people have for centuries written of Scots, spoken and written, as 'the Scots language' as if it had an identity of its own, they never appear to do so in the same breath as they talk of Gaelic, to which it is harder to deny the identity and status of a language. The first person I have noticed equating Scots and Gaelic in this way is, not too surprisingly, Hugh MacDiarmid in 1934, when he writes of 'English, Gaelic and Scots' (MacDiarmid 1934, p.182) or 'Scots, Gaelic, English' (p.186). Burns's reference in the *Address to the Deil* to 'Lallan tongue' and 'Erse' is not, I think, in the same spirit. Though it would not surprise me if I have missed other references from Scottish Renaissance writers, it is not until the 1970s that I know of frank declarations that Scotland is a multilingual nation in a number of allusions to its 'three languages' (Fraser 1974; Low 1974, p.21). The book *Languages of Scotland* (Aitken and McArthur 1979) was similarly the first ever, to my knowledge, to treat all three tongues on a more or less equal footing, though except for one article the treatment of Gaelic on the one hand and Scots coupled with English on the other is separate, which is how things have always been in the past.

So since MacDiarmid and especially recently, it appears that some of us have been thinking of Scotland as a multilingual country. I regret therefore to have to point out that according to the typology devised by William Stewart (1968), Scots qualifies as no more than a Dialect and neither as a Standard nor a Classical language. Using Stewart's terminology, its functions are marginal to the patterns of communication within the polity: in fact it has unquestionably only one of the functions (*literary*) which Stewart takes into his reckoning, unless we consider it has the *group* function within the working-class. As a spoken language it lacks 'standardisation'; it is heteronomous with – bound up in a sociolinguistic continuum with and constantly influenced by – Standard English, and therefore conspicuously lacking in the crucial attribute of 'autonomy'. It has indeed only two of the four 'attributes' used by Stewart in assessing language-type. It does possess the attributes of 'historicity' and, though perhaps questionably, 'vitality' – questionably, because by some definitions of Scots it could be said not any longer to be spoken by more than a tiny minority. This makes it what Stewart calls a Dialect.

Equally, of course, there is no sense at all in which Scots could count as a national or an official language according to the terminology proposed in the 1951 Unesco report on Vernacular Languages (Fishman 1968, p.689). In official pronouncements, the public media, advertising, religious services, even in oral use in public speaking, it is all but unheard of.

Scots is not, either, a medium of education or even, more than quite marginally, a school subject, and it is never learned, except in the most casual way, by foreign learners. As W. A. Craigie said about 1924: It has never been regarded as a necessary part of the education of any Scot that he should have even an elementary knowledge of the history of his own language and literature (Craigie *c.* 1924).

So it is not really surprising that Scots receives no formal official recognition whatever: it is not a language which is admitted by government authority to exist and towards which there exist some declared policy and specific official provisions, as there do towards the Celtic languages in the United Kingdom and Ireland or towards Frisian in the Netherlands. Even educationists, who confront Scots speech every day, have until this decade given it only the most cursory and passing attention, and that almost always hostile (Withrington 1974; Aitken 1979b, p.139; McClure 1980, pp.13–15). To be fair, some of the Scottish Universities have recognised since 1949 that there is a Modern as well as a Middle Scots, and Scots now exists as a minor sub-discipline in three of the Universities. And there has always been some, and recently more, research into Scots, centred especially in Edinburgh University (Aitken 1972 and 1979b).

Perhaps all this negativity or non-entity of Scots follows predictably enough from its past history. Down to the middle of the sixteenth century it had been gradually growing apart from the developing Standard English of England, the latter broadly a variety of London English; and for that period, the age of the Stewart Kings of Scotland and the Tudor Kings and Queens of England, it is often described as an autonomous 'full national language showing all the signs of a rapidly developing, all-purpose speech, as distinct from English as Portuguese from Spanish (etc.)' (Murison 1979a, p.9). 'As a spoken and written language [it] stood on a level with English', according to Craigie in 1921 (Craigie 1924, p.4); and many other similar assertions could be cited. But it could also be said and indeed has been said in effect by Gordon Donaldson (Donaldson 1961, pp.287–94) that its autonomy was never quite complete. For one thing it was commonly referred to by either of two names: one, *Scottis*, had been in use only since 1494 and was, as yet, less commonly used than the older name *Inglis* or 'English' which embraced the Anglo-Saxon vernaculars of both the Scottish and the English kingdoms. Thereafter the two names remained in competition: by the eighteenth century this competition was all but won by 'Scots' in the Lowlands but continues to this day in the Gaidhealtachd. In any case, between the Union of the Crowns in 1603 and of the Parliaments in 1707, whatever autonomy Scots had possessed disappeared and the situation which essentially is still with us came into existence.

Today the national and official language of Scotland is Standard English, shared with, and of course having originated in, England. Standard English, too, is the language of the literature most people mostly read. (The audience for serious Scottish literature is probably only a few thousand, though of course the Scots of the comic strip and comedian's patter has a huge audience, and serious drama in Scots is increasingly successful.) Standard English is also the language of all forms of what David Abercombie (1963) calls 'spoken prose'. In speech there is a continuum between varieties of Standard English, spoken either with R.P. or with more or less Scottish accents at one pole and non-standard Scottish dialects at the other pole.

Speakers with R.P. and other English accents are quite numerous in some places and their proportion of the total population has increased noticeably in this century: in 1971 (Census, 1971) 5 per cent of the population of Scotland (279,340 × 5.5 million) had been born in England, as against 1.5 per cent in 1851 and 3.2 per cent in 1911. R.P.-accented Standard English is the variety spoken universally by the upper class of the Scottish landed gentry; still favoured by the broadcasting media, though admittedly a little less so than, say, thirty years ago; and, perhaps since some time in the last century, the variety of greatest social cachet, albeit not universally liked by those who do not speak it themselves (Aitken 1979a, p.110).

But the accent spoken by most middle-class Scots is a different one. This middle-class Scots accent shares many, though by no means all, of its features with local working-class Scots speech; and its speakers also make very occasional use, some much more than others, and men more than women, of various sorts of Scotticisms of vocabulary and idiom and in some cases also of selectional form (see Aitken 1979a, pp.99–110). But these Scotticisms remain, in middle-class Scottish speech, only rare interlopers in the stream of Standard English. At the opposite pole of the continuum working-class Scots speakers offer a noticeably higher type and token frequency of lexical and especially formal Scotticisms (like *hame* and *doon* for *home* and *down*) and speak in accents marked by stigmatised features, some publicly recognised as stereotypes, others noticed and reacted to, but not identified, by other speakers. But the situation is a continuum, so there are intermediate varieties, much room for idiosyncratic variation, and much obvious inconsistency in performance. Both dialect-switching and what I have called style-drifting occur. And all varieties share a very large common core.

The three following passages illustrate the working-class end of the continuum. All are transcribed verbatim from tape-recordings made about 15 years ago.

1) Two speakers from Auchterless, Aberdeenshire:

Far wist e come fae?

Aboot e Black Hills. He wis feet it at big ferm i Yokies Hill, near Mintla.
Oh, a great big toon, e gid hame for orra man. There wis een i the horsemen
took ill an he had to tak e pair. Oh, he vrocht awaw. An the wis ae day at e
foreman an him they were gin to tak is ploo to e smiddy.

2) Speaker from Middleton, Midlothian:

Well that wis the case long ago, where a man always had tae have the two
horses in the hey time away tae Croalls i Shawfair – or – cairtin hey. Two
horses, one wi the half moon at the back, an the other wi the half moon at the
front. An the horse wis completely enclosed, in the twae cairts o hey. The back
o the furst yin, an the front o the second yin.

3) Speaker from Fraserburgh, Aberdeenshire:

For the month i April, May, June, July, August and September they caught
aboot two hundred thousand crans. So that's how the fishing is now by it was
when they startit in the sail-boat days.

Ignoring features of accent and considering only grammar, word-form, vocabulary and idiom, on a rough count I reckoned the first passage as containing thirty-five Scotticisms in seventy words, the Scotticisms fairly evenly distributed between content and function words and between idioms and distinctive cognate forms, with the rest common core items. So this passage differs from Standard English much more than the Nynorsk does from the Bokmål in the specimens in Einar Haugen's 1959 article 'Language Planning in Modern Norway' (Haugen 1959 in Fishman 1968, pp.685–6). But Aasen's Landsmål, as exemplified by Haugen, scores almost identically in its difference from Riksmål (twenty-six Landsmålisms in fifty-one words in the first paragraph). At any rate, the sort of Scots exemplified in the first passage is quite distinctive.

It is also very rare. You will see that the other two passages, which are more widely typical, score very much lower for distinctiveness. The general run of even working-class Scottish speech no doubt has a token frequency of Scotticisms comparable with the second and third passages – though I hasten to add that no-one so far as I know has as yet actually tried to count Scotticisms as tokens in passages of this sort. I would also guess that not many Scots, other than literary and philological pundits, command as extensive a repertory of non-literary Scotticisms as types as our speaker of the first passage does.

So the Scots speech which most people in Scotland hear most often is, in McClure's terminology (McClure 1979a, pp.29–31), quite 'thin' Scots, that is, it displays a low token-frequency of Scotticisms. In effect it is English spoken in some Scottish accent and with an occasional distinctively Scots form or word sprinkled through it. Most such Scots indeed contains far fewer and no more frequent Scots words and idioms than does the narrative prose of John Galt's *Annals of the Parish*. But most critics of the *Annals*, who include Douglas Young, David Murison and J. D. McClure, deny to this the designation Scots, calling it instead 'Scotticised English'. Now the habitual speech of many Scots today probably contains more distinctively Scots *forms* than Galt's narrative prose, like *hame* and *doon* as against *home* and *down*, but far fewer distinctive words and idioms. Should we not also then be labelling it Scotticised English rather than Scots?

This is my rough estimate of what Scots speech is like now. You may think it conforms to my assessment of its place in Stewart's typology and the Unesco symposium's terminology. You may even feel that our officials and educationists have been justified in granting it no different treatment from that commonly accorded to non-standard English elsewhere in Britain: that is, neglect, leavened by occasional denigration, especially of the urban varieties or some of their stereotyped features, and, conversely, nostalgic concern for the archaic and regional words and forms of the rural dialects. Over the past two centuries there have been many, though not always a majority, of those Scots who concerned themselves with such matters, whose position was very like this.

And yet some Scottish philologists and other Scots writers have either, like Craigie (*c*.1924, p.1), been willing to entertain the notion, or have positively argued, not only that Scots once was a national language on an equal footing with English, but that in some sense it still has, or ought to have, its own distinct identity as the national tongue of the Scots nation. To be sure, only one of those I am thinking of, Lord Brougham in his Installation Address as Chancellor of the University of Edinburgh in 1860 (Ramsay 1872, pp.89–90), actually states that Scots is 'a national language, used by the whole people in their early years, by many learned and gifted persons throughout life, and in which are written the laws of the Scotch, their judicial proceedings, their ancient history, above all, their poetry'. Brougham is echoed by J.Logie Robertson in 1878 (p.48). Later, in 1946, Douglas Young insists on 'the national status of Lallans' (Young 1946, p.3) and in 1979 Murison rates Scots and Standard English as 'two distinct historic speeches' (Murison 1979b, p.62).

These and other writers do seem to imply the identity of Scots. The trick is to begin by undertaking to dispel what they describe as a widespread popular misconception or 'the amount of nonsense talked about Scots' (Murison 1971, p.171; McClure 1980a, pp.12–13), to wit, that Scots is 'a mere dialect of English' (Young 1946, p.3) or merely bad English or 'Standard English corrupted by uneducable Scots' (Murison 1971, p.171) or corrupt English or slang (Templeton 1973, p.4), and, having denied this, then go on to say that none of this is true because Scots is not English at all: it is a separate language with its own distinct history. William Graham does this succinctly (1977, p.9): 'It is remarkable how many people regard Scots as merely a degraded form of Standard English, when the fact is that each is derived from a distinct dialect of the Germanic tongue.'

How far, one wonders, is the Scots whose separate origin is being extolled the same linguistic system as the Scots which is the subject of popular misconception. Just as one wonders, can the Scots which is one of 'Scotland's three great languages' be the same as the Scots one hears about one in the streets (against which, I hasten to say, I have no complaints)? Or perhaps it is what one reads in Scots literature, or maybe only some Scots literature? The fact is that the term 'Scots' has for long presented a chameleon-like character in use and that its users have been apt to conflate rather different applications of it. At times it is used for 'a group of low-prestige dialects' (McClure 1979b, p.93), at times for an archaistic literary variety, at times for the perfect Ideal Scots which if it is not ought to be, and at times for a conflation of two or three of these. In order to disambiguate this, in what follows I shall be introducing a few qualified terms of my own.

The principal arguments of those who have claimed some kind of separate identity for Scots have been its separate origin (the most common), as well as the copiousness of its distinctive vocabulary, and, less common, the great antiquity of its original separation from English. Among those who have argued on these lines have been John Jamieson in 1808, R. de B. Trotter in 1901, Douglas Young in 1946, Janet Templeton in 1972, David Murison in 1971, 1977 and 1979, William Graham in 1977. J. D. McClure in 1980 (Letter to *The Scotsman*, May 7, 1980) adds to this the possession by Scots of a non-dialectal literature (that is, it has a mainstream literary tradition represented by such writers as Burns, Scott and Hugh MacDiarmid, as opposed to 'dialectal' literatures in more localised forms of Scots); or, again, Scots 'is a rich and flexible language, with a large vocabulary and an abundance of expressive idioms' (McClure 1980a, p.12). Douglas Young in 1946 thought there was a case in that 'Lallans' was formerly a national and a copiously literary language (see Young 1946, p.9–10), and David Angus in 1980 points to the fact that there once was a national Standard of Scots (Letter to *The Scotsman*, May 7, 1980).

A. J. Aitken has added his mite to this (1976, pp.50–1). Although it is quite true that many of the features popularly supposed by Scots to be distinctive of Scots are in fact shared with the northern English of England though not with Standard English, there are many others, phonological, grammatical, and especially lexical, which are unique to Scots. Scots is a dialect island in Britain, and (I guess) the largest and most important bunch of isoglosses in Britain is that around the Scots–English Border. Some of Beat Glauser's findings on Borders vocabulary appear to support the view that Scots speakers have, recently at least, displayed greater dialect loyalty than their English neighbours across the Border. The following items are found in use just north of the Scots–English Border (and in Scotland generally of course): *ay* (always), *poke* (bag), *redd* v. (comb), *kame* (comb), *filler* (funnel), *ingan* (onion), *pooch* (pocket), *speeder* (spider), *steek* (stitch), *soop* v. (sweep), *twaal* (twelve), *gaed* (went), *kye* (cows), *shuin* (shoes), *een* (eyes), *nicht* (night). South of the Border only the Standard word is found. In most of these cases too it can be shown that northern English has only quite recently given up the 'dialect' word (Glauser

1974, pp.286, 292–3). Converse cases – of Scots having a Standard word and northern English a 'dialect' one – also occur, but much more rarely. (From what I have been and will be saying, of course, it would be natural to expect greater dialect loyalty from the Scots towards their national tongue than from the English towards their provincial dialect.) Judging from the contents of the *Scottish National Dictionary* – which, even leaving out the special case of Orkney and Shetland vocabulary, has upwards of 30,000 main entries, many of them with numerous sub-senses and idioms, and few marked obsolete – general and local Scots presents a very large list of distinctive word-types, larger than regional dialects such as those of England or the United States are likely to boast. The predominant part played by Scottish material in the *English Dialect Dictionary* also supports this. Unfortunately, Scots is let down as an autonomous language by the comparatively low token-frequency with which these numerous types are actually used in speech.

And Scots *does* possess an archaic literary variety of long history which is broadly standardised, as well as several other varieties of more recent origin based on various regional dialects and stereotypes. The orthography of literary Scots is also fairly standardised – admitting variation but strictly limited variation. In recent times Scots literature has ranged from sophisticated poetry by Hugh MacDiarmid to the dialogue of the comic strips of the D.C.Thomson and Outram presses and the stereotypes of the Scottish music-hall comic.

J.D.McClure (e.g. 1980a, p.12) has rightly stressed the great bulk, distinction and variety of Scots literature, which incomparably outshines any other of the English vernacular literatures, such as the dialect literature of the English regions, in both quantity, quality, celebrity and influence outside Scotland. This is certainly a very important plank in the platform of those claiming a distinct identity for Scots.

To some extent Scots has had its own philological discipline of Scots language since 1710 (Ruddiman 1710), which has lately flourished more than ever before, though perhaps less than we might think proper or desirable. In consequence, Scots has already been to some extent codified – certainly far more fully than any other non-standard vernacular of English (e.g. in Grant and Dixon 1921, *The Scottish National Dictionary*, Murison 1977, Graham 1977).

So Scots has all these attributes which have been thought to entitle it to claim the status of 'a language distinct from English' (McClure 1979b, p.97), or at least much more than that of a mere regional dialect. The English, it is true, do not accept this. The National Portrait Gallery in London has recently (1980) acquired a bust of Hugh MacDiarmid, who is described on the caption as a nationalist who often wrote in dialect. A Scot would have known to say 'in Scots'. On 24 April 1980 the newspaper *The Scotsman* carried a letter in slightly imperfect Lallans by the leading Scottish Nationalist, William Wolfe, arguing for more of the Scots leid on the wireless, including a daily news-reading in Scots: the caption read 'Scots ilk day on

B.B.C.' This brought a reply in excellent and copious Lancashire dialect, arguing that the latter shared all the attributes implied by Mr Wolfe for Scots and that both were equally dialects of English. But much earlier than this (*The Scottish Review*, 1907, 5, p.521) Professor W.W.Skeat pointed out 'how misleading it is to talk about "the Scots language"'. No doubt it would be possible to seek out still earlier dissentient English voices, between the sixteenth century (when they are first heard) and the present century.

But some Scots at any rate hold and have long held a different view. A favourable and defensive attitude towards something called variously Scots, our own tongue, our own language, our native language, our own dialect, broad Scots, Lallans, the Scots or Scottish tongue, the good Scots tongue, the old Scottish tongue, good old Scots, the Scots language and no doubt other terms I have forgotten, has been held by many Scots, and at times probably a majority of Scots, from the sixteenth century to the present. These attitudes have been expressed in writing by poets, novelists, authors of reminiscences, commentators on local life, literary historians, philologists and others. There are indications too that this attitude has not been confined to littérateurs like these, though I am afraid I can only offer hearsay evidence to this: but I take it that Long Rob of the Mill's celebrated defence of 'Scotch' in Lewis Grassic Gibbon's *Sunset Song* (1950 ed., p.123) is meant to typify the common man's position in this. The term 'Scots language' or 'Scottish language', is perhaps the term most often used, and sometimes, as in the title of John Jamieson's *Etymological Dictionary of the Scottish Language* (1808), this is intended to claim for Scots the standing of an actual or potential national language or, popularly, a 'language' rather than a mere 'dialect'. In section II (a), Works of Antiquarian Interest, of J.S.Woolley's *Bibliography for Scottish Linguistic Studies* (Edinburgh: James Thin, 1954), the name 'Scottish Language' appears in eleven titles as against different designations like 'the Scottish Dialect' or 'the Scoto-English Dialect' in only eight other cases. A number of publications of the present decade have implied similar claims in their titles (and of course in their content as well). In 1966 the University of Glasgow founded a lectureship which it elected to call a Lectureship in Scottish Language, and in 1976 a society founded in 1972 as the Lallans Society renamed itself as the Scots Language Society, and in neither case to the best of my knowledge did anyone protest or suggest that the denominations were preposterous. So there are and have been many Scots ready to dignify the national vernacular with the designation 'language'.

However, even when they uphold the claim of Scots to national language or national dialect status, virtually all commentators, philologists and laymen alike, immediately go on to, as we might suppose, sell the pass by revealing that the Scots people are failing to uphold their language as they should or have allowed it to fall on evil times or alternatively that they have allowed it to be encroached upon by the hostile tongue of the south. I interpret this as an admission that when we say portentous things about the

Scots language we are talking of an imaginary Ideal Scots which may perhaps have corresponded to something more actual in the recent or less recent past, but that the present reality of what Scots people actually now do falls in various ways short of this Ideal.

What the criterial characteristics of Ideal Scots are we learn partly from direct descriptions and partly by inference from accounts of the short-comings of actual Scots. An important characteristic is that Ideal Scots is consistently fully Scots: it possesses a large repertory of Scotticisms and selects them invariably and exclusively in preference to the corresponding Standard English options. It is homogeneous, maximalist, consistent, pure. A leading complaint about what I shall be calling Bad Scots is that it is not homogeneous. So when Duncan McNaught in 1901 (p.27) tells us that 'nine-tenths of so-called modern Scots is a concrete of vulgarised, imperfect English, in which are sparsely embedded more or less corrupted forms of the "lovely words" with which Burns wove his "verbal magic"', we conclude that Ideal Scots is the opposite of this: *it* is not imperfect English and lovely words are *not* sparse in it.

As well as being homogeneous, Ideal Scots is also very conservative. Morphological innovations are disallowed. Murison well indicates both these requirements – homogeneity and grammatical conservatism – in his textbook *The Guid Scots Tongue* (Murison 1977, p.56): 'Modern Scots rarely matches up to the description and criteria we have been prescribing [*sic*] above. Like dialects everywhere, it is under the severest pressure from the standard language and is rapidly losing its historic forms and structure through constant confusion with the official speech. Scots and English forms are jumbled up haphazardly so that a clear and consistent pattern can no longer be traced, and a systematic grammar has gone out of the window.'

People who have very good Scots and speak good or rich Scots (as commented on by Dean Ramsay (e.g. 1872, p.87), W.A.Craigie (1924, pp.16–18), and many since) approach these Ideals. Of course it is true that English and other dialectologists often speak approvingly (Harold Orton and Stanley Ellis, for example) of 'good speakers' of English dialect in the same way. 'Good' English dialect too is meant to be homogeneous and conservative.

But, as everyone agrees, Scots is unhappily falling away from this perfect condition of Ideal Scots. It is evanescent (George Paton, 13 May 1776, in *Percy Letters 6*, 133), decaying (Hugh Haliburton in *Scottish Rev.* 1907, p.522), receding (Craigie 1924, p.10), declining (Craigie 1924, p.12), dying or dying out (Craigie 1924, p.12), or going out as a spoken tongue every year (Cockburn (1838) in 1874, 1, p.189), while apparently still vigorous in written use. This belief could be exemplified in hundreds of quotations between 1776 or earlier and now. More colourful metaphors have also been employed: Scots, it is said, is being 'bludgeoned out of existence' (W. Will in MacDiarmid 1926, p.239), is undergoing 'hammering and attrition' (Murison 1979b, p.59), or is 'suffocating under a mountain of ignorance and prejudice' (McClure 1978, p.1). The malign influences responsible for this may be identified. 'What "the mail-coach and the Berwick smacks" have left undone', says J. H. Millar in 1903, quoting Lockhart's *Life of Scott* (Millar 1903, p.314), 'has been achieved by the railroad and the locomotive'. In 1960 the minister of Old Deer (in *Third Statistical Account*) singled out the travelling cinema as the chief enemy. Maurice Lindsay (1962, *Preface*) was incautious enough to allege that 'during the 50's the Scots tongue receded more rapidly than ever before under the impact of television and has now been reduced to a mere matter of local accent'. Both David Murison and J. D. McClure are very severe on the Scottish Education Department (Murison 1979b, pp.59, 62; McClure 1980a, p.13f.), even though that Department has existed only since 1872 and the alleged diminution of Scots is constantly mentioned long before then. The 'big battalions of state and bureaucracy, press, radio, television, education, social cachet' are of course often mentioned (Murison 1979b, p.59 and compare Murray 1873, *Preface* and Craigie 1924, p.12). Less metaphorically, what all this presumably means is that the number of distinctive Scottish lexical types in use by Scots is declining, and also, presumably, that their frequency of use as tokens is going down. Fewer Scotticisms are being used less often by fewer people. To some degree and in some ways this is doubtless true.

This process of dying out of Scots is often felt to be inevitable and sometimes desirable (*Third Statistical Account*, 1962, Dumfries, p.112). Whether this is so or not, statements about it are commonly accompanied by regret that as Scots dies, so in consequence 'many fine old words which once salted and adorned conversation' (*Third Statistical Account*, 1964, Ashkirk, Roxburghshire) will no longer be heard and that we will lose 'countless expressive phrases with no exact equivalent in Standard English' (Craigie 1924, p.24) or many 'soft and beautiful words untranslateable into any other language' (Oliver 1902, p.12); sometimes these are exemplified, e.g. 'westlin and eastlin winds, loaning for lane, yestreen in the gloaming' (Oliver 1902) or 'compluther, devaal, go by and re-by' (*Third Statistical Account*, 1964, Ashkirk). Of these only *compluther* may now in fact be obsolete. The delightfulness of the threatened words and expressions, which is regularly stated, is presumably a consequence of the fact that they are stylistically marked for Standard English speakers or in a situation in which Standard English is the unmarked variety; whether they would carry the same overtones in an exclusively Scots-speaking situation seems doubtful. The idea that there is a threat to the existence of 'many ancient and emphatic terms, which now occur only in the conversation of the sage of the hamlet, or are occasionally mentioned by him as those which he has heard his fathers [*sic*] use' (Jamieson 1808, p.vii) goes back to 1768 or earlier (Aitken 1979a, pp.16–17 [note 6]). All this stuff has a strangely timeless quality about it. This particular notion is repeated many times thereafter; also, for example, by Dean Ramsay in 1858 or Lewis Grassic Gibbon as Long Rob of the Mill in 1932. Whether this myth was true when it was first invented (whenever that was), or merely due to faulty generalisation from observed differences in the vocabularies of a few contemporaries, I do not know. It is now a very firmly held and constantly repeated belief, despite the fact that some of us are given to pointing out that if Scots has been dying since, say, 1768, it is taking a long time about it. I agree with Craigie in his 1921 lecture (1924, pp.15–18) that the experiments which purport to prove the dwindling of Scots by comparing the knowledge of selected vocabulary items of speakers of different generations are fallacious (see Will 1930 for a report of one such experiment).

As well as allegedly declining internally, externally Scots is being used by fewer Scots less often. Statements to this effect exist from the eighteenth century onwards, particularly that it is being abandoned by 'the higher and better educated classes', or that it is only now heard 'in the more retired parts of the country' (Ramsay 1872, pp.91–2), and so on. There is, I dare say, some truth in this.

How does one explain this long-standing and abiding interest in and concern for the diminution of the old national tongue and its encroachment by the language of the more powerful nation to the south? I suppose it is relevant to this that *not* all Scots or even most Scots are much concerned in this way, though many of course have heard about it and feel a lukewarm concern – often confused with more or less opposite attitudes due to the current sociolinguistic situation of Scots. The misconception that Scots is merely a corrupt dialect of English has been held since some time in the eighteenth century at least, and hostile feelings towards Scots are frequently very strongly expressed between about 1750 and 1850. About the middle of this period a desire for the total extinction of modern Scots was the normal establishment position (Aitken 1979a, pp.96–7). As late as 1845 the minister of Kelso wrote that his parishioners 'speak the Scottish tongue in the most Doric of its forms; nor does there appear any prospect of a speedy improvement in this particular' (*New Statistical Account*). That this hardheaded, practical attitude to Scots continues – after all, the *useful* dialect in our society is Standard English – is shown *inter alia* by the continuation into the nineteenth (*Scotticisms corrected* 1855) and the present century (Masson 1929, pp.40–52) of the old tradition launched in 1752 of publishing lists of Scotticisms for Scots to learn to avoid (Aitken 1979a, pp.96 and 117 [note 7]).

Conversely, those Scots who are unhappy or distressed at the steady reduction of the lexical resources of Scots and its encroachment by English are no doubt a different breed from those we have just been considering, a backward-looking, soft-headed lot – antiquarians, poets, philologists, schoolmasters a lot of them, whose business is old forgotten far-off things, not the practical economic issues of the present day. When, between the sixteenth and the eighteenth centuries, actual and Ideal Scots as it were parted company, some Scots people of this kind resented the submergence of 'gueed auld Scots', the Scots' 'ain leid', by the tongue of the nation to the south: these people included Alexander Ross (1768) (see Aitken 1979a, pp.95 and 117 [note 6]) and the author of 'An Address in Scotch on the decay of that language' (1788 in Shirrefs 1790, pp.xxiv–vii). They looked back to a happier time when Scots was both autonomous and unmixed with 'Southren gnaps', when all Scots was Ideal Scots. Adherents of Ideal Scots then and since have been encouraged by the presence of surviving national institutions of local government, law, the church and the rest, and the persisting concept of Scottish nationhood sustained within the long-standing disciplines of Scottish history, literature and philology. These have reinforced the notion of a *national* tongue, one which bears the nation's name – something that no mere provincial dialect of England can claim.

It is almost certainly also true that more people have felt more strongly about the plight of Scots in this century and particularly since Hugh Mac-Diarmid than ever before. No doubt many of those have been Scottish Nationalist activists and sympathisers, such as MacDiarmid himself and some of the other authors cited in this paper. The increased concern for the Scots language is in this and no doubt in other ways thus linked with the expansion of political Scottish Nationalism since the First World War.

The beliefs I have been considering are apparently free of social comment or value judgement, except that the facts they allege are mostly held to be regretted. Another body of comment on the fallen state of Scots does introduce social prejudice and other value judgements.

I mentioned that in the second half of the eighteenth century most of the Scottish establishment viewed Scots as a 'very corrupt dialect of the tongue we make use of' (David Hume 1757, in Smith 1970, p.107). This disapproval of Scots by the intelligentsia and the middle classes at this period is also sometimes stated in explicitly social terms. In 1763 James Boswell attended a tea-party in London where he met some fellow-Scots. Complaining of 'the common style of company and conversation' and the 'coarse gibes of this *hamely* company', he felt that 'the Fife tongue and the Niddry's Wynd address were quite hideous' (Boswell 1952, p.120). Again, in 1800 James Sibbald describes 'Scottish' as 'the familiar dialects of the meanest vulgar' (Sibbald 1802, 4, p.xlv); and for other evidence of a middle-class feeling, dating from 1710 onwards, that Scots was 'the language of the common people' rather than of 'the more polite people', see Aitken 1979a, pp.93–8.

Quite early in the nineteenth century, however, the establishment, influenced no doubt by the work of Burns, Scott and other writers in Scots, by the revelation provided by John Jamieson's *Dictionary* (1808), and by the expansion of Scottish antiquarian and historical research from Register House, the publishing clubs and the Universities, seems to have revised some of its views on Scots and begun to regard it with nostalgic regret for a dying but richly expressive tongue. At the same time the social rejection of Scots is on occasion ruefully commented on (e.g. Cockburn 1874, 2, p.302, in 1853; see p.87 below). More recently this lack of social prestige has been seen as a serious problem by would-be restorers of Scots of our own time, such as W. A. Craigie (*c.*1924, p.25), David Murison (1971, pp.178–9;

1979b, pp.58–9), J.T.Low (1974, pp.17, 25; etc.) and J.D.McClure (1974, pp.68–9; 1980a, p.16; etc.). 'We have to find means,' says Low in 1974 (p.26), 'of breaking the social-status barrier. If Scots were to regain something of status in society, the problem of teaching and encouraging it in schools would lessen considerably.' The means most often suggested for breaking this barrier are to encourage more teaching and study of Scots in schools and Universities (e.g. Craigie 1924, pp.37f.; McClure 1974, pp.68–9; Aitken 1976, pp.52–5; McClure 1979b, p.94). In this way Scots would be given the respectability due to its long independent history and that of a serious subject of academic study. Ignoring the circularity of this whole argument, one may agree with the great desirability of such a course of action, while continuing to doubt whether it can conceivably have more than the slightest effect on powerfully entrenched social attitudes. The same motivation seems to lie behind a proposal which appears to have been made more than once early in the present century for founding University chairs in Scots for its 'preservation' (see p.87 below). Though the details require qualification since attitudes vary among different social groups and since individuals hold apparently ambivalent or self-contradictory positions, it is of course true enough in broad terms that many Scotticisms are of generally low repute in spoken use, albeit some of these are perfectly acceptable in traditional literary environments (for amplification and any necessary correction of this point, see the forthcoming studies by K.I.Sandred and I.K.Williamson briefly mentioned in Aitken 1979b, p.148).

As we noted a moment ago, many eighteenth- and nineteenth-century commentators on Scots appear to associate any kind of Scots indiscriminately with the lower orders. By the nineteenth century, some commentators are aware of more than one sort of Scots: one sort, it is hinted, is more vulgar? and so? less attractive? than another sort. In 1800 John Ramsay of Ochtertyre launched the myth of an 'old court Scots' of the Scottish gentry at the time of the Union Parliament which 'differed as much from the common language as the language of St. James's from that of Thames St.' (Currie 1800, 1, pp.280–2). In 1814 Walter Scott alludes to 'broad Scots of the most vulgar description' (*Waverley* ch.39). In 1818 he took up Ochtertyre's myth, as the Duke of Argyll speaking (c.1740) of Lady Staunton's Scots: 'You must suppose it is not the broad coarse Scotch that is spoken in the Cowgate of Edinburgh, or in the Gorbals. This lady . . . speaks that pure court-Scotch, which was common in my younger days; but it is so generally disused now, that it sounds like a different dialect, entirely distinct from our modern patois' (*Heart of Midlothian* ch.48). Then in 1827 he narrated an anecdote of his own, parallel to that on which Ramsay founded his myth (for this and other references see Craig 1961, p.315). This belief is occasionally revived (e.g. in *Scottish Rev.* 1907, p.540); I have heard it asserted more than once myself.

In still more recent times many of the commentators who are given to lamenting the decline of Scots themselves decry certain varieties of current

Scots speech, in fact those very varieties which the great majority of their compatriots actually speak. The model of Scots speech most commonly expressed in print (and in middle-class and educated spoken comment) in this century comprises three different varieties: Standard English, accepted by everyone (so long as pronounced in an acceptable, that is, not a fully urban working-class, accent); what I will call Good Scots, professedly approved (in the abstract) by many of those who discuss it, though perhaps less universally and wholeheartedly accepted when heard from speakers unprotected by a middle-class accent; and Bad Scots, which nearly all commentators between 1900 and very recently excommunicate.

This model seems to have been the one favoured by Scottish educationists until recently and it appears in a number of mid-century Scottish Education Department reports (Aitken 1979a, pp.98–9; 1979b, p.139). A number of adherents of the model locate Bad Scots in Glasgow, others equate it with urban working-class speech more generally. Several, including David Murison, refuse to dignify Bad Scots with the name of Scots at all: this is in print; in oral communication this attitude (that Bad Scots is no Scots) is very commonly expressed. One writer in 1901 (Trotter, pp.23f.) describes Bad Scots as a 'wonderful gibberish which now passes current for Scotch', spoken by the young in Glasgow and so likely to replace completely the Scotch (apparently Good Scots) of their parents in 30 years. In 1907 the editor of *The Scottish Review* (p.540) distinguishes between 'the way in which most people in Scotland talk today' which is 'in the main misspelt and mispronounced English' and 'what we may call *classic* Scots – the speech full of racy idioms and felicitous words, a speech in which great literature has been produced, and which in certain landward parts is still spoken'. In 1915 John Buchan (in his Preface to Violet Jacob's *Songs of Angus*) distinguishes Good and Bad Scots. Violet Jacob's Scots, he says, 'is good Scots, quite free from misspelt English or that perverted slang which too often nowadays is vulgarising the old tongue.' (The 'old tongue', itself, is presumably Ideal Scots.) (Cited in Young 1946, p.24). In 1971 Murison describes Bad Scots as a 'debased industrial variety which, as we have seen, can hardly be described as Scots – we must guard against the all too frequent assumption that any form of speech used in Scotland that is not standard English is *ipso facto* Scots' (He has forgotten Gaelic, of course.) (Murison 1971, p.178: compare also his description of current Scots cited on p.80 above).

This position, perhaps most explicitly expressed by Murison in the previous quotation, that Bad Scots is no Scots, evidently arises because Bad Scots fails to measure up to the requirements of Ideal Scots. It is a position which seems to approach very close to the 'popular misconception' already mentioned (p.76 above), namely, that there is no such thing as Scots, that Scots is merely bad English, a 'misconception' which Murison himself and others find it necessary to repudiate quite firmly. The latter misconception presumably arose because popular observers noted little that was distinctively Scots about actual Scots speech and noted at the same time that it contravened the established prescriptive norms of 'correct English'. And these popular observers failed to bring into their reckoning Ideal Scots, which for them, after all, exists at best only as an ideal. Yet the two positions – that Bad Scots is no Scots, strongly asserted by some protagonists of (Good) Scots, and, on the other hand, that there is no such thing as Scots, equally strongly repudiated by the same protagonists of Scots – do seem to come perilously close, and no doubt for many others they merge.

So we have on the one hand Good Scots spoken, according to Murison (1977, p.62) '*diminuendo* in familiar circles, especially in the outlying areas', and Bad Scots spoken in the industrial areas, 'but one may question how far it is Scots at all and not merely a kind of broken English', says Murison (Murison 1977, p.56). According to this view, it seems, we have Good or Ideal Scots spoken if at all only in remote parts in a diminished way, and Bad Scots – really non-Scots, according to Murison and the others – which is the Scots that the majority of Scots actually speak.

The shibboleths of Bad Scots are itemised and exemplified in a number of sources, most fully in Trotter 1901, also in Murison 1977, pp.56–7. They turn out in fact to be the well-known stereotypes of urban working-class Scots speech, which do indeed include some distinctively Scottish features of vocabulary, word-form and grammar as well of course as others common to non-standard English generally (currently the fullest single description of the features of working-class as against middle-class Scots speech is in Aitken 1979a, pp.102–4, 108–10, and notes on p.118). And of course Good Scots is just Ideal Scots under another name or the nearest we get to Ideal Scots in this imperfect world. It has or should have a fairly high token frequency of Scotticisms – it will not be the 'watered down version of Trongate Glesca' deplored by Murison (1971, p.177), it will contain few or none of the Scots and general non-standard vulgarisms of lexicon or grammar which exist in working-class non-standard dialects of English, and it will display a low incidence of the pronunciation features which are among the shibboleths of Bad Scots.

Now I must have deeply disappointed you by failing to prove that Scots has an identity. One crucial lack is that of autonomy from Standard English. This applies to actual Scots, of course. Ideal Scots is by definition autonomous, since it is homogeneous or pure. But as for actual Scots, many of its attributes and the phenomena surrounding it differ not much in kind from those of provincial regional dialects of England, as the denigrators of Scots have always said.

Yet the Scots linguistic situation does contain one unusual? extraordinary? attribute, in both degree and kind, in the elaborate and copious mythology we have been considering, which has grown up around the good old Scots tongue since it ceased to be a national language and which appears to have as many or more enthusiastic adherents today than it ever had. The fundamental tenet of this mythology is that there really exists a distinctive and noble national Scots language, however diminished or debased this may be today, and that this once existed in its full glory, let us say before the diaspora.

Since this is 'the national tongue' (Craigie 1924, pp.16f. *passim*), and 'has a national value' (Craigie 1924, p.11) and its effacement will imply 'a denationalization of the Scottish people' (Craigie 1924, p.20), and since its use is 'an assertion of Scottish identity' (McClure 1980a, p. 18) it should be restored to spoken use and given official status. That it can be so restored we may see if we look at the exampes of Norwegian, Frisian, Catalan and various other languages which have had reputedly successful revival movements. If this restoration is not carried out, the Scots will end in the humiliating position of being unable to read their national literature without a glossary – a fear that has haunted us for a century and a half now (e.g. 1844 in Cockburn 1874, 2, pp.88–9; *Scottish Rev.* 1907, p.540) – the lexical riches of a 'rich, euphonious and expressive tongue' (Craigie 1924, p.25) will have perished, and the Scots will have been still further divorced from their native linguistic and cultural roots. The people whose ideas I am travestying are three distinguished colleagues: William Craigie in 1921 (Craigie 1924), David Murison in 1971 and 1977, Derrick McClure in 1978 (McClure 1980a) and 1979 (McClure 1979b).

These ideas for the restoration of Scots belong to the present century. Before then the decline of spoken Scots seems always to have been regarded as natural and inevitable, albeit, from some time in the nineteenth century, also sad. In 1853 Lord Cockburn, commenting on the formation of a new 'National Association for the Vindication of Scottish Rights', stated that 'the gradual disappearance of the Scottish accent and dialect is a national calamity which not even this magniloquent association can arrest' (Cockburn 1874, 2, p.296). Later in the same year, with reference to the Association's first meeting, he asks: 'how can we retain our language respectably after it has become vulgar in the ear of our native gentility?'; but adds resignedly 'This is all very sad, but it is the natural course' (Cockburn 1874, 2, p.302).

But in 1901 (McNaught 1901, p.20) and 1907 (*Scottish Rev.* 1907, p.22) we hear of suggestions for establishing university chairs for the preservation of Scots, still not quite dead, it was agreed, and a suggestion for concocting a 'classical vernacular' out of the dialects: neither of these, needless to say, came to anything. Somewhat later Hugh MacDiarmid (e.g. Grieve 1926, pp.315–6; MacDiarmid 1934, pp.185–6) and Douglas Young (1946, 1949) put forward equally vague suggestions for strengthening literary Scots ('Synthetic Scots' or 'Lallans') by enriching its vocabulary and employing it in narrative prose as well as verse.

The proposals of the philologists whom I mentioned first, Craigie, Murison and McClure, are rather more far-reaching. The first two give as at least one of their leading motives for wishing to 'restore' Scots that of halting the decline of the spoken language, but in fact the prescriptions of all three are directed primarily to the written language and various forms of pedagogy. So are their expedients for giving back social respectability to Scots (p.84).

J. D. McClure hopes to persuade the Scots to extend the range of Scots prose into general purpose and utilitarian prose and urges further prescriptive codification of Scots. But he feels that we will need to exert unremitting pressure to see that progress is continued. One step in this direction has already been taken in the shape of the magazine *Lallans*, the journal of the Scots Language Society, dating from 1973. This is written almost entirely in Scots, and mostly Good Scots or Ideal Scots at that, including prefaces, reviews and notices of meetings and competitions. As McClure says, the resistance met by this sort of thing now – and there are many people who find all this preposterous and unnecessary – would quickly disappear as people accustomed themselves to it. I would not like to deny value to this, both as an interesting development in the Scottish literary tradition and as helping a little to counter existing prejudice against any native Scots spoken forms.

But it does seem to me a round-about, laborious and in the end unrealistic way of tackling what I see as the real linguistic ills of the Scottish people, which are those of other socially disfavoured non-standard varieties, namely linguistic intolerance. (Apart from the many writings on this for English in general by social dialectologists such as William Labov and Peter Trudgill, see the following in the Bibliography to Aitken 1979b for comments on this subject in the Scottish setting: Trudgill 1974; Macaulay 1974, 1975, 1976 and 1977; Aitken 1976 and 1979a.) I find it impossible to believe that what McClure hopes for could possibly happen either without compulsion or in continued competition with Standard English, as he claims.

But anyway, Murison says all this is up to the Scots themselves (Murison 1979b, p.62): '[Scots] cannot be restored until the Scots know what it is and want it so' (Murison 1977, p.62). Does this mean: until they know the rules of Ideal Scots and want their Scots to be Ideal Scots?

McClure, it appears, has a gradualist plan for restoring Ideal Scots to the Scots people by unremittingly extending its range (and, one hopes, popularity) in the written medium, presumably with a spin-off one day to the spoken tongue. Murison appears to await the day when the Scots will undergo a spontaneous conversion to Ideal Scots by a kind of Pauline revelation.

And yet if, by some chance, such as political independence for Scotland, we did achieve political conditions which favoured a revival of Ideal Scots, we still possess at least one useful prerequisite of this – the mythology of an imaginary Ideal Scots, passionately believed in by some, more vaguely and inconsistently entertained by many.

References

Abercrombie, D. (1963) Conversation and spoken prose, *English Language Teaching 18*, No. 1. Reprinted in *Studies in Phonetics and Linguistics*. Oxford 1965.

Aitken, A. J. (1972) The present state of Scottish Language studies, *Scottish Literary News* (Association for Scottish Literary Studies) March 1972, pp.34-44.

Aitken, A. J. (1976) The Scots language and the teacher of English in
    Scotland, in *Scottish Literature in the Secondary School*, pp.48-55.
    Edinburgh: Scottish Education Department.
— (1979a) Scottish Speech: a historical view, in Aitken and McArthur
    (1979) pp.85-118.
— (1979b) Studies on Scots and Scottish Standard English today,
    in Aitken and McArthur (1979) pp.137-58.
Aitken, A. J. and McArthur, T. (1979) *Languages of Scotland*.
    The Association for Scottish Literary Studies Occasional Papers
    No. 4. Edinburgh: Chambers.
Boswell, J. (1952) *Boswell's London Journal 1762-1763*.
    London: Reprint Society.
Cockburn, H. (1874) *Journal, 1831-1854*. Edinburgh:
    Edmonston and Douglas.
Craig, D. (1961) *Scottish Literature and the Scottish People 1680-1830*.
    London: Chatto & Windus.
Craigie, W. A. (1924) The Present State of the Scottish Tongue (1921),
    in *The Scottish Tongue, A Series of Lectures on the Vernacular
    Language of Lowland Scotland*, by W. A. Craigie, John Buchan,
    et al. London: Cassell.
— (c.1924) *The Study of the Scottish Tongue*. MS. lecture,
    penes A. J. Aitken.
Currie, J. (1800) *The Works of Robert Burns*. London.
Donaldson, G. (1961) Foundations of Anglo-Scottish Union, in
    *Elizabethan Government and Society: Essays Presented to Sir John
    Neale* (ed. S. T. Bindoff), pp.283-314. London: Athlone Press.
Fishman, J. A. (1968) *Readings in the Sociology of Language*.
    The Hague, Paris: Mouton.
Fraser, K. C. (1974) The Rebirth of Scots, *Scotia Review 6*, 32-5.
Glauser, B. (1974) *The Scottish-English Linguistic Border: Lexical
    Aspects*, The Cooper Monographs. Bern: Francke Verlag.
Graham, W. (1977) *The Scots Word Book*. Edinburgh:
    Ramsay Head Press.
Grant, W. and Dixon, J. M. (1921) *Manual of Modern Scots*.
    Cambridge: University Press.
Grieve, C. M. (1926) *Contemporary Scottish Studies: First Series*.
    London: Leonard Parsons.
Haugen, E. (1959) Language Planning in Modern Norway,
    Anthropological Linguistics 1, 3, pp.8-21; reprinted in
    Fishman (1968), pp.673-87.
Jamieson, J. (1808) *An Etymological Dictionary of the Scottish
    Language*, in Two Volumes. Edinburgh.
Lindsay, J. Maurice (1962) *Snow Warning and Other Poems*.
    Arundel: Linden Press.
Low, J. T. (1974) Scots in education: the contemporary situation,
    in McClure (1974), pp.17-27.
McClure, J. D. (ed.) (1974) *The Scots Language in Education*,
    Association for Scottish Literary Studies, Occasional Papers No. 3.
— (1978) Review of Murison 1977, *Scottish Literary Journal*
    Supplement No. 8, Autumn 1978, pp.1-3.
— (1979a) Scots: its range of uses, in Aitken and McArthur (1979),
    pp.26-48.
— (1979b) The concept of Standard Scots, *Chapman 23, 24*, pp.90-9.
— (ed.) (1980) *The Scots Language: Planning for Modern Usage*.
    Edinburgh: Ramsay Head Press.
— (1980a) Developing Scots as a National Language, in McClure
    (1980), pp.11-41.
MacDiarmid, Hugh (1934) The Case for Synthetic Scots, in *At the Sign of
    the Thistle*. London: Stanley Nott, N.D.

McNaught, D. (1901) The raucle tongue of Burns, *Annual Burns Chronicle 10*, pp.26-37.

Masson, R. (1929) *Use and Abuse of English: a hand-book of composition*, Fifth Edition, revised. Edinburgh: James Thin. (First Edition, entitled *Elements of English Composition*, 1896.)

Millar, J. H. (1903) *A Literary History of Scotland*. London: T. Fisher Unwin.

Murison, D. (1971) The future of Scots, in *Whither Scotland?* (ed. D. Glen). London: Gollancz.

— (1977) *The Guid Scots Tongue*. Edinburgh: Blackwood.

— (1979a) Scotland's Languages: the Historical Background, in Aitken and McArthur (1979), pp.2-13.

— (1979b) The future of Scots, *Chapman 23, 24*, pp.58-62.

Murray, J. A. H. (1873) *The Dialect of the Southern Counties of Scotland*. London: Philological Society.

Oliver, J. (1902) Teviot and District, *Transactions of the Hawick Antiquarian Society*, 1902, pp.7-14.

Ramsay, E. B. (1872) *Reminiscences of Scottish Life and Character*, Twenty-first edition (First edition, 1857). London: Gall and Inglis.

Robertson, J. L. (1878) On the Decadence of the Scots Language, Manners and Customs, in *Poems*, pp.42-62. Dundee: John Leng & Co.

Ruddiman, T. (1710) 'General Rules for Understanding the Language of Bishop Dowglas's Translation of Virgil's *Aeneis*' and 'A Glossary', in *Virgil's Aeneis* by Gawin Douglas, A new edition [ed. by T. Ruddiman]. Edinburgh: Andrew Symson & Robert Freebairn.

Scotticisms corrected (1855). London: John Farquhar Shaw.

Scottish Rev. (1907) 'The Future of the Scots Tongue' by Walter W. Skeat, William Wallace, Neil Munro and 'Hugh Haliburton', and 'The Scots Tongue', *The Scottish Review 5*, July 4 to Dec. 26, pp.521-2 and 540.

Shirrefs, A. (1790) *Poems, chiefly in the Scottish Dialect*. Edinburgh and London.

Sibbald, J. (1802) *Chronicle of Scottish Poetry, . . . to which is added a Glossary*, 4 vols. Edinburgh.

Smith, J. A. (1970) Some eighteenth century ideas of Scotland, in *Scotland in the Age of Improvement* (eds N. T. Phillipson and R. Mitchison), pp.107f. Edinburgh: University Press.

Statistical Accounts of Scotland: 1. [*Old*] *Statistical Account of Scotland, drawn up from the communications of the ministers of the different parishes* (ed. J. Sinclair), 21 vols. Edinburgh, 1791-9. 2. *The New Statistical Account of Scotland, by the ministers of the respective parishes* (ed. J. Gordon), 15 vols. Edinburgh, 1845. 3. *The Third Statistical Account of Scotland* (various eds), 20 vols. published to 1979. Various publishers, 1951-.

Stewart, W. A. (1968) A Sociolinguistic Typology for describing National Multilingualism, in Fishman (1968), pp.531-45.

Templeton, J. M. (1973) Scots: an outline history, in *Lowland Scots* (ed. A. J. Aitken), Association for Scottish Literary Studies, Occasional Papers No. 2, pp.4-19.

Trotter, R. de B. (1901) The Scottish Language, *The Gallovidian 3*, pp.22-9.

Will, W. (1930) *Our Persistent Speech. An Enquiry into the Life of Certain Aberdeenshire Words*. Aberdeen: William Smith & Sons.

Withrington, D. J. (1974) Scots in education: a historical retrospect, in McClure (1974), pp.9-16.

Young, D. (1946) *Plastic Scots and the Scottish Literary Tradition*. Glasgow: W. Maclellan.

— (1949) *The Use of Scots for Prose: The John Galt Lecture for 1949*. Greenock: Papers of the Greenock Philosophical Society.

8. The Synthesisers of Scots

If it should be thought that a discussion of the written language is out of place here, I base my defence first on the general point that in the language of any literate society the relationship between the written and the spoken languages, and specifically the part played by men of letters in establishing linguistic standards, is a matter of extreme interest; and secondly on the fact that in the case of Scots the issues have manifested themselves in an extraordinary, perhaps a unique, form. Developments in written Scots during the present century demonstrate at once the enormous potential which the language affords for a planned development programme, and the practical sterility of such a programme when undertaken on the literary level alone and without reference to social and political conditions.

The general history of Scots, at least in outline, is well known. The point relevant here is that until the present century the status of Scots as a written language was roughly predictable from its status in Scottish society. As the official government language of an independent state, it was the vehicle for the full canon of literary genres which existed at that time. Later, as the domestic speech of the rural and urban working classes, superseded by English as the language of government, education, commerce and the professions, it declined to being the medium of a literature limited in range and cultivating a rustic, homely and jocular tone. Scots had diminished from a fully-developed language to what Kloss (1952, 102ff.) calls a *Halbsprache*. With the twentieth-century literary revival, however, this close relationship between the spoken and the written languages ceased to exist. This is true in reference to actual resemblance: the literary idiolect of, for example, Douglas Young is far less like any spoken form of Scots than those of Charles Murray or Logie Robertson. It is also true of relative status: Scots-writing poets in recent decades have achieved work of a distinction that seems to belie the low degree of respect accorded to their medium. The group of poets of whom Hugh MacDiarmid is the unchallenged leader has undertaken the enormous task of upgrading the language: restoring it (as they saw the situation) to its place among the established vehicles for international culture. I propose to illustrate and discuss their methods of extending the vocabulary of the language; I will not be concerned with literary evaluations.

The least obviously innovative, though not the least enterprising, practice of modern Scots poets has been to use individual words in unfamiliar contexts, thus abrogating their established connotations. Many Scots words – indeed, the written language as a whole – had come by the nineteen-twenties to be associated with literature of a romantic and sentimental cast, deliberately unimposing and unheroic – indeed, taking a perverse pride in emphasising the humbleness of the community depicted. (This association is to a large extent perpetuated, even today, by popular entertainment: songs in the 'Granny's heiland hame' mode are the staple of amateur and professional music-hall performers.) When Tom Scott in his translation of Ulysses' story from Dante's *Inferno* applied the word *crouse* (translating *lieta*) to Penelope, he must have been fully aware that this word to many people would instantly recall the domestic comedy of Burns's *Duncan Gray* ('Now they're crouse and canty baith'), or the tearful sentimentality of Lady Nairne's *The Auld Hoose* ('Oh, the auld laird, the auld laird, sae canty, kind and crouse!'): that it had built-in overtones as inappropriate to this particular passage as they could be. Similarly, in the same translation the sea *synds* (for *bagna*) the islands: *synd* is wash or rinse, as a vessel or one's face; and its use here is a considerable departure from its normal meaning. The most extreme example in this translation is Scott's use of the word *plunk*, normally applied to children playing truant, of Ulysses' companions (*dalla qual non fui diserto* – 'that hadnae plunkt and left me on my lane'). In all these cases the words are, in intention at least, being (so to speak) promoted, by the deliberate ignoring of their normal limited and undignified range of collocations. Other examples are Scott's use of what might have been thought a hopeless cliché in translating Villon's *Mais où sont les neiges d'antan?* as 'Ay, whaur are the snaws o langsyne?'; Douglas Young's application of the double diminutives *wifikie* and *bairnikie*, immediately suggestive of humour or playfulness, to Andromache and Astyanax in his translation from Homer; and, in Alexander Scott's renderings of Old English poetry, his use of *Sassenach* (a word generally used facetiously in Scots, though not in its native Gaelic) in *Makar's Lament* (an adaptation of *Deor*), and his references to *drams* ('a wee dram' being a phrase associated by innumerable songs and jokes with the stereotype of the Scot as a drunken buffoon) and *lairds* ('the laird' in literature is more often a comic character than a figure of power or dignity) in his versions of *The Wanderer* and *The Seafarer*.

These examples have been drawn from writings of a particular kind – poetic translations of literary classics – for the reason that in such works the intended tone of the Scots text is 'given' by the original: there can be no doubt that the poets expected their work to be read in entire seriousness, with the overtones of hameliness, couthiness, pawkiness which those words and others tend to evoke being wholly absent. Of course the device is not restricted to poetic translations; but in many other instances the issue of verbal upgrading could be obscured by debate on the precise effect which the writer intended to produce: a literary question beyond our present scope.

An observation frequently made of twentieth-century Scots poetry is that it utilises obsolete or obsolescent words. The frequency with which this charge has been brought suggests an insufficient awareness of the fact that the death of a word is not always easy to date; and in reality the poetic use of unquestionable archaisms is almost certainly less frequent than is sometimes thought. Sydney Goodsir Smith (1948) cites *antrin* (occasional), *smittel* (contagious), *waukrife* (wakeful), *begrutten* (tear-stained) and *wanchancy* (unlucky) as words which can readily be heard in colloquial Edinburgh speech, and elsewhere (1964–5) offers the enormous public success of his play *The Wallace* as evidence that its language presented no barrier to widespread appreciation – though it must be admitted that *The Wallace* is written in a far less contrived Scots than much of Smith's other work. *The Scottish National Dictionary*, too, shows from its recent attestations that a very large number of words were at least passively known to its live informants; and they were presumably not unique. The following is a small selection from the words which, though known to the present writer only from literature, are shown by the *SND* to have been 'alive' within the last few years: *knabrie* (gentry), *nesh* (soft, tender), *outrug* (backwash of a wave), *puggie* (monkey), *rack* (storm-clouds), *scurl* (scab), *scarroch* (shower of rain or snow). A further side to the question is suggested by the consideration that many words may well have been kept alive precisely by virtue of their use in earlier literature: the undiminishing popularity of Burns and several lesser writers has probably resulted in the wide distribution and preservation of some words which might otherwise have remained limited in space and time: *houghmagandie* (fornication) is an example that springs to mind. At least one dialect scholar has noted that he found it expedient to treat with particular care information elicited from known Burns enthusiasts (Riach 1978). All allowances being made, however, there is no doubt that a recourse to the vocabulary of earlier periods has been a device frequently used by recent Scots poets to enrich their language.

The exact source of a particular word is, in the nature of things, often impossible to verify. For *riggin-tree* (roof), used by Goodsir Smith and Douglas Young, the only literary precedent is Walter Scott. Smith's *aroint* (expel) is unique to Shakespeare except for a rare imitative use by Walter Scott (whose fondness for Shakespearean borrowings is well-attested: Roberts 1953) and others. Smith also follows Scott in misusing *warison* to mean a war-cry. *Laillie*, a reduced form of *laithlie* (loathsome), was apparently taken by Smith from a ballad, and *misgate* (mistake) from P. Hately Waddell's 1871 translation of the Psalms.

It is common knowledge that John Jamieson's *Etymological Dictionary of the Scottish Language* was a happy hunting ground for Scots Renaissance poets; and many words are almost conclusively shown to have been obtained from that source by the fact that their citation in 'Jamieson' is the only instance of their use recorded in the *SND*. Some examples from MacDiarmid's early poetry are *amplefeyst* (sulky humour), *barrowsteel* (barrowshaft, but used in the phrase *tak your barrowsteel* – co-operate), *eemis* (unsteady), *knedneuch* (smelling of musty bread), *reeze* (pull about sharply, as by wind), *whuram* (slur or quaver in singing), and a group of words that appear together in an alliterative section at the end of the poem *Gairmscoile*: *datchie* (penetrating, of wit), *drote* (uppish yeoman or cocklaird), and *druttle* (emit small quantities of dung). Jamieson is Douglas Young's apparent source for *braal* (fragment), *braikit* (speckled), *brub* (check, restrain), *cowzie* (boisterous), *dullyeart* (of a dirty dull colour), *slamber* (delicate), and *vivuallie* (used by Young to mean 'vividly', though Jamieson's definition is 'in life'); and Goodsir Smith's for *blyte* (storm-gust), *dronach* (punishment), *gleemoch* (dim light as misty sun), *hammerflush* (sparks from an anvil), *larry* (farmer), *pultrous* (lascivious), *rambaleuch* (tempestuous), *ramskeerie* (restless, irresponsible), *rankreenging* (lawless), *scubble* (spoil), *spear-wund* (tempestuous rage), *stramyulloch* (turmoil, skirmish), *tregallion* (beggar band), and *wudwise* (a bitter yellow weed). In the case of a rare word like *reithe* (fierce, ardent), used by Goodsir Smith, though I would risk a bet that the poet's source was in fact Jamieson, the word does occur in James Hogg's *The Brownie of Bodsbeck* and Andrew of Wyntoun's *Oryginale Chronykil of Scotland*; and it is, for all I know, quite probable that Smith had read the former and not impossible that he had read the latter too. The pertinent fact is that many words in the literature of the last half-century are obsolete in speech, and have come, via Jamieson or directly, from writings of earlier periods.

Instances from MacDiarmid are *skrymmorie* (terrifying), for which Jamieson's authority is Gavin Douglas, *mapamound*, *crammasy*, and (from the poetic vocabulary of a more recent era) *pitmirk* (pitch dark), *derf* (bold), *swith* (quick), and *thring* (shrug). Goodsir Smith revives, among others, *allhail* in the mediaeval sense of 'mistletoe', *barla-fummil* (pax), *besprent* (sprinkled – though this was occasionally used as an archaism also by some English Romantic poets), *bluidwyte* (bloodshed fine), *campion* (champion), *elfame* (fairyland), *emerant* (a Middle Scots form of 'emerald', also used by Hogg), *endyte* (write), *fairheid* (beauty), *fantice* (vision), *gaincome* (return), *hautand* (haughty – the *-and* is probably an error but the form is attested in Dunbar), *kingrik* (kingdom), *redeless* (careless), and *traiterie* (treachery). (Not all of those words, it will be observed, are peculiar to early *Scottish* literature.) Douglas Young, perhaps the most linguistically inventive of all recent Scots poets, in a corpus only a fraction of the size of Smith's has proportionally far more archaisms: some examples are *bassanat* (helmet), *bestial* (cattle), *blasounrie* (charge on a shield), *blee* (complexion), *chaudron* (cauldron), *crangle* (twist), *doungang* (sunset), *flesche* (a rare MSc form for 'fleece'), *forvay* (wander), *fruct* (a MSc Latinism for 'fruit'), *gumphion* (funeral banner), *helmonte* (helmet), *musardry* (pensiveness, attested only in Gavin Douglas), *nichtartale* (by night: a word familiar from Chaucer but used by Young with its MSc spelling), *orlege* (clock), *orpheling* (orphan), and *renay* (deny).

Perhaps the most interesting, as well as the most controversial, method of augmenting the vocabulary employed by the modern Scots poets is that of outright invention. Here too, the device is probably less frequently employed than is sometimes imagined; and the category of verbal invention is unquestionably a dubious one. Many words which occur in recent Scots poetry are not to be found in any dictionary; but on the other hand nearly all of them are not absolute inventions but are derived from existing words or morphemes and formed in accordance with established principles. There are exceptions: I can find no precedent whatever for Young's *wint* (pupil of the eye), Smith's *buck-tree* (beech), or *spase*, a word used frequently by both those poets to mean 'open sea'. However, most neologisms of modern Scots are firmly rooted in the attested forms of the Scots language.

The weakest form of lexical innovation is a simple variation on the sense of an existing word. Thus *crottle*, originally a noun meaning 'crumb', is used by MacDiarmid as a verb meaning 'sprinkle', and *doonsin*, a rare word glossed by Jamieson as 'very', becomes an adjective meaning 'dazzling' – and here, since in Jamieson's only illustrative quotation for the word it appears in the phrase 'doonsin white', MacDiarmid's interpretation of it is arguably as legitimate as Jamieson's own. Goodsir Smith takes the meaning 'supreme' for *owerhailan*, part of a verb glossed by the *SND* as 'overtake'; and by a combination of metaphor and pun gives a sexual sense to *cundy* (for which one of Jamieson's definitions is 'concealed hole'), and uses *widdreme*, traditionally 'state of confusion' (and not related to the modern English word *dream*) to mean 'nightmare'. Douglas Young alters *aflocht* from 'agitated' to 'flying', perhaps in reminiscence of MSc *on flaucht* for 'in flight', demotes *breve* (in Older Scots, an official missive from King or Pope; in modern Scots Law, a legal writ) to mean simply 'book', transfers *gaig* from hacks in the skin to fissures in a glacier, and uses *owerset* to mean 'translate' – presumably in imitation of the German *übersetzen* – instead of 'overturn'. *Gesserant*, a favourite word of Young's meaning 'gleaming' or 'glittering', is derived from its original sense of 'light plate armour' (that the scholarly Young innocently swallowed Jamieson's patently absurd proposal to interpret the word in James I's line 'As gesserant ay glitterit in my sight' (*The Kingis Quair*, stanza 153) as meaning 'sparkling' is to me inconceivable; and the fact that he also uses *begesserant* with the same meaning suggests that he recognised the word as primarily a noun). *Machicolate* (indented or serrated like battlements), by which Young translates Sorley Maclean's *eagarra*, a somewhat literary but by no means recondite word meaning 'ordered' or 'regular', is a nonce use of a word (with no Scottish attestations in the *Oxford English Dictionary*, incidentally) referring to the openings between the supports of a projecting stone parapet.

Variations on not only the meanings but the forms of existing words have also been produced. Goodsir Smith changes *accumulate* to *accume*, *centripetal* to *centripetant*, *heaven* to *hovenum*, *langour* to *langorie*, and *tumulus* to *tumle*, none of which is attested elsewhere. More significant than these seemingly random and arbitrary mutations are a number of derived forms, which, though their roots are easily recognisable as existing words, are in themselves new coinages. This is a device favoured by Smith: *commell* (mix), *dumfounrous* (dumbfounding), *fellrife* (fey or unlucky), and a redundant *quietlinswise* (peacefully); and still more by Young: *cordinant* (of Cordova leather: the noun *cordain* appears in a ballad), *flownrie* (fragile, apparently from *flowin*, a small quantity of grains or particles), *keethanlie* (apparently), *sainless* (incurable), *trullerie* (foolishness), *untwynable* (inseparable), *thraipfu* (famous). Young's *flather* (foamy pouring) appears to be an altered form of *fluther* (a confused fluttering mass), and Smith's *clopperin* (bottle rattling) to be a variation on *clap*.

New compound words have also been introduced. The large group of forms in Scots having the pattern adverb–verb is the model for Smith's *doungae* (descend) and Young's *dounharl* (drag down) and *upfraith* (send up in froth). *Yearhunder* for 'century' appears to be Young's concoction, again no doubt modelled on the German *Jahrhundert*. Smith uses *ayebydan* for 'everlasting', and Young derives a noun *everbydandness*. *Hailisted* for 'Heaven' is a nonce invention of Smith's, and his *shilpiskate* (non-entity) is a combining of two insult terms into a single word. Young, from the archaic *flume* meaning 'river', concocts *ice-flume* for 'glacier'. Loose compounds of this kind are a feature of Young's style: other examples are *fuddrie-leams*, *licht-bumbazit*, *swaw-pouther*, *water-flads*, *ferly-potency*, *glamarie-licht*, and – based on a favourite word, itself a fanciful coinage, of the Scots Renaissance poets – *howedumbdeidsunsheen*.

Still another category of 'invention' is illustrated by the neo-aureate diction of Smith: his use, following the mediaeval poets, of nonce words derived from Latin or French. Examples are *granderie* (pride), *scelartrie* (infamy), and *orsplendant* (which Smith does not gloss, but it is etymologically self-explanatory). Finally, in such coinages as MacDiarmid's *heichskeich*, Smith's *flichterie-fleeterie*, and Young's *weeferty-wafferty*, we have examples of a type always plentifully represented in Scots: impressionistic words employed for their phonaesthetic force.

The literary effectiveness of such neologisms in their actual poetic contexts is a matter for the attention of literary critics; but from a linguistic point of view there is no debate on the status of the words: their 'legitimacy' or 'authenticity' cannot be disputed on any linguistic grounds. It is unnecessary to point out that changes on all levels, including the lexical, occur in living languages: that diachronic change is indeed virtually a diagnostic sign of life in a language. And though it is neither logically consequent on this nor necessarily true in practice that the more innovative a language the greater its degree of vitality, it is often found that periods of rapid and extensive linguistic innovation coincide with periods of drastic social change affecting a language. The intention of the Scots Renaissance writers has been to promote Scots from a group of declining low-prestige dialects to a national language: a major social change by any reckoning. A further point is that all the techniques of innovation used by MacDiarmid, Smith, Young and other poets are in full accordance with precedents established in earlier stages of the language, and paralleled in other languages. Even the mere fact of producing fanciful and in many cases ephemeral words appears to have been peculiarly characteristic of Scots throughout its history. The linguistic inventiveness of the Makars is common knowledge (*Ane Ballat of Our Lady* alone contains at least a dozen words used by Dunbar for the first or only time, of which only one, *serene*, has passed into the general speech); and from the Scots of a later period the *SND* records an astonishing number of words, some extremely imaginative, which have been attested once or twice only: *mabbie, macglashanite, machamore, madwullie, mahoofanat, mahugger, maicherand, maizle, malapavis, malheurius, manfierdie, magluntew, manyogl, maroochan, maulhoozle* and *mazerment* occur within the space of sixty pages.

On a level less easy to discuss in concrete terms, the achievement of the Scots Renaissance writers is of profound theoretical interest. George Steiner (1975, chapter 5) discusses the implications of translation for both the original and the new languages of the translated work. Actual translations from poetry in many languages have appeared with notable frequency in recent Scots writing; but in a sense there is an element of translation in all the work we have been discussing, for though many people speak Scots it is not the Scots of *Under the Eildon Tree* or *A Braird o Thristles*: the language used by the 'Lallans' writers is to some extent a learned language even for the poets themselves. From this point of view, such writers as MacDiarmid, Smith and Young can be seen as exercising what Steiner (p.339) calls 'the unique authority [of translation] against time and the banal contingency of historical fact'. Scots in the twentieth century *is* a low-prestige and undeveloped (or rather, degenerate) speech-form ill-equipped for discourse on abstract or intellectual topics; but it *might have been* otherwise – if the language had continued to develop as it was developing in the early sixteenth century and had not fallen victim to social disrespect and literary stagnation. In deliberately reviving words from earlier and more flourishing periods of the language, and coining new words on principles which obtained then, the Scots Renaissance writers have, so to speak, realised a might-have-been Scots. Steiner's phrase 'a part of one's own tradition temporarily mislaid' (p.347), referring to the effect of a good poetic translation in an archaising style, is an exact description of the effect that MacDiarmid and his successors, in their best work, have achieved.

However, the success of twentieth-century Scots poets when considered with reference to the general situation of the Scots language today turns out to be less than an unequivocal triumph. The first of two fundamental defects in their contribution to the development of Scots is that they have strengthened the language where it was already strong, and left its areas of weakness untouched. The most impressive characteristic of Scots, its large stock of semantically and phonaesthetically powerful words relating to the senses and the emotions, has been splendidly developed and increased, with the result that Scots, formerly a potentially good poetic language, has now become a demonstrably superb one. On the other hand, Scots is as totally lacking in words from the domains of physics, biology, astronomy, electronics and the other sciences as it was fifty years ago: there are vast areas of modern knowledge on which it is simply impossible to speak using a distinctively Scots vocabulary. Poets have been fully aware of this: MacDiarmid's use of English for his later 'scientific' poetry has often been remarked on; and Tom Scott found it impossible, despite protracted efforts, to write *The Tree*, his long poem on animal evolution, convincingly in Scots. The obvious retort is that it should not be the business of men of letters to attend to the scientific register in a language; and this, despite the unusual prevalence of esoteric interests among some recent Scots poets, is no doubt true. But the fact that neither they nor anybody else has attempted to supply this register has ensured that Scots, with all its remarkable literature, is still a *Halbsprache*.

The second flaw in the achievement of the 'Lallans' poets is that their work on the language has been conducted in isolation from the actual social, political and educational situation. Fishman (1980) distinguishes between two aspects of language planning: corpus planning (the process of equipping a language with an adequate word stock) and status planning (the process of persuading people to use the language for some or all purposes). 'Corpus planning without status planning is a linguistic game, a technical exercise without social consequence' (p.12). The truth of this is clearly demonstrated by the present state of Scots. The corpus planners, if our poets may be so designated, have not only brought about an actual increase in the expressive power of Scots, but also demonstrated the potential which the language holds for future developments. But because their efforts have not been complemented by any planned programme affecting the social status of the language, they have achieved little beyond the addition of some excellent poems to the corpus of Scottish literature. Faced with the fact that Scots has no official standing, is largely ignored or discouraged by the schools, and is the object of entrenched social prejudice, they have not attempted to combat this situation on its own terms: they have simply defied it. The boldness of their stance is no more to be questioned or denigrated than the value of its results from a literary point of view; and indeed their achievement in the educational field is not negligible: it is surely beyond doubt that the hints of a greater degree of attention to Scots literature, and even a more liberal attitude to the language, that are appearing in the educational system are due in part to a belated recognition of the merit of some recent Scots writing;

and some (admittedly very limited) data in Macaulay (1977, 55–6) suggest that certain traditional Scots words are rather better known to professional-class than to working-class speakers. But the development of Scots which the poets have achieved remains essentially a literary development.

Whether it will always remain so is impossible to predict: certainly it has had the effect, alluded to at the beginning of this paper, of establishing a dramatic gap between the spoken and at least some registers of the written language. (Of course, there are many Scots writers who employ a language far closer to actual speech than those of MacDiarmid, Smith and Young.) I have discussed elsewhere (McClure 1980) the possibility of a planned development programme for Scots: this may eventually be put into practice, though the political situation at present is far less encouraging than when that paper was written. If not, post-MacDiarmid Scots will no doubt still prove to be good for a few more decades as a literary language. And the case of a language of which the development is entirely in the hands of men of letters, though extraordinary, is at least better than total extinction.

References
Fishman, J. A. (1980) Bilingual education, language planning and English, *English World-Wide* 1:1, 11-24.
Kloss, H. (1952) *Die Entwicklung Neuer Germanischer Kultursprachen von 1800 bis 1950*. München.
Macaulay, R. K. S. (1977) *Language, Social Class, and Education: a Glasgow Study*. Edinburgh.
McClure, J. D. (1980) Developing Scots as a national language, in *The Scots Language: Planning for Modern Usage*, J. D. McClure, A. J. Aitken and John T. Low. Edinburgh.
Riach, W. A. D. (1978) *A dialect study of comparative areas in Galloway*. Edinburgh University PhD thesis.
Roberts, P. (1953) Sir Walter Scott's contributions to the English vocabulary, *PMLA* 68, 189-210.
Smith, S. G. (1948) In defence of 'Lallans', *The Scots Review*, May 1948, 23.
— (1964) Trahison des clercs: the anti-Scots lobby in Scottish letters, in *Studies in Scottish Literature*, vol. II, no. 2, October 1964, 71-86.
Steiner, G. (1975) *After Babel*. Oxford.

9. Language Fragmentation in Scandinavia:
Revolt of the Minorities

Rights are things we get when we are strong enough to claim them.
                                                    Helen Keller (1915)

The world is full of minorities, from the individual or minority of one, to the largest of nations, which is still a minority in relation to mankind as a whole. The same holds for languages, whether they are spoken by only one person or by millions.

Here, however, the focus is more limited: a minority is defined in relation to an administrative unit, which in the modern world is generally the nation-state. Even here there are various kinds of minorities, some of them *dominant* (like the Norman conquerors of England in 1066), others *dominated*. We may call the former *élite* minorities, the latter *non-élite* or *submerged*. To put it another way, a *demographic* minority need not be a *functional* minority (Connors 1979).

We are chiefly concerned with the functional minorities, but we need also to see them in relation to the dominant groups, whether they be demographic minorities or majorities. The key concept is *power* and especially the means of *access to power*. A minority language is one that denies or hampers the access of its users to power. In general usage today the term 'minority' is little more than a euphemism for 'non-élite' or 'dominated' (Schermerhorn 1964, Holmestad and Lade 1969, Skutnabb-Kangas 1975a, Dorian 1979, Poole 1980, Giles and St Jacques 1979, Gal 1979, Adler 1977).

If there is anything we can learn from the Scandinavian experience, it is the importance of political power in establishing languages. The fragmentation of Scandinavia is a reflection of its political history. Scandinavia is more Balkanized than even the Balkans themselves. Since I cannot assume that all my readers are familiar with this history, I shall take them on a short guided tour of the power struggles that have in the end led to the present diversity-within-unity of the Nordic countries. Scandinavia today is a miniature Europe, with all the problems of minority groups that beset other parts of the world. It may be instructive to see what solutions, if any, have emerged and what problems still bedevil them. They may be more transparent in a smaller sample, such as Scandinavia. I can only sketch the main contours; others will take up the details of specific problems.

Scandinavian Languages

A recent headline in the *Boston Globe* (21 April 1980) described Scandinavia as 'five Nordic nations in search of a mother tongue'. The curious fact about Scandinavia is that its linguistic fragmentation exists within an overall cultural unity in which language plays a major role. What Scandinavians call *Norden* – the North – consists of five sovereign nations, three central (Denmark, Norway, Sweden), and two marginal (Iceland, Finland). Between them they have six official standard languages of Germanic origin (Icelandic, Faroese, Nynorsk-Norwegian, Bokmål-Norwegian, Danish, Swedish) and one of Finno-Ugric origin (Finnish). None of these is strictly a minority language today; but we shall return to this problem later.

The four languages of the central area are mutually intelligible (with a little good will), and in practice they function as dialects of a common Scandinavian 'language' (Braunmüller 1979). They are what Kloss has described as *Ausbau* languages, i.e. languages by virtue of separate standardization. Finnish is clearly an *Abstand* language, while Faroese and Icelandic are somewhere between (Kloss 1978). Within the central area there are also mutually unintelligible dialects, which often share features with other standard languages than their own. The national borders are determined by past historical conflicts, in which military power was more significant than linguistic self-determination. National sovereignties have created artificial linguistic boundaries within what was once a linguistic continuum. (For surveys see Haugen 1976, Sigurd ed. 1977, Bandle 1979.)

International Communication

Scandinavians are perhaps more aware than the citizens of larger countries of their vulnerable position. In a talk given in 1969 by the well-known linguist Hans Vogt, speaking to the First Congress of Nordic and Modern Linguistics in Reykjavík, he pointed out that all the Nordic countries are 'small language societies which, in a world that is constantly being more and more internationalized and standardized, are exposed to increasing pressure from the outside world, from the great languages of culture' (Vogt 1970). His plea for Scandinavian cooperation came as an especially apt conclusion to a conference where nearly all the papers were given in English although nearly all the speakers were Scandinavian (Haugen 1978).

The overwhelming importance of English as a channel to the outside world is reflected in the teaching of the primary schools. The consequent availability of English is reflected in heavy borrowing of words and turns of phrase in all the central languages. This influence is a matter of deep concern to many serious thinkers in the North (Sutton 1979). But English was not the first medium of international communication in Scandinavia. The first

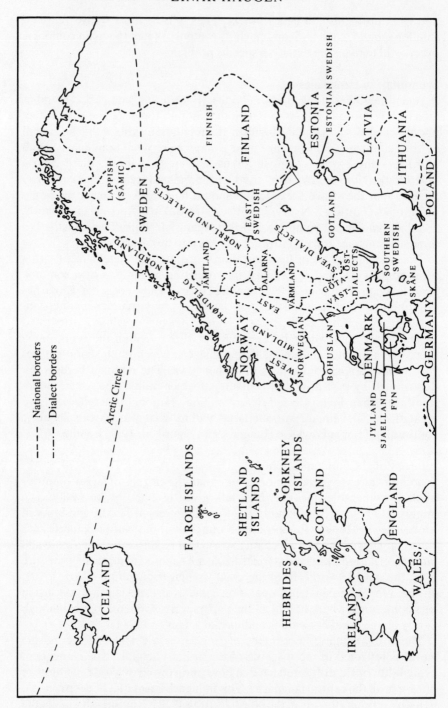

Figure 9.1. Scandinavia: countries, languages, dialects.

foreign language introduced was Latin. Christian missionaries of the tenth and eleventh centuries accomplished what Roman legions had failed to do, the establishment of Latin on Nordic soil. The first schools were Latin schools, in which clerics not only trained new clerics but also bureaucrats for the budding royal chanceries. In so doing, they brought Scandinavia within the orbit of European culture. But at the same time they deprived the vernaculars of part of their natural domain. They set up a functional diglossia, in which the native languages played the role of 'low' (L) languages against Latin as the 'high' (H) language (Ferguson 1959).

Even so, the Scandinavian languages were written in Roman letters on parchment by these same missionaries and clerics, more so in the west where Christianity was introduced from the British Isles. It is characteristic that the Danish Saxo Grammaticus (*fl. c.*1200) wrote his history of Denmark in Latin, while his Icelandic contemporary, Snorri Sturluson (1178–1241), wrote his history of Norway in the vernacular. In a recent study of the classical tradition in Norway, Sigmund Skard has pointed out that Latin extended far beyond its role as a link with Europe: 'In certain areas of life the use of Latin soon became a matter of course . . . not only in international correspondence, treaties and negotiations of court and clergy, but in the formulation of important state documents and at many solemn or special occasions' (Skard 1980, 29).

The Reformation may be regarded as the first minority revolt against the dominance of Latin. By rejecting the authority of the Roman Church and introducing the vernaculars into the service, the Germanic nations at one blow eliminated one of the major domains of the Latin language. In the sixteenth century, after the model of Luther, the Nordic nations not only established national churches, but also translated the Bible into the vernaculars: primarily Swedish (1541) and Danish (1550), secondarily Icelandic (1584) and Finnish (New Testament by Mikael Agricola 1548) (Groenke 1978).

Even after the Reformation, however, Latin remained a window to the world. Humanism established Latin as the language of learning. I quote Skard once more: 'In Norway, as in all nations of Germanic tongue, Latin became a mark of social standing, the insurmountable barrier between the cultured and others. More important, it symbolized the distant and supernational [*sic*] character of an education only tenuously connected with real life. In their most formative years generation after generation of European youth were to devote their best energy to the study of a civilization long passed away, and its dead languages, while hardly any attention was paid the past and the present, including the language of the country in which they were to live their lives' (Skard 1980, 57. On Denmark see Skautrup 1.194–207; 2.29–31, 170–4, 301–2; on Sweden Tengström 1973, Wennås 1966).

The gradual restriction of Latin began in the Middle Ages: Queen Margaret of Denmark issued her first law in Danish in 1396. But by this time another language was threatening Scandinavian autonomy, viz. the Low

German of northern Germany. This language was spread by the powerful Hanseatic League, by the involvement of Danish and Swedish courts with German rulers and noblemen, and by the influx of thousands of German craftsmen and merchants to the cities of the North. According to Skautrup, historian of Danish, Denmark between 1325 and 1425 was well on its way to becoming bilingual (Skautrup 2.31). Low German charters were written before Danish ones, especially in relation to the border duchies of Schleswig and Holstein. At one time the kingdom of Denmark embraced so many native speakers of German that they constituted one-third of its entire population (Brems 1979, 428). In 1864 Germany retrieved the German speakers and a number of Danes as well, most of whom were returned to Denmark after the First World War. But the border is ragged and there are still small minorities on both sides of it (Søndergård 1978, 1980).

The linguistic jumble in Denmark around 1700 was summed up by Wilster, a nineteenth-century wit, as follows:

> Each man who plunged deeply in learning
> Wrote nothing but Latin on paper,
> Spoke French to the ladies, German to dogs,
> And Danish alone to his servant.

Neo-Scandinavian

Actually, by 1700 the new Danish and Swedish standards had been firmly established for most internal purposes. Their complete victory would not come until the nineteenth century, when universal school systems were established for the teaching of the native languages. But these new native norms were strikingly different from the medieval writing traditions (Haugen 1976, 313–23). For a single century prior to the Reformation Danish had had a fleeting chance to become the standard language of all Scandinavia, as it did in fact in Norway. But the Swedish secession of 1523 under Gustavus Vasa meant the rise of a formidable rival, political as well as linguistic, to Danish supremacy. As late as 1506 prominent Swedes could acknowledge that they and the Danes were 'all of one language', but by 1554 they had discovered that the Danes 'do not trouble to speak like other people, but force their words out as if they wish to cough' (Haugen 1976, 326; Dahlstedt 1976; for comments on Danish problems of today see Larsen 1977).

When the Swedes established their norm for official writing in the sixteenth century, they made it as different from Danish as possible. After 1658, when they secured sovereignty over the Norwegian and Danish provinces of what is now western and southern Sweden, they instituted a policy euphemistically known as *uniformiteten*, i.e. uniformity. In a single generation they turned the written language of these provinces from Danish to Swedish, although with little effect on the local dialects (Ingers 1974, Ohlsson 1978–9). The most striking feature of the new Danish and Swedish norms alike is their formal transformation from the norms known as Old

Danish and Old Swedish. They had ridden out the threat of Latin and Low German, but only at the expense of absorbing many of their features. They were flooded with thousands of Low German and Latin loanwords. The synthetic grammatical structure, with its many morphological suffixes and relatively free, oral syntax had been turned into an analytical morphology with few suffixes and a relatively rigid word order, clearly influenced by Latin.

The leap from Old to New was closely parallel to that from Old to New English. It is not fanciful to attribute the change in part to foreign influence: French in England, Low German in Scandinavia. For centuries these languages had played the role of minority languages in their own countries. What the Norman Conquest did for English, the Hanseatic dominance did for Scandinavian. Continuity with the past was broken, less as a natural development, Jespersen's 'progress in language', than as a linguistic mutation. The proof of the pudding is the survival of the old structure in distant Iceland, which is equivalent to what the survival of an Anglo-Saxon-speaking community in England might have been.

Once these new norms had been established by the combined forces of government and church, with the schools and the printing press as new and powerful weapons, it was only a matter of time until they had become the chief means of unification within their respective realms. Once both God and his representative on earth, the King, began speaking Swedish and Danish, these languages acquired the aura of sacred as well as secular veneration. The process was completed in the nineteenth century by the universal public school, which gradually mobilized the entire population into more or less active participation in the lives of the nations.

The New Nations

The French Revolution and the Napoleonic wars created new political alignments that shook the established position of Danish and Swedish. In 1809 Finland was lost to Sweden; in 1814 Norway was lost to Denmark. Movements for linguistic autonomy arose in both countries, partly under the influence of the established patterns of national linguistic sovereignty and partly through the ideology of national identity as taught by the German romantics. By the middle of the nineteenth century similar movements gathered force in Iceland and the Faroes, eventually resulting in independence for Iceland (1918, 1944) and home rule for the Faroes (1948).

In the modern period we also observe the establishment of active organs for language cultivation, the most famous being the Swedish Academy of 1786, whose purpose was declared to be to work for 'the purity, strength, and sublimity' of Swedish. It is not at all clear just how much it contributed to these laudable goals. By the end of the nineteenth century, at least, the maintenance and cultivation of the norms were actually in the hands of the ministries of education of the respective nations, under advice from *ad hoc* committees of linguistic and pedagogical specialists.

With the growing spread of the schools to encompass the entire population, and the rise of new standards in the liberated areas, cultivation expanded into conscious planning. This was especially crucial in countries like Norway, but also in Iceland and the Faroes, in Finland and in Greenland. These procedures come under the term 'language planning', for which I suggested a four-point model as long ago as 1966. For the established languages, like Danish and Swedish, the process had been stretched out over a long period. But even here it involved (1) selection, (2) codification, (3) implementation, and (4) elaboration. The models *selected* at the time of the Reformation were the traditions of speech and writing current in the capitals Copenhagen and Stockholm, seats of the court, of trade and finance, breeding places of the bureaucracy. They were *codified* by rule-of-thumb grammarians, who were dominated by their latinity, mindful of propriety, biased by doctrines of correctness, subservient to throne and church. They were *implemented* by schools under the thumb of the clergy, who took centuries to reject the umbrella of Latin and make the native languages central in their teaching. They were *elaborated* in edifying writings, textbooks for the folk, and eventually by literature in every genre that could find an audience (Haugen 1966b).

In a recent essay I have incorporated some of the terminology proposed by colleagues in the field of language planning (Haugen 1980). Primarily this consists of recognizing a distinction between *status planning* (which includes my 'selection' and 'implementation') and *corpus planning* (including 'codification' and 'elaboration'). Following distinguished precedent, I have ventured to call this my 'extended standard model' and present it here without further comment:

	Form (Policy planning)	Function (Language cultivation)
Society (Status planning)	1. Selection (Decision procedures) a. Identification of problem b. Allocation of norms	3. Implementation (Educational spread) a. Correction procedures b. Evaluation
Language (Corpus planning)	2. Codification (Standardization procedures) a. Graphization b. Grammatication c. Lexication	4. Elaboration (Functional development) a. Terminological modernization b. Stylistic development

The new languages that required the attention of language planners were carved out of Swedish and Danish territory: Finnish, Icelandic, Faroese, and Norwegian. I shall sketch the process briefly for each, recognizing that others will fill in or correct the details.

Finland
Finnish was a minority language, demographically as well as functionally, as long as Finland was a part of the Swedish kingdom. Within Greater Sweden the Finns were a minority and were treated accordingly. Since all major administration was in Swedish, any Finnish speaker who wished to get ahead had not only to learn Swedish, but to some extent disguise or deny his Finnish identity. The tables were turned in 1809 when Finland became a Grand Duchy within Russia, with considerable autonomy. In the course of the century Finnish was encouraged to take over new functions. A national-istic 'Fennoman' movement worked to raise its status. With the publication of the national classic, the *Kalevala*, in 1835, it not only became a symbol of nationality, but even widened its linguistic base to include eastern Karelian dialectal features absent from the old Biblical standard. The elaboration included a rapid expansion of vocabulary as well as the elimination of many traces of Swedish influence which reflected its subordinate position.

For Swedish in Finland the result was to be pushed into minority status, though within a system of official bilingualism. A Fenno-Swedish movement sprang into being to protect its status. Since most of its speakers were located in western Finland, along the coast, a kind of regional segregation could be enforced, with a separate Swedish school system as one of its most powerful forces (Paulston 1977, 1980). Another strategy was a strict purism to keep Fenno-Swedish as much like mother-tongue Swedish as possible and free of Finnish influence (Loman 1977a). The manuals of Hugo Bergroth (1917ff.) are famous guardians of the 'purity' of Finnish Swedish. A third strategy was the organisation in 1906 of a Swedish political party, to bridge the varied social backgrounds of the Swedish population. Active contact with Sweden was encouraged, and Swedish was supported as a link with the rest of Scandinavia. For both populations the other language was a required second language in the schools, though in recent years the requirement has been relaxed in favor of English. The core population of Swedish speakers is static today at around 300,000, which is no more than 6.4 per cent of the total population (in 1975; see Laurén 1978, 1980; Reuter 1977; Loman 1977b; Gröndahl 1977).

The changing economy of Finland is bringing more and more Swedish speakers into contact with bilingual or with monolingual Finnish groups, where Swedish is useless and unpopular. Many young Swedish Finns are today transitional bilinguals on their way to Finnish (Finnish National Commission 1979, article by K. Liebkind and R. Broo). Even in Åland, where Swedish is protected by law, the Finnish-speaking population is growing.

Across the border in northern Sweden, however, there is an area where the opposite movement is going on. This is the valley of Tornedalen, which for strategic reasons was retained by Sweden in the treaty of 1809. Like the Mexicans who suddenly found themselves living in the United States after the annexation of Texas in 1846, the people of Tornedalen landed on the wrong side of the border. The Swedes made it part of their national mission either to ignore them or to assimilate them. In recent years Tornedalen has become a subject of contention. After more than a century of melting-pot treatment, the people of Tornedalen are now enjoying a taste of schooling in the language many of them still use in daily life. But mixture of population and gradual acculturation have left many of them uncertain whether they want their children to study a language that only handicaps them in the new competitive society of modern Sweden. The Swedish scholar Hansegård has raised a controversial issue by describing their bilingualism as 'dual semilingualism', meaning that they master neither or at most one language (Hansegård 1974). His views have been attacked or modified by several scholars, including Erling Wande, who is a native of Tornedalen and denies the contention that his compatriots are only semi-lingual (Wande 1977).

Iceland

The promotion of Finnish from dominated to dominant position was paralleled by the cultivation of Icelandic in the late eighteenth and early nineteenth centuries. From the half-Danicised Icelandic of the 1584 Bible the language was recodified by reference to the classic models from Old Icelandic, which had never been wholly forgotten, although Danish dominance had for a time submerged them. Among the factors that made this possible were the remoteness of Iceland from the mainland, the unbroken tradition of writing, the absence of urban centres of linguistic influence, and the admiration of Nordic and German scholars. The enthusiasm of men like Rasmus Rask stimulated Icelanders to emphasise their uniqueness through a form of corpus planning intended to save Icelandic from the grammatical and lexical Germanisation of the mainland languages.

Techniques of adaptation of foreign terms to the native vocabulary are now so well established and well known that I need not go into them further. I mention them only as part of the process that Icelandic went through in establishing itself as autonomous from Danish and eventually, with independence, as fully dominant. It became a model and an inspiration for others, especially Faroese and Nynorsk-Norwegian (Haugen 1976, 32–3, 332–4; Jónsson 1977).

The Faroes

While Icelandic, thanks to its solid base in the old Bible translation, only needed to be rediscovered, these languages had to be created. The first language planner of Faroese was the fabulous but neglected J. C. Svabo, who began writing down its traditional ballads in 1773, using a Danish-based orthography. He was convinced that it was doomed and advised his countrymen to spend their time learning Danish. It is a classic example of negative status planning, which involved leaving Faroese in the position of a Danish dialect, as most people thought of it then. But in the mid-nineteenth century the times demanded a different solution: it became an *Ausbau* language when Hammershaimb in 1846 codified its orthography after the pattern of Old and Modern Icelandic. By disguising the dialectal differences and clearly revealing its structural relationship to other Nordic languages, Hammershaimb established a norm that was nobody's speech, but everybody's language.

Repeated attempts have been made to make it more orthophonic, but in essence it has survived as the language of Faroese writing. Today it is the language of internal government and a symbol of Faroese home rule (Djupedal 1964). Danish remains the language of outside contact, and the small size of the Faroese community makes full independence unrealistic. So far the best-known writers (e.g. William Heinesen) are still using Danish. And there is still controversy over its elaboration: shall it follow Danish or shall it emulate the creativeness of the Icelanders? (Clausén 1978, Poulsen 1977).

Norway

The case of Norwegian was more complex. Norway is usually said to have lost its language in the late Middle Ages and to have replaced it with Danish between 1450 and 1540. Norwegian did lose the complex of writing traditions that we call Old Norwegian, but so did Swedish and Danish lose their old forms. The crucial differences were: (1) No new Norwegian standard language was created at the time of the Reformation. In contrast with Iceland, the writing traditions were interrupted; no Norwegian Bible was produced; and the post-Reformation writers had learned to write a fairly pure Danish. (2) More important still, a Norwegian speech norm arose, which was partly dependent on Danish writing. One may speculate on the reasons for the strength and independence of this new norm, which was not clearly identified until the time of Knud Knudsen in 1840. He called it 'cultivated daily speech' (*den dannede dagligtale*) and advocated that it become the model for Norwegian spelling reform. Its strength had something to do with the existence of urban centres in Norway, where a new ruling class of bourgeois and bureaucrats could set the standards. A new, supra-local speech norm developed, in origin perhaps a provincial Danish, but with Norwegian independence in 1814 the unquestioned élite dialect of the country (Haugen 1975).

A series of respellings in the twentieth century have brought out its predominantly Norwegian character. Whatever traits of Danish it may have retained, its nature as a living language produced in Norway makes it unmistakeably Norwegian. In spite of all attempts to reject or reshape it, it is still the most prestigious form of Norwegian speech and writing. Its government-controlled form is known as *bokmål*, 'book language', while its more conservative form, favoured by private enterprise, is known as *riksmål*, 'national language'.

Nevertheless, its written form remained predominantly Danish for nearly a century after 1814, a thorn in the flesh to all good patriots. The alternative solution proposed by Ivar Aasen, that genius of language planning, was closely parallel to Hammershaimb's for Faroese. He succeeded in codifying a norm that should remedy the failure of Norwegians to establish a New Norwegian at the time of the Reformation. The norm he produced by a comparative study of the dialects was in effect a reconstructed language, in Stewart's terms a 'classical' language. It was a kind of Middle Norwegian from which each dialect speaker could derive his dialect by a set of transformational rules. Like Faroese, it was to be nobody's dialect and everybody's language, worthy to stand as an instrument of culture alongside Danish, Swedish, Icelandic, and Faroese. His first grammar appeared in 1848, and was revised into definitive form in 1864.

Aasen's norm was noble, but too archaic; its further development has brought his *landsmål*, since 1929 known as *nynorsk*, closer to *bokmål* and the dialects of the midland and eastern regions. Since 1885 it has enjoyed official status, and is available as a first language of writing to any community that adopts it. After reaching a high point of nearly one-third of the school children just before the Second World War, it has retreated to about one-sixth. Its failure to become the unique symbol of the nation, as have Icelandic and Faroese, is due to the existence of the dominant élite dialect, which in a modern urbanised society has proved to be stronger. Aside from this very real stumbling block, there is nothing in its form to prevent Nynorsk from becoming the only Norwegian language. It has a well-entrenched position, especially in western and midland Norway, but has made no headway in urban and eastern Norway. Yet its very existence is something of a miracle and an enrichment for the nation (Haugen 1966a, Gundersen 1973, Steblin-Kamenskij 1977, Vannebo 1979, Haugen 1980, Vinje 1977, Kristiansen 1977).

The Marginal Minorities
In all their zeal to establish national language norms, the Scandinavians of the nineteenth century showed little concern for the marginal or semi-colonial speech groups. The general policy of all the new school systems was to unify the people by requiring that all children learn to master the standard language. Old ethnic groups like the Greenlanders, the Sámi (Lapps), and the Gypsies were expected to learn and use the Nordic language of their country. The probems could generally be ignored, except for missionary purposes, since these people remained relatively underdeveloped or extraneous and were located in remote areas. In each country the dominant policy alternated between periods of benign neglect and hardhanded assimilation (*Scandinavian Review* 1978).

Greenlandic
Greenland as a Danish colony became the object of missionary attention in 1721, when the Norwegian Hans Egede led an expedition to find the old

Norwegians who had settled there in 986 and built flourishing settlements. Egede found that *they* were all gone, but he stayed to convert the Eskimo. His son Paul wrote the first grammar in 1760 and translated the New Testament in 1766. The modern orthography, however, is the work of Samuel Kleinschmidt (1814–86). Only recently, with the Home Rule Act of 1979, have the Greenlanders reached a stage of development that calls for a fully functional standard language. Until a few years ago the Danes did not even realise that they had a minority problem here.

It is a remarkable fact that the Greenlanders have their nearest linguistic kinsmen in Canada and Alaska, most of whom have mutually intelligible dialects. In recent years these 'Bedouins of the North', as Jean Malaurie has called them, have reached out to each other for contact and mutual support (Hatle 1980). In July of this year a conference was held at Godthåb in Greenland, where delegates of what they now wish to call the 'Inuit' peoples met from Greenland, Canada, and Alaska. The second of its kind, it called for an end to white exploitation of the Arctic and for the establishment of an Inuit university, where an Eskimo language would presumably be the medium of instruction (*Adresseavisen*, Trondheim, 4 July 1980). The number of Greenlandic speakers is estimated at about 37,000 (in 1968: *Aschehougs Konversasjons-leksikon*, vol. 8, 1974). Even the use of Greenlandic in the elementary schools and the production of books and newspapers in the language has not protected the Greenlanders from social and economic assimilation to modern society (Hoëm 1971). In fact, it may have promoted it, by putting them in touch with the rest of the world.

Sámi (Lappish)

The Lapps, or Sámi, as they now wish to be known, have long been neglected or discriminated against. They have been treated much like our American Indians, as a picturesque but primitive people of nature. In modern times they have been largely limited to the occupation of reindeer herding, which in Sweden has even been legalised as their exclusive domain. Attempts to create a group bond within a population of perhaps 50,000 have been frustrated by lack of resources and general neglect, as well as their being split among four national jurisdictions, each with its own policies. Bernt Thomassen, the first school inspector of Norwegian Finnmark (appointed 1902) wrote in 1903 to the Norwegian pastor in Kautokeino, 'You and I will make Kautokeino a Norwegian town, if we keep it up' (Hoëm 1980, 47; see also Dahl 1957, 319–23). They failed to reach this goal, however hard they tried, and Kautokeino is today a centre of Sámi activism. But only half of the Sámi stock can still speak the language (see Keskitalo, present volume). It is also split by dialectal differences great enough to offer serious problems of codification. Since 1956 there has been a Nordic Sámi Council, functioning as an inter-Scandinavian Sámic parliament. One of its functions is to produce textbooks and other instruments for the teaching and development of the language.

Among the many steps taken in recent years on behalf of Sámi may be mentioned the Sámi radio station at Karasjok in Norway, the establishment of a Sámi Institute at nearby Kautokeino, and the secondary schools in the same towns (News of Norway, Washington, D.C., March 14, 1980; Finnish National Commission 1979, 51–97; Nesheim 1966; Sámiráđđi 1980). A number of regulations have been aimed at protecting their culture, as the picturesque resource it is. But their territory and their separateness are constantly being encroached upon, so that outside observers have raised the question: are they being protected to death? (Beach 1980, Hoëm 1971, Vorren and Manker 1976).

Romany

A minority that by and large asks only to be left alone is the Gypsy population, which is said to be especially numerous in Finland. They have been known in the North at least since 1500, and they still tend to be peripatetic. Attempts by the government to make them settle down have met with only moderate success. This old Indic tribe is highly endogamous and retentive of its way of life. They still speak Romany, though often in a debased form as a mere secret vocabulary within the framework of the local idiom. There is an international movement for creating a written form of Romany, but I do not know whether it has reached Scandinavia (Finnish National Commission 1979, 99–103; Arnstberg 1974).

Immigrants

The most recent and possibly the most acute minority problem in modern Scandinavia is the one created here as elsewhere by the immigration of exiles and laborers. Children with home languages from Italian and Spanish to Turkish and Pakistani are faced with school systems that are geared to teach only Scandinavian. It is a novel experience for Europeans, though it is only too familiar to Americans. The u.s. Bilingual Act of 1968 with amendments of 1974 attempts to cope with a similar influx from our Spanish and Portuguese-speaking neighbors as well as some of the indigenous minorities (Schneider 1976).

In Sweden, where the number of workers is largest and the problem most acute, a special magazine has sprung up, called 'Immigrants and Minorities' (*Immigranter och Minoriteter*), edited by David Schwarz. Conferences of experts have been hastily called to discuss the problems. The newspapers carry articles discussing measures adopted by school authorities and teachers. There have been clashes between immigrant and native youth. One Norwegian parliament member has recently declared that 'immigrant policy will be one of our most important problems in the coming decades' (Petter Thomassen, *Adresseavisen*, Trondheim, 4 July 1980). In discussing a bill before the Norwegian parliament in 1980, the member cited has declared: 'One can't play blind man's buff in questions that have such profound human aspects as this one.' A recent Norwegian book, *The Immigrants and Their*

Children, exemplifies what can be done to enlighten both teachers and parents (Sætersdal 1978). In Sweden a special research project (FUSKIS) has been organised at the University of Uppsala to study the language problems of Finno-Ugric speakers and another (MESK) to coordinate research on 'Sweden as a multi-ethnic society' (*Sverige Multietniskt Samhälle* 1980, Skutnabb-Kangas 1975b, Kramer 1976, OMEP n.d., Projektet FUSKIS).

For the first time Scandinavian teachers have begun to take an interest in the problems of teaching their languages as second languages (cf. the American TESOL).

Dialects

In recent years there are rumblings of discontent over the enforcement of the national standards in school. As long ago as 1961, a teacher in northern Sweden, Tore Österberg, wrote a dissertation on the language-learning problems of his dialect-speaking pupils. He concluded on the basis of experiments that the pupils should learn reading from writings in their own dialects. For many rural and working-class speakers in these countries, except possibly Iceland and Finland, learning the written standards is virtually equivalent to learning a foreign language. Standards that were established after the Reformation by élite groups dominating the school system are often a poor match for the current speech in town and country. The usual approach has been to stamp such speech as 'incorrect', 'degenerate', or 'vulgar' (on corresponding American discussion see *Dialects and Educational Equity* 1979).

In Norway, where the movement is strongest, the advocates of New-Norwegian have rallied under the slogan, 'Speak your dialect, write New-Norwegian' (Jensen 1974, Jahr 1980, *Dialekt* 1979). Sociolinguist Bengt Loman in Swedish Finland has advised the speakers there to be less concerned about 'correct' Swedish, lest the dialect speakers turn to Finnish (Loman 1977a, b). In 1979 a Nordic symposium recommended that greater attention be paid in schools to the dialects, as the 'real mother tongue'. This appears to be in line with Robert A. Hall's well-known book title, 'Leave your language alone!' If this turns out to be more than a passing fad, it would represent the ultimate fragmentation of Scandinavian.

Nordic Unity

So far I have deliberately stressed the centrifugal trends: one minority after the other is knocking on the doors of the school system. There are also centripetal trends, conscious or not, strengthening the unity that remains. Mass media play a central role in bringing people together, now reinforced by planning for Nordic unity. In 1978 a Nordic Language Board (*Nordisk språkråd*) was established, with Bertil Molde as chairman and a secretariat in Oslo. On this board are seated, for the first time, representatives for Sámi and Inuit, along with each of the major or minor languages so far discussed.

The Nordic Council, parent of the Language Board, has declared 1980 as

'Nordic Language Year'. Special efforts are being made through propaganda and research to keep the central languages from drifting apart. Successful efforts have been initiated to adopt identical terminology for new concepts. Advice is being given on how to adapt one's language for easier communication (Nordiskt språksekretariat 1977, *Att tala nordiskt* 1980).

All this activity is in the name of self-preservation. The real threat to Scandinavian, as mentioned, is felt to be English. The teaching of English in the lower grades, the overwhelming media exposure to Anglo-American entertainment, and the military and commercial dependence of Scandinavia on the English-speaking world has created a pressure on their languages that is directly and obviously threatening. The wheel has come full circle. The dominance of Rome and its Latin, under whose shadow Scandinavian lived for so long, has been replaced by that of its heir, the Anglo-American empire and its Latinised English.

Observations

In conclusion, I would like to make some remarks about the problems of protecting a minority language. The process has much in common with the protection of endangered species of plants and animals; we need, as I have pointed out elsewhere, an ecology of language (Haugen 1972). Languages and species can die, as Cornish did in Cornwall and as the passenger pigeon did in America.

Wherever languages are in contact, they are in competition for users. They may be seen as commodities on a *language market*, and they will live only as long as they find customers who will buy them. Language competence is a skill with a market value that determines who will acquire it. The price of a language is the effort required to learn it, and its value is the benefits its use will bring to the learner. Even our so-called mother tongue, the first language we learn willy-nilly from our environment, will be maintained only if it serves as a medium of communication with speakers with whom we wish to communicate (cf. Lundén 1977).

The value of a language involves both material and spiritual aspects. It is obviously more profitable to learn English than, say, Israeli, unless one happens to be an Israeli. For other Jews the value is likely to be more purely spiritual, in that it gives access to the heritage of a great tradition. Languages like English are referred to as Languages of Wider Communication (LWC), but for most people the highest value lies in their Language of Intimate Communication (LIC). Everyone needs such a language, but not everyone needs a second language, and unless they do, they may be unwilling to pay the price of learning it (cf. Sigurd 1977).

One price that most speakers of minority languages have to pay is that of becoming bilingual. There is no evidence that bilingualism as such is harmful, any more than any other intellectual exercise. Quite the contrary. But it does require time and effort to acquire and maintain – time and effort that not everyone is willing (or able) to put in.

In a bilingual society the children are faced with a conflict of values. They are expected by their parents to maintain the values of the old, and by their peers to adopt the values of the new. In this age-old conflict between tradition and innovation, the result depends on the degree of *separateness* the old speech group can maintain. Performing successfully in two groups requires a constant vigilance that many are not willing to exert. The ideal is to preserve the best of the old while gaining the best of the new, but in practice the result can be to lose the best of both. The alternative is segregation or isolation, terms that are not popular these days. Yet they are practised by every nation through the language teaching of its schools and by every religion that maintains a sacred language. Languages set borders to ethnicity and communication; they form enclaves – ghettos, if you will – within which intimacy can prosper, while efficiency languishes.

Visionaries have dreamt of a world in which all such boundaries would be dissolved by the introduction of a world language. As far as I can see, the world is not yet ready for it. On the other hand, most men and women are in no need of it, since their lives are lived face-to-face within the immediate neighborhood of their birth or occupation. But those who would preserve all the minority languages of the world are equally visionary.

In studying the ebb and flow of the language market, we have been impressed by the importance assigned to the school systems. These have as their primary goal to socialise and thereby guide the rising generation, so that the young will be able to function effectively and happily within the nation and the world. Among other things this means to master the national written and spoken language, and in the case of small nations, a world language as well. When there are groups whom we choose to call 'minorities', whose language is neglected by the nation, the schools become a major battleground of language conflict. We assume, perhaps too lightly, that those who master the teaching of the young are also masters of the linguistic future.

The experience of foreign language teachers everywhere has confirmed that languages *can* be taught and learned in schools, given enough time and resources. But competence does not of itself motivate the learner to make use of his language. Survival in the present and (for some) in the hereafter is a more powerful incentive. Political autonomy, the creation of language enclaves, helps to protect a language. But, as the Irish have learned to their distress, the autonomous nation-state is no longer a guarantee of linguistic autonomy.

A language is a precious treasure so long as it serves as a reservoir of wit and wisdom from the past that will help to guide our future. We are here to ponder the means that will enable our leaders and our peoples to look less at the cost of maintaining small languages, and more at the values that are lost if we let them die. We know what those means are: to mobilise the power to claim our rights. But do we have the will to do so?

References

Adler, Max K. (1977) *Collective and Individual Bilingualism:
A Sociolinguistic Study.* Hamburg: Buske.

Arnstberg, Karl-Olov (1974) *Zigenarens väg: Essä om en minoritet.*
Stockholm: L. T. 's Förlag.

Att tala nordiskt – språkråd till nordbor i nordiskt samarbete (1980)
Nordisk råd och Nordisk språksekretariat. Oslo.

Bandle, Oskar (1979) Soziolinguistische Strukturen in den nordischen
Sprachen, in *Standard und Dialekt,* 217-38. Bern: Francke Verlag.

Beach, Hugh (1980) On Being Culturally Protected to Death: The
Lappish Case, in *Cultural Survival,* 4.1.4. Cambridge, Mass.

Bergroth, Hugo (1917) *Finlandssvenska: Handledning till undvikande
av provinsialismer i tal och skrift.* Helsingfors: Schildt.

Braunmüller, Kurt (1979) Mehrsprachigkeit, Diglossie und Sprach-
probleme in Skandinavien, in *Current Issues in Linguistic Theory*
(ed. B. Brogyanyi), vol. 11, 139-57. Amsterdam Studies in
Linguistic Science IV.

Brems, Hans (1979) The Collapse of the Binational Danish Monarchy in
1864: A Multinational Perspective, *Scandinavian Studies 51,*
428-41.

Clausén, Ulla (19978) *Nyord i färöiskan: Ett bidrag till belysning av
språksituationen på Färöarna.* Stockholm: Studies in Scandinavian
Philology, N.S. 14.

Connors, Kathleen (1979) Review of William F. Mackay [*sic*],
Bilinguisme et contact de langues (Paris: 1976), *Language in
Society 8,* 453-63.

Dahl, Helge (1957) *Språkpolitikk og skolestell i Finnmark 1814 til 1905.*
Oslo: Universitetsforlaget.

Dahlstedt, Karl-Hampus (1976) *Societal Ideology and Language
Cultivation: The Case of Swedish.* Umeå: Dept. of General
Linguistics, University of Umeå (Publication 11).

Dialects and Educational Equity (1979) 5 vols. Arlington, Va.:
Center for Applied Linguistics.

Dialekt og riksspråk i skulen (1979) Rapport frå eit nordisk symposium
på Lysebu 2.-5. april 1979. Oslo.

Djupedal, Reidar (1964) Litt om framvoksteren av det færøyske
skriftmålet, in *Skriftspråk i utvikling,* 144-86. Oslo:
Norsk språknemnd.

Dorian, Nancy (1979) Review of Max K. Adler: *Welsh and the Other
Dying Languages of Europe: A Sociolinguistic Study* (Hamburg:
Buske, 1977), *Language in Society 8,* 70-1.

Ferguson, Charles (1959) Diglossia, *Word 15,* 325-40.

Finnish National Commission for Unesco (1979) *Cultural Pluralism and
the Position of Minorities in Finland.* Helsinki.

Gal, Susan (1979) *Language Shift: Social Determinants of Linguistic
Change in Bilingual Austria.* New York: Academic Press.

Giles, Howard and B. Saint-Jacques (eds) (1979) *Languages and Ethnic
Relations.* Oxford, etc.: Pergamon Press.

Gröndahl, Aulis (1977) Statistik och prognoser om svenska språkets
framtid i Finland, in [Sigurd] 1977, 69-80.

Groenke, Ulrich (1978) Mikael Agricola und Åbo. *Mitteilungen,*
Deutsch-Finnische Gesellschaft in Köln 10.3.1-2.

Gundersen, Dag (1973) Successes and Failures in the Reformation of
Norwegian Orthography, in *Advances in the Creation and Revision
of Writing Systems* (ed. J. Fishman), 247-65. Mouton.

Hansegård, Nils-Erik (1974) *Tvåspråkighet eller halvspråkighet?,*
4. ed. Stockholm. (Article with same title: *Nordisk Minoritets-
forskning* 1975.)

Hatle, Liv (1980) Jyväskyla sommar. *Dag og tid* (Oslo),
    4 September 1980.
Haugen, Einar (1966a) *Language Conflict and Language Planning:
    The Case of Modern Norwegian.* Cambridge, Mass.: Harvard.
    (Norw. version, tr. by Dag Gundersen: *Riksspråk og folkemål,*
    Oslo: Universitetsforlaget, [1969].)
— (1966b) Dialect, Language, Nation, *American Anthropologist 68,*
    922-35.
— (1972) *The Ecology of Language: Essays* (ed. Anwar S. Dil).
    Stanford: Stanford University Press.
— (1975) Språket: en sosiolingvistisk profil, in *Det norske samfunn*
    (ed. N. Ramsøy and M. Vaa), 620-57. Oslo. (English version in
    Michigan Germanic Studies 1, 9-46.)
— (1976) *The Scandinavian Languages: An Introduction to Their
    History.* London: Faber and Faber/Cambridge, Mass.: Harvard.
— (1978) The English Language as an Instrument of Modernization
    in Scandinavian, *Det modärna Skandinaviens framväxt* (Acta
    Universitatis Upsaliensis, Symposia 10), 81-91.
— (1980) Language Problems and Language Planning: The Scan-
    dinavian Model. *Sprachkontakt und Sprachkonflikt (etc.),* ed. by
    P. H. Nelde (Wiesbaden: *Zeitschrift für Dialektologie und
    Linguistik,* Helft 32), 151-7.
Hoëm, Anton (1971) National Schools and Ethnic Minorities: A Com-
    parison, *Tidsskrift for Samfunnsforskning* (Oslo) *12,* 211-30.
— (1980) *Etnopolitikk som skolepolitikk.* Oslo: Universitetsforlaget.
Holmestad, E. and Lade, A. J. (eds) (1969) *Lingual Minorities in
    Europe.* Oslo: Det Norske Samlaget.
Ingers, Ingemar (1974) Uniformiteten och Skånes folkmål,
    Ale: Historisk tiddskrift för Skåneland, Nr. 3, 31-43.
Jahr, Ernst Håkon (1980) A Rationale for Language Planning Policy in
    Norway, *Nordlyd* (Tromsø University Working Papers), 67-82.
Jensen, Martin Kloster (1974) Vårt forhold til dialektene, *Norsk
    tidsskrift for logopedi,* 134-8.
Jónsson, Baldur (1977) Isländskans situation, in [Sigurd] 1977, 81-9.
Kloss, Heinz (1978) *Die Entwicklung neuer germanischen Kultur-
    sprachen,* 2. ed., revised. Düsseldorf: Schwann.
Kramer, Jane (1976) The Invandrare, *New Yorker,* March 22, 43-84.
Kristiansen, Bjarne (1977) Språkstrid og politikk, in [Sigurd] 1977,
    41-57.
Larsen, Mogens Baumann (1977) Sprogsituationen i Danmark –
    en betragtning, in [Sigurd] 1977, 19-25.
Laurén, Christen (ed.) (1978) *Finlandssvenskan: Fakta och debatt.*
    [Helsinki]: Söderström and Co.
— (1980) Finland-Swedish Language Cultivation Strategy during
    Hundred Years. Paper, Society for Advancement of Scandinavian
    Study, May.
Loman, Bengt (1977a) Högspråk och dialekt i den Finlandssvenska
    skolan, *Dialectology and Sociolinguistics* (Acta Universitas
    Umensis, Studies in the Humanities 12), 71-82.
— (1977b) Svenska språkets framtid i Finland, in [Sigurd] 1977, 58-68.
Lundén, Thomas (1977) Språket, samhället och geografin, in [Sigurd]
    1977, 4-18.
Nesheim, Asbjørn (1966) *Samene: Historie og kultur,*
    2. ed. Oslo: Tanum.
Nordiskt språksekretariat (1977) Nordiska rådet och Nordiska
    Ministerrådet. Oslo.
Österberg, Tore (1961) *Bilingualism and the First School Language.*
    Diss. Umeå.
Ohlsson, Stig Örjan (1978-9) *Skånes språkliga försvenskning,* 2 vols.
    Lund: Lundastudier i nordisk språkvetenskap, Serie A, nr. 30, 31.

OMEP (n.d.) *Små indvandrerbørn i det danske samfund.* Copenhagen.

Paulston, Rolland G. (1977) Separate Education as an Ethnic Survival Strategy: The Finlandssvenska Case, *Anthropology and Education Quarterly 8,* 3, 181-8.

— (1980) The Swede-Finn Movement for Ethnic Separation in Finland, in *Other Dreams, Other Schools,* 140-69. Pittsburgh: University of Pittsburgh Press.

Poole, Jonathan (1980) Review of William M. O'Barr and Jean F. O'Barr (eds), *Language and Politics,* Mouton and Co., 1976, *Language in Society 9,* 104-8.

Poulsen, Jóhan Hendrik W. (1977) Det færøske sprogs situation, in [Sigurd] 1977, 90-102.

Projektet Fuskis (Finsk-ugrisk språkkontakt i Sverige) (n.d.) Stencilled report from Finsk-ugriska institutionen, Uppsala.

Reuter, Mikael (1977) Svenskan i Finland och finlandssvensk språkvård, *Språkvård 4,* 5-14.

Sætersdal, Barbro (1978) *Innvandrerne og barna deres.* Oslo.

Sámiráđđi (1980) *Bibliografia sámiid birra 1960-1969.* Ohcejohka.

Scandinavian Review (New York) (March 1978) Special issue on minorities, pp.7-77 (17 articles and poems).

Schermerhorn, R. A. (1964) Toward a General Theory of Minority Groups, *Phylon 25,* 238-46.

Schneider, Susan Gilbert (1976) *Revolution, Reaction or Reform: The 1974 Bilingual Education Act.* Arlington, Va.: Center for Applied Linguistics.

Sigurd, Bengt (ed.) (1977) *De nordiske språkenes framtid.* Oslo: Norsk språkråd, skrifter 19. (Articles by T. Lundén, M. Baumann Larsen, F.-E. Vinje, B. Kristiansen, B. Loman, A. Gröndahl, B. Jónsson, J. H. W. Poulsen, N. Hasselmo, B. Sigurd.)

— (1977) Språk och framtid – några spekulationer, in [Sigurd] 1977, 132-47.

Skard, Sigmund (1980) *Classical Tradition in Norway.* Oslo, etc.: Universitetsforlaget.

Skautrup, Peter (1944-70) *Det danske sprogs historie,* 5v. Copenhagen.

Skutnabb-Kangas, Tove (1975a, repr. 1978) *Om tvåspråkighet och skolframgång.* Svenska Litteratursällskapet i Finland.

— (1975b) Bilingualism, Semilingualism and School Achievement. Fourth International Congress of Applied Linguistics, Stuttgart.

Søndergård, Bent (1978) Tosprogethedsproblemer i det dansk-tyske grænseområde. *Mødet mellem sprogene i det dansk-tyske grænseområde,* 58-67. Åbennå: Institut for grænseregionsforskning.

— (1980) Sprogkontakt i den danske-tyske grænseregion: Interferensproblematikken. Fourth International Conference of Nordic and General Linguistics (Oslo, June 23-27, 1980), Abstracts, 127.

Steblin-Kamenskij, M. I. (1977) Is Planning of Language Development Possible? The Norwegian Language Movement at an Impasse, in *Soviet Contributions to the Sociology of Language* (ed. T. A. Luelsdorff), 99-111. The Hague.

Sutton, Geoffrey (1979) Cultural and Socio-economic Factors in the Formation of Foreign Language Education Policy in Sweden – with a Comparison with the Finnish Case, *Language Problems and Language Planning 3,* 9-24.

Sverige Multietniskt Samhälle: Rapport (1980) Uppsala.

Tengström, Emin (1973) *Latinet i Sverige: Om bruket av latin blant klerker och scholares, diplimater och poeter, lärdomsfolk och vältalare.* Lund: Bonniers.

Vannebo, Kjell Ivar (1979) Omgrepet 'samnorsk', *Maal og Minne,* 165-81.

Vinje, Finn-Erik (1977) Språksituasjonen i Norge, in [Sigurd] 1977, 26-40.
Vogt, Hans (1970) De små språksamfunn: Noen betraktninger, in *The Nordic Languages and Modern Linguistics* (ed. Hreinn Benediktsson), 306-10. Reykjavík: Vísindafélag.
Vorren, Ørnulv and Manker, Ernst (1976) *Samekulturen*, 2. ed. Oslo: Universitetsforlaget.
Wande, Erling (1977) Hansegård är ensidig, *Invandrare och Minoriteter*, 44-51.
Wennås, Olof (1966) *Striden om latinväldet: Idéer och intressen i svensk skolpolitik under 1800-talet*. Stockholm: Almquist och Wiksell (Skrifter utg. av Statsvet. Föreningen i Uppsala, 45).

10. Is Nynorsk a Minority Language?

Is Nynorsk a minority language? It has been said that it is a majority language with the problems of a minority language. This statement is of course paradoxical, but it contains an element of truth which I shall try to make clear by looking at the social status of the language in relation to the other Norwegian standard language and to the dialects. I have chosen to approach the subject through a survey of the terminology used in the Norwegian language debate. By defining the terms we use and discussing their appropriateness I hope to bring you one step closer to an understanding of our complicated linguistic situation.

First of all I have to point out that I am not an impartial or unbiased observer. No Norwegian who has given any thought at all to our language problems can have avoided forming an opinion of his own, and every opinion is at least partly based on emotional factors. This is a very important point. Many Norwegian linguists who believe themselves to be objective have, in reality, been partially guided by their likes or dislikes. I do not accuse any of them of having misrepresented or distorted facts, but some of them have selected and used facts to support their preconceived ideas, especially with regard to 'Norwegian-ness': has such and such a phenomenon developed independently on Norwegian soil, or is it due to influence from Denmark? I am a former propagandist for the cause of Nynorsk and have still a strong emotional attachment to this form of Norwegian. I also prefer to use Nynorsk in speech and writing, although there are occasions where I have to, or feel I ought to, use Bokmål.

Before going any further it is necessary for me to give you some basic definitions. This is especially important because the linguistic struggle in Norway has often been made more confused and more abortive by inaccurate terminology and occasionally also by conscious speculation, for propagandistic purposes, in the accuracy of certain terms.

The first concept we have to define is the term *standard language*. I do not propose to define the term *language* and shall attempt not to use it here except in a loose and general manner. A standard language is a system of writing and speech which is recognised as official by a national or provincial government. By this definition we have four Nordic standard languages in Scandinavia today: Danish, Swedish, Norwegian Bokmål and Norwegian Nynorsk (I do not include Icelandic and Faroese, which are standard languages, or rather *have* standard languages, but are not spoken in Scandinavia if by this geographical term we understand only the Scandinavian peninsula and Denmark; nor do I include the obvious ethnic minority languages Lapp and Finnish or such new minority languages as Urdu, Turkish and English). A standard language may also be a written norm only, without a spoken equivalent. This may, with some justification, be said about Nynorsk. In a standard language the written norm dominates, and is usually invoked in discussions about the 'correctness' of spoken forms.

A *dialect* is, in contemporary linguistics, often defined as a linguistic system peculiar to a given locality or a given social group. By this definition the standard languages are dialects as well as the non-standard linguistic systems. While, in a different context, I might very well use this definition myself, I choose, for the present purpose, to use the term dialect only for non-standard linguistic systems. This is necessary, or at least desirable, because in any discussion of the linguistic situation in Norway the opposition between dialects and standard languages has to be taken into consideration. Each locality in Scandinavia, urban or rural, has its own geographical dialect; and in the towns and cities there are also social dialects which vary according to such factors as occupation, education and income class. All these are non-standard (here I am talking of *dialects* which, in the towns, are spoken *beside* Standard Bokmål). I hesitate to use the term 'substandard' because it suggests that the dialects are qualitatively inferior, which in my view they are not. They are all chiefly spoken rather than written: although many dialects are occasionally used in writing, they have no *norm-providing* written form. The local dialects in Scandinavia melt gradually into one another so that there are few very clear language boundaries in the sense of thick bundles of isoglosses. Most of the clear boundaries that exist are due to the influence of the various modern standard languages and are accordingly identical with the political boundaries. They are also of fairly recent date. One example will suffice to show what I mean. I have of recent years had occasion to spend a good deal of time in an area of West Värmland in Sweden, close to the Norwegian border. A middle-aged farmer I talked to only a few weeks ago told me that the true local word for 'pail' was *bötte*, but the young people would hardly understand what it meant, he said, their word for 'pail' being *hink*. Now *hink* is the Standard Swedish word for 'pail', and this is the word the children learn at school and hear on radio and television, while *bötte* stretches across the border and is found all over Norway as the normal word for 'pail'. This shows a linguistic border in the making, corresponding with the boundary of the Swedish political sphere of influence.

It should be noted that the Scandinavian dialects are not dialects 'of' the modern standard languages in the sense of being derivations or deviations from them. The dialects are developments from older language stages and sometimes preserve features that the standard languages have lost. One example: Standard Swedish has lost the three-gender system in nouns, the masculine and feminine having converged into a so-called common gender, so that modern Standard Swedish has only two genders in nouns, common and neuter, while many dialects have preserved the original three, masculine, feminine and neuter. When I use the term Norwegian dialects I simply mean Nordic dialects in Norway; by Swedish dialects I mean Nordic dialects in Sweden, etc.

This concludes my basic definitions. Let us now turn to my main subject, the terminology we use in our debates on language policy and language planning in Norway. The first and also the most important problem in terminology is the naming of the two standard languages.

To begin with I shall call them Language A and Language B. The Old Norwegian literary language was forgotten during the Danish reign from about 1400 to 1814. Up to about 1850, an almost pure Danish was the only written language in Norway and accordingly needed no specific name. It was indiscriminately called 'Danish', 'the written language' and, as a school subject, even *modersmålet* although it was hardly anybody's real mother tongue in Norway. In the larger towns a spoken counterpart of this written language had developed. This spoken language was originally a reading language, based on the Norwegian reading pronunciation of written Danish, to which had been added some items of dialectal Norwegian vocabulary and also a few Norwegian inflectional features. This enriched reading language eventually became the spoken language of a minority among the populations of the larger towns – some but not all of the rich and the educated. It has not been clearly established when this took place, but at any rate this type of language must have been in daily use to a certain extent before 1814, the year of Norway's secession from Denmark; and it is an irony of history that Danish influence on the Norwegian language was never so strong during the centuries of Danish rule as it was after the liberation. This, of course, was among other things a consequence of an improved educational system where illiteracy was eradicated by the teaching of written Danish – the only written language that was available for this purpose at the time.

Language A, the language I have just been dealing with, is accordingly the one which is chiefly derived from written Danish. Language B is the one that is based on Norwegian dialects and was 'created' towards the middle of the last century. Even this simple statement would enrage some people. I shall have more to say about this a little later on; at the moment I am only concerned with an identification of the two languages. Language A was eventually named *riksmål* and Language B *landsmål*, which two terms are probably to this day the best known internationally. Language A is also often called Dano-Norwegian; Language B is also, but less frequently, termed simply Norwegian. In 1929 the two languages were officially renamed *bokmål* (Language A) and *nynorsk* (Language B). These are still the official terms, but many people continue to use the older terms *riksmål* and *landsmål*. What is important to remember is that *Dano-Norwegian*, *riksmål* and *bokmål* are synonymous and denote Language A, while *landsmål* and *nynorsk* both denote Language B. Both languages have changed constantly and rapidly during the brief span of their existence, so that either of the two can be observed in a variety of evolutionary stages.

I shall now make a few comments on the terms and definitions I have presented so far, beginning with the terms for Language A. The term *Dano-Norwegian* (*dansk-norsk*), used by many writers in the last century and also by some foreign linguists even today, is a good term because it describes the language as accurately as can be done in one word (although *norsk-dansk* is conceivably a trifle more accurate still). Unfortunately it is unacceptable to users of Language A because of its emotional load. Above all, Bokmål people do not want to be regarded as un-national or un-Norwegian. It is also a common notion among Norwegians that Danish is a slightly comical language when spoken. It is perceived as a sort of broken Norwegian: the Danes write almost the same as we do, but their pronunciation of the letters is quite wrong, almost like a speech defect. This is hardly ever asserted openly, and any Norwegian with a minimum of education will reject this line of reasoning, but nevertheless I think this attitude is quite common on a lower level of consciousness. Occasionally the aversion to Danish speech betrays itself. An acquaintance of mine, a doctor of medicine and a specialist in occupational diseases, once told me: 'Danish is not a language, it is a disease of the musculature of the throat'. The aversion to spoken Danish is not linked with any unfriendly feelings towards the Danish people. On the contrary, Danes are very popular in Norway (and vice-versa), and the Danish supremacy over Norway which came to an end in 1814 is very definitely a thing of the past.

The term *riksmål* for Dano-Norwegian or Language A was created in order to provide a term without reference to Danish, as a counterpart to the term *landsmål* for the other language. It was in 1853 that Ivar Aasen launched *landsmål* as a designation for his newly-constructed Norwegian standard language. *Riksmål* as a name for Dano-Norwegian was first used in the 1870s. It is of some interest to see how *riksmål* is defined in *Norsk Riksmålsordbok*, the largest and most authoritative dictionary of Riksmål. I quote in translation: '*Riksmål* (1) = *rikssprog* (national language), (2) Norwegian language form, one of the two official language forms of the country, used of both the Dano-Norwegian written language (especially at the end of the nineteenth and the beginning of the twentieth century) and the spoken language that has arisen by an amalgamation between the so-called intermediate language of the towns and the formal or ceremonious language with influence also from an older Norwegian reading-language tradition (characterised among other things by two genders, and mono-phthongs where many Norwegian dialects have diphthongs), a language form which, through the Government's modifications of 1907 and 1917, has been adopted as the basis for the written language, which, in its turn, through the modifications of 1938, has been the object of attempts to carry it further in the direction of East Norwegian dialects and Landsmål.' This part of the Dictionary was written in the 1940s, as far as I am able to ascertain. It may be noted that the authors, all of whom were of course supporters of Riksmål but conscientious linguists, did not try to avoid the term Dano-Norwegian in the definition of their language.

The invention of the term *riskmål* was a psychological masterstroke. The word suggests officialdom. *Riksmål* 'Language of the Realm' is associated with, e.g. *Riksarkiv* 'Archives of the Realm', 'State Archives', *Rikstryg-deverk* 'State Social Security Administration', etc. By implication the term *landsmål* sounds less official, in spite of the fact that the Storting or Parliament granted equal status to the two languages in 1885.

It was mainly opposition from the Landsmål side to this terminological advantage of Riksmål – an unfair advantage, in their opinion – that led to the official renaming in 1928 when *riksmål* became *bokmål*. The new term is as bad as the old one, both because it suggests that Language A is exclusively a written or bookish language and because it hints that Language B has no literature.

The nomenclature used for Language B has also been misleading. Before it received a specific name it was often called *Folkesproget*, *Folkemålet* or *Almuesproget*, all meaning approximately 'language of the common people' and modelled on the German *Volkssprache* – language of the common people as opposed to such classes as the gentry, the rich and the educated. It was quite appropriate to use this term for the dialects on which Language B was based and for which it was intended to be a common denominator, but it would have led to confusion to continue using it for the new *standard* language because a standard language is by definition not a dialect or *Volkssprache*. The term *landsmål* was therefore invented. It did not, like the Swedish term *landsmål*, mean 'local country dialect', but quite the opposite: it was a language intended to be valid for the whole country *as opposed to* local dialects. The term *landsmål* is not to be compared with *landsbygd* 'countryside' or with *landsfolk* 'country people', but rather with *landsfor-bund* 'countrywide organisation', *landsnamn* 'name of a country', *landslag* 'national team' or *landsgyldig* 'valid for the whole country or nation'. In fact, it was intended to express practically the same idea as the term *riksmål*, and it is tempting to speculate on the hypothetical course of events that might have ensued if Ivar Aasen had chosen *riksmål* as the name of his standard language. The term had not yet been used by anybody as early as 1853, and if Aasen had known anything about modern advertising he would have rea-lised the enormous sales potential of the term *riksmål* with its ring of officialdom. The term *landsmål* turned out to be about the worst label he could have put on his product. It has largely been misunderstood as 'rural' or even 'rustic language' – an interpretation that was not unnatural, since Language B was in fact based on the dialects of country districts while Aasen rejected the town dialects, not necessarily as inferior in themselves but as unsuitable for the purpose because they had developed into forms too remote from their common Old Norse origin. This misinterpretation has also to a great extent been made by the *supporters* of Landsmål, to the great detriment of the movement. The opposition between the two standard languages became part of the opposition between rural and urban culture, and it was almost taken for granted that a supporter of Landsmål was also a supporter of the use of folk costumes, folk music, folk food, etc. Consequently townspeople, and country people who wanted to emulate townspeople, rejected Landsmål along with the local dialects. In our days Language A, Bokmål or Riksmål, is almost a part of the modern standard of living, a status symbol like an expensive car, a colour television set or a pedigree dog. This is still largely so in spite of some new tendencies which have begun to appear during the 1970s, the 'green wave' and the various environmental and populist movements. Many of the young people who have embraced these ideas have become ardent supporters of Nynorsk, and so have many people of the political Left, from moderate Communists to revolutionary extremists, who consider Nynorsk the language of the oppressed masses and Bokmål an instrument of the corrupt establishment.

When *riksmål* became *bokmål* in 1928, *landsmål* became *nynorsk*. The latter change of names had more success than the former. The term *landsmål* is now used only by some very old people and by a few who reject the name *nynorsk* on principle. But *nynorsk* is not a very good term, either. It means 'New Norwegian' and is equivocal because it can also mean Modern Norwegian dialects as opposed to Old or Middle Norwegian, which were earlier stages in their development, as if one would call English *New English* every time it were mentioned. The only satisfactory pair of terms that has been proposed and used is *Dano-Norwegian* for Language A and simply *Norwegian* for Language B; but the pair is politically impossible, as you will readily understand from what I have said.

I would like to insert a little remark here: *nynorsk* is often translated into English as *New Norse*. This is completely wrong. It suggests a resuscitation of the Old Norse language of the sagas, which is Icelandic rather than Norwegian. Nynorsk is definitely not a language arisen from the dead, like Modern Hebrew for instance. It is a norm based on the living dialects *descended* from Old Norse, dialects that survived the four centuries of Danish cultural and political domination. It is true, as Einar Haugen has pointed out (present volume, p.110) that Ivar Aasen's first norm was 'a kind of Middle Norwegian from which each speaker could derive his dialect by a set of transformational rules', but this retrogression in time was not a goal in itself, only a means to achieve the goal which was democratic rather than nationalistic.

The official terms today, then, are *bokmål* and *nynorsk*, misleading and unsatisfactory as they are. But we now arrive at a new chapter of terminology, the terms that concern the different varieties of present-day Bokmål and Nynorsk. For there *are* different varieties, and they have played an important part in the discussion during the last few decades. The reforms of 1907, 1917, 1938 and 1957 have, among other things, resulted in a *radical* and a *moderate* variety of either language. As practically all reforms have partly codified actual changes in which the two languages have come closer to each other and partly even anticipated such changes, radical Bokmål and radical Nynorsk are more similar than are moderate Bokmål and moderate Nynorsk. These are the official varieties. But many conservative people on both sides refuse to accept the latest changes and have, through their organisations, established private norms which they recommend to writers and to the public. As these norms are more conservative than the official moderate forms (although their advocates dislike the term conservative) it seems reasonable to call them so, and we may visualise the state of affairs like this:

(Private)	Conservative Bokmål	Conservative Nynorsk
(Official)	{ Moderate Bokmål	Moderate Nynorsk
	Radical Bokmål	Radical Nynorsk

Schools have the choice between the four official varieties. The language of each school is determined by vote among the parents in the school district.

In practice there are no strict boundaries between the conservative, moderate and radical varieties. Many writers use some forms from one variety and some from another, so that it is often quite impossible to tell whether a given writer, in a given piece of writing, intends to use one variety or another, or indeed if he wants to conform to a norm at all.

The authorities, against strong opposition from conservatives on both sides, have attempted to promote and at times to accelerate the natural development towards a total convergence of the two languages into one standard language. This hypothetical future language is often called *samnorsk* 'Common Norwegian'. There is even an organisation called *Språklig Samling* 'Linguistic Unification' which demands that a Samnorsk alternative to Bokmål and Nynorsk must be given *now*, and they have set up a tentative norm for this alternative. This norm, however, remains private and has not very many followers in spite of the fact that many people sympathise with the idea in theory.

The intricacies of our terminology have made it easy for obscurants to confuse the issues. Thus, conservative supporters of Language A have refused to acknowledge the equation of *riksmål* with *bokmål*. They reserve the term *riksmål* for conservative and moderate Bokmål and use *bokmål* as a term of abuse for radical Bokmål, which they also equate with the non-existent Samnorsk.

I shall now return to the question posed in the title of this paper. Nynorsk *is* a minority language in the sense that it is preferred as a standard language by a minority of Norwegians. The percentage of this minority can only be estimated, as there are no statistics of preferences, only some opinion polls in which the questions have been completely inadequate. Even if adequate questions were prepared – or indeed could be prepared – the results would be unreliable because a large percentage of the interviewees would only have very dim ideas on the subject, as you will readily appreciate after my discussion of the confusing terminology. Further, a preference may be many things. I may *like* one language better personally, but prefer my child to learn the other language in school because I think it will be more useful for the child.

But why talk about preferences? Wouldn't it be better to ask people which language they actually speak or write? In Norway this cannot be done, because a majority of the population do not speak a standard language habitually, but a town or country dialect. Very many dialect users are able to speak a standard language as well, but do so only on special occasions. When people are interviewed on radio or television, they may answer the questions in dialect, in Bokmål or in Nynorsk, but perhaps more often than not they use a haphazard mixture of dialect and one or both standard languages. When people with little formal education write, they do try to write one or the other of the standard languages, but the result is very often a mixture which it is difficult to place under any one heading.

In the heated language debate in Norway it has often been maintained by Bokmål supporters that Bokmål is spoken by seventy-five or eighty or ninety per cent of the Norwegian population. This is downright nonsense, and people can only be brought to believe it because the city of Oslo and the densely populated areas on the Oslo Fjord are assumed to be Bokmål-speaking. This assumption is quite incorrect. The majority of the population in these areas, the working classes, speak Norwegian dialects descended mainly from Old Norse. The confusion results from three facts: (a) these dialects have been strongly *influenced* by Oslo Bokmål, more strongly than many town dialects in other parts of Norway; (b) conversely, the Dano-Norwegian Bokmål, especially as spoken in Oslo, has been very strongly influenced by precisely these dialects which form its Norwegian substratum; (c) these same dialects have again and again been denounced as debased varieties of Bokmål. On the Nynorsk side it is often maintained that all the dialects of Norway are Nynorsk dialects because they are neither Danish nor Old Norse, another fallacy made possible by the equivocality of the nomenclature, this time the term *nynorsk*, which is here taken to mean both the standard language and a stage of development of the dialects.

In the light of what I have just said it must be clear that we cannot use number of speakers as a criterion except for a relatively small number of people, those members of the educated classes who speak the standard languages. Among these an overwhelming majority speak Bokmål. I must, however, stress here that very many educated people, unlike the educated classes in many other European countries, speak dialect deliberately and with a certain pride in everyday life and turn to a standard language only on certain formal occasions.

The number of speakers of Standard Nynorsk is still smaller than it might have been if the speaking of Nynorsk had been encouraged more. As it is, there is very little such encouragement. Nynorsk is regarded by many as the written counterpart of the spoken dialects. In fact, the latest slogan from *Noregs Mållag*, the countrywide organisation for Nynorsk, runs: 'Speak dialect, write Nynorsk!'. The largest concentration of speakers of Standard Nynorsk is probably found in the capital itself, where Nynorsk is spoken by many University people and civil servants, most of them immigrants to Oslo.

In trying to work out a numerical ratio between the two standard languages we are accordingly forced to work with preferences. And even here we have to use guesswork to a great extent. One fairly good criterion was, in earlier days, the number of children in primary schools who received their education in one or the other of the standard languages according to the wish of the district's voters. In the late 1930s about one-third of Norway's children learned Nynorsk at school. The Nynorsk organisation *Noregs Mållag* published a map of Norway on which the Nynorsk areas were coloured red. The map showed that the total Nynorsk area was far larger than the Bokmål one. This, of course, looked very encouraging until you realised that the Nynorsk area included vast stretches of mountain and forest where no one lived at all, but which belonged to districts that had chosen Nynorsk. Today the percentage of primary schoolchildren who receive their education in Nynorsk has dropped to about sixteen, and it is generally assumed today that about one-sixth to one-fifth of the country's population prefer Nynorsk, the rest Bokmål. This setback for Nynorsk has many reasons. One is the rapidly rising standard of living during the post-war period (as I mentioned, Bokmål is to many people a status symbol); another is an enormous amount of propaganda arranged by the Bokmål people who are backed by money from industry and shipping, traditional strongholds of conservatism; but a third and weighty reason is our policy of closing down all the small schools in out-of-the-way areas and sending the children to large central schools, which are often located in industrial centres where it is easy to get a majority vote for Bokmål. (The latter phenomenon is well known in other parts of the world.)

The two standard languages of Norway have been granted equality by the Storting since 1885, but this equality is very limited and has been interpreted in many ways. In theory a government official is required to master both languages and always to answer letters in the language in which they are written, but in practice this is largely limited to officials whose own preferred language is Nynorsk. They usually comply with the law and answer Bokmål letters in Bokmål. But officials who normally use Bokmål will, as a rule, answer *all* letters in that language, and if they do answer a Nynorsk letter in Nynorsk they will usually make so many mistakes that a Bokmål answer would have been preferable. They do this with complete impunity: the law provides no penal measures for offences of this kind.

Post offices and other Government services are required to provide forms in both languages. But in most such offices only Bokmål forms are in sight. If you want a Nynorsk form you have to ask for it, and as often as not it cannot be found.

All the daily newspapers are edited in Bokmål. The relatively few Nynorsk newspapers are small and appear once, twice or three times a week, and they mostly contain local news. On the other hand, practically all the large Bokmål-edited newspapers print some material in Nynorsk, both letters to the editor and articles by specialists in various fields who happen to be users of Nynorsk. Very occasionally one may also come across an editorial in Nynorsk in certain large papers, mostly when the subject is agriculture – which of course helps to nourish the belief that Nynorsk is a peasant language.

When foreigners want to learn Norwegian it is automatically Bokmål they are offered, often without even being told that there *is* another Norwegian standard language. This practice is, in a way, fair to the foreigners, who will undoubtedly, for practical purposes, find more use for Bokmål than for Nynorsk; but I have more than once heard linguistically-minded foreigners deplore it because they find Nynorsk more interesting, some of them because they know Danish already and would prefer to learn a Norwegian more different from that language, others because they would like to be able to read Nynorsk literature, which is surprisingly rich and in some ways more representative than Bokmål of the typically Norwegian side of our complex culture.

The reply to the question asked in the title of this paper is yes, Nynorsk *is* a minority language, with some qualifications. It has nearly all the problems of a minority language, and it is preferred by a numerical minority of the population. But it has one advantage which most minority languages lack: it is understood immediately and perfectly (or almost perfectly) by supporters and users of the majority language. If some Bokmål people claim not to understand Nynorsk, it is only pretence. It is the usual expedient of making a virtue out of ignorance, with the added ingredient that in this case the ignorance is not even genuine.

Another advantage Nynorsk has over many other minority languages is the fact that it is in no immediate danger of extinction. If the present trends continue it is possible that Nynorsk will disappear as a separate language in two or three generations, but in the meantime it will have influenced Bokmål to such an extent that it cannot be said to have existed in vain.

11. The Status of Swedish in Finland
in Theory and Practice

It is questionable whether Swedish in Finland should be considered a minority language. Historically, it was a dominant language, and it is still an official language. However, it reveals many features that are typical of a minority language; and in many respects its position is weakening in practical life, regardless of the official language regulations. Swedish is the mother tongue of slightly more than 300,000 or 6.3 per cent of Finland's population of 4.8 million inhabitants. According to the Constitution of 1919, Finnish and Swedish are the national languages of the Republic, and thus Finland is officially a bilingual country. The Lappish or Sámi population of some two to three thousand people enjoys no constitutional linguistic rights. The Swedish-speaking population of Finland is concentrated in two coastal regions: the west coast of Ostrobothnia from Kokkola/Karleby in the north to Siipyy/Sideby in the south, and the south-western archipelago and south coast from the Aaland islands in the west to Pyhtää/Pyttis in the east. Fewer than ten thousand Swedish-speaking Finns live outside these traditionally Swedish or bilingual regions.

No absolutely dependable information exists as to how long there has been a Swedish-speaking population in Finland. The first large-scale settlement, however, took place during the thirteenth century, in connection with the so-called Swedish crusades, when the southern and western coasts of Finland were colonised by Swedish settlers. This colonisation was followed by several other population movements from Sweden to Finland during the six hundred years in which Finland was part of the Kingdom of Sweden. Although at times areas with a Swedish-speaking population were slightly larger than they are today, it is a striking fact that the language borders have as a whole been stable through the centuries. It is only in the present century, with increasing industrialisation, that there has been a considerable influx of Finnish speakers into the formerly predominantly Swedish areas. This has resulted in the strong and often dominant influence of Finnish in many districts that were traditionally unilingually Swedish.

It has been estimated that about 70,000 or as many as 17 per cent of Finland's population were Swedish-speaking in the seventeenth century (Allardt and Miemois 1979, 21). The Swedish-speaking population increased in size until about 1940, when the number of Swedish speakers was over 350,000. In relation to the whole population, however, there has been a continuous decrease, due to the much more rapid growth of the Finnish-speaking population. Since the War the absolute number has also decreased, mainly as a result of emigration, low birth-rates and Finnisation through mixed marriages. During the large waves of emigration from Finland to America around the turn of the century, a highly disproportionate number of the emigrants were Swedish-speaking, and the same holds true for the post-war emigration to Sweden (Allardt and Miemois 1979, 46 and 68). Approximately 60,000 Swedish Finns are now living in Sweden, and perhaps 10,000 in the United States and Canada. These speakers, of course, are not included in the 300,000 Swedish Finns mentioned above.

Finland was part of the Kingdom of Sweden for approximately six hundred years, until the Russian conquest of 1808–9. Although hardly any attempts were made to increase the knowledge of Swedish or to enforce the use of Swedish instead of Finnish among the general population, it is natural that to a large extent Swedish became the language of administration and formal education from the seventeenth century onwards (Allardt and Miemois 1979, 9). After 1809, Finland became an autonomous Grand Duchy within the Russian Empire. The laws from the Swedish era remained in force, however, and the Swedish language held its dominant position in official life. Only in the mid-nineteenth century, with the growth of nationalistic consciousness all over Europe, was the need to give the Finnish language a stronger official status acknowledged. In 1863 the first actual language statute in Finland was promulgated. It laid down that the Finnish language was to be placed on an equal footing with Swedish. A transitional period of twenty years was stipulated. When Finland became independent in 1917, attempts were made in certain quarters to establish Finnish as the only official language, but the Constitution of 1919 and the Language Act of 1922 granted to Swedish the position of an official language on equal terms with Finnish.

The present situation of the Swedish language in Finland is influenced by three principal factors: the historical development, the present close and continuous contacts between Finland and the Scandinavian countries, and the Swedish-speaking population in Finland. Were it not for exigencies of a historical and geographical nature, the position of Swedish as a minority language would certainly be much weaker. Without a considerable domestic Swedish-speaking population, on the other hand, it is not very likely that Finland would allow Swedish to retain the position it still has in education and in communications with Sweden and the other Nordic countries. Swedish is a compulsory language in all Finnish schools, although most pupils nowadays choose English rather than Swedish as their second language. It has been estimated that perhaps as many as twenty per cent of the Finnish-speaking Finns have at least some knowledge of Swedish. The fairly strong position that Swedish occupies in the educational system is supported by the findings of a research project carried out at the unilingually Finnish University of Turku. The results of the project clearly showed that Swedish is the most important language after Finnish both in trade and commerce, tourism and different kinds of services.

As regards their linguistic environment, the Swedish Finns live under very varied conditions. Approximately one-third live in what are for practical purposes unilingual Swedish districts, where they only rarely come into direct contact with Finnish. One-third live in clearly bilingual areas with a Swedish-speaking population of between twenty-five and seventy-five per cent, where both languages are used in most sectors of life. The final third live in predominantly Finnish areas – most of them in the Helsinki area. However, only a few thousand Swedish Finns live in districts which are officially unilingually Finnish and lack public services in Swedish. Under the Constitution, the cultural and economic needs of the Finnish-speaking and Swedish-speaking populations are to be 'satisfied on the basis of equality'. The citizens have a right 'in court or before administrative authorities to use either their Finnish or Swedish mother tongue in their own cases'.

All laws and ordinances are written with parallel Finnish and Swedish texts, and Government proposals to Parliament, as well as Parliament's replies, are written in both languages. In practice this generally means that the texts are first written in Finnish and then translated into Swedish by the Government Translation Office or the Translation Office of Parliament, but the translation must be carried out before such laws or proposals are dealt with by the Government or passed by Parliament. Statutes of the Language Act of 1922 prescribe the use of Finnish and Swedish in court and before administrative authorities, and stipulate the principles that determine when an administrative district is to be officially unilingual or bilingual. A special law from the same year prescribes certain language examinations for higher civil servants in order to ensure service from the authorities to both language groups. State officials are supposed to have a 'complete' knowledge of the language spoken by the majority of the inhabitants in the district where they are working, and, if the district is bilingual, a 'satisfactory' knowledge of the language of the minority. There are official examination boards for each language, the members and associate members of which have the right to issue certificates of knowledge of the respective languages. The requirement of 'satisfactory knowledge' should be the same for both languages, but in practice the level of knowledge required tends to be lower for Swedish and the certificates do not always guarantee a working knowledge of that language.

The basic unit of language policy is the municipality ('commune'), a town or a rural district forming the primary unit of local government. The linguistic status of a municipality determines the use of language or languages within the local administration, but it also affects all the larger administrative bodies in which the municipalities are included and also the state authorities operating within the municipality. In a bilingual municipality citizens have the right to be administered in Finnish or Swedish by both local and state authorities. The authorities are required to publish documents and announcements that affect the general public in both languages. The internal administrative language of a municipality is the language of the majority. In principle, state authorities should communicate with the municipalities in the principal language of the municipality. A municipality is considered unilingual – Finnish or Swedish – when the entire population speaks the same language or when the number of inhabitants who speak the minority language is less than eight per cent. If the minority exceeds eight per cent or numbers 3000 persons, the municipality is bilingual. A bilingual commune is not declared unilingual until the minority falls below six per cent.

At the beginning of 1980, 399 municipalities were unilingually Finnish, 17 were bilingual with a Finnish majority, 22 bilingual with a Swedish majority and 26 were unilingually Swedish – 16 of them on the autonomous and constitutionally unilingual Aaland Islands. The linguistic status of the municipalities is determined by the Government every tenth year on the basis of official statistics, in which the question of which language group the individual belongs to depends on his own report. In 1960 and 1970 citizens were requested to report what they considered their main language, whereas the statistics are now based on what language is reported as being the individual's mother tongue. It is estimated that this will result in a considerably larger number of Swedish speakers than would a question about the individual's main language, since so many originally Swedish-speaking persons live in a more or less completely Finnish environment and thus for practical purposes consider Finnish their main language.

From the point of view of language maintenance, one of the most important consequences of official bilingualism is that education in Swedish is available at all levels, although there are several fields of higher education where instruction is given only in Finnish. On the academic level there is a unilingual Swedish university in Turku/Åbo and a Swedish School of Economics in Helsinki; besides, at the University of Helsinki and the Helsinki University of Technology there are several chairs with Swedish as the language of instruction. Many institutional spheres and central governmental boards have Swedish divisions or sections devoted to the affairs of the Swedish-speaking population. The Lutheran church has a Swedish diocese with a Swedish-speaking bishop and with Swedish as its internal language. The National School Board has a Swedish section for the administration of Swedish schools. The Finnish Broadcasting Corporation has a Swedish programme unit producing programmes in Swedish for both radio and television. The Swedish language press comprises some thirty daily or weekly newspapers, and about two hundred new Swedish books are published in Finland every year.

133

It must be stressed that the Language Act only regulates the use of language within *public* agencies and institutions. In the private sector there has been in the last twenty years or so a rapid decline in opportunities for using Swedish, not only in the predominantly Finnish areas but also in districts with a considerable Swedish-speaking population.

The language law in Finland is one of the most generous in the world with respect to the status and the rights of the minority language, but the practical application of the law is not always equitable. Especially in the urban areas with Swedish minorities of ten per cent or less, it is becoming more and more difficult to use Swedish in practical situations: not only in private but also in the public services or before administrative authorities; or, to mention a very important sector, in hospitals and health centres. In the public services it is possible, at least in theory, to insist on service in Swedish; but because so many public employees do not have a working knowledge of the language in spite of the official language knowledge requirements, communication is often possible only if Finnish is accepted. For practical purposes, most Swedish Finns with a sufficient knowledge of Finnish tend to accept this. In the long run this may have a very negative effect, however. Finnish-speaking officials will easily become accustomed to the fact that they need not offer service in Swedish, which in turn makes communication with the authorities more difficult for those numerous Swedish speakers whose knowledge of Finnish is limited.

In written communications, authorities and courts are obliged to use both languages wherever relevant. But if no-one in the organisation in question has a good enough knowledge of Swedish, what often happens is that letters or reports in Swedish are written in such poor language or are so short that they are of no practical use. Thus, even in courts, people who want their cases satisfactorily dealt with often prefer to use Finnish instead of Swedish. In practice there are no legal sanctions that can be invoked to ensure that the language stipulations are being observed – no state official has so far been punished for violating the Language Act.

A recent study made by the Research Group for Comparative Sociology at the University of Helsinki, under the supervision of Professor Erik Allardt, showed that there is a considerable gap between the importance that Swedish speakers in the Helsinki region attach to being served in Swedish and their actual chances of receiving such service. This gap is illustrated in the following table (Miemois 1980, 56, abridged):

Public agency	Swedish important	Swedish primarily used
Hospitals	72 per cent	28 per cent
Internal revenue offices	60	32
Libraries	60	48
Post offices	51	24

The table shows that the discrepancy is greatest for hospitals and smallest for libraries. Thus the need is satisfied most incompletely in the area of medical care, where service in the mother tongue is considered most important, while the libraries seem to meet the need rather well.

I have heard of several cases in the medical sector that support these findings. A few examples may suffice. A certain doctor had spoken only Finnish to a five-year-old Swedish-speaking child, until the boy, who understood nothing, burst into tears. The doctor then switched languages – and started talking English instead – English, to a Swedish-speaking child in Finland who had not even started school! Another child from a predominantly Swedish rural area had been admitted to hospital in Helsinki for treatment for some neurological disturbance. The doctors spoke only Finnish to him, which he did not understand. When he did not reply to their questions, they sent him home with a diagnosis of mutism. In many cases even adult unilingual Swedish speakers have misunderstood the instructions given to them, and have, for instance, returned home instead of going to the laboratory or to another department of the hospital. Remember that in all these cases the doctors studied Swedish at school for at least seven years, and that many of them had passed the official examination for 'satisfactory' knowledge of Swedish.

These problems are now generally acknowledged by society. For about a year now the municipalities and in certain cases other authorities, too, have been able to pay an extra bonus to employees with a good knowledge of both national languages, and many courses in Swedish are arranged for the administrative personnel of municipal and state authorities. It is therefore likely, or at least possible, that the services in Swedish offered by *public* bodies will maintain their present level. One important prerequisite, however, is that there should be a clear demand for it, in other words that the Swedish Finns should really insist on using their own language when they come into contact with the authorities and other public bodies. The same is true, of course, of the services offered by the private sector: shops, for instance, and banks and insurance companies. Here the use of language is not regulated by law, but it goes without saying that a greater demand for service in Swedish will make it more profitable for such concerns to employ bilingual people. The decline in the Swedish service in the private sector has been so rapid, however, that it is not likely that the service can be maintained even at the present level.

One of the most important issues for the Swedish Finns today is how to sustain the will to survive as a group and maintain the Swedish language as a living means of communication. There is no problem in the predominantly Swedish-speaking areas, but the pressure from the Finnish-speaking majority in the Helsinki area, for instance, is very great. One of the most important questions is that of school language. It is often very tempting, especially for a bilingual family, to place the children in a neighbouring Finnish school, when the nearest Swedish school is so far away that the children have to travel long distances by bus. But this almost invariably tends to give the children a Finnish-speaking identity, besides of course affecting their proficiency in Swedish. The language used outside school and the home is also extremely important. As a matter of fact, Professor Allardt's research group has shown that one of the greatest single factors governing linguistic identity in adult years is the linguistic milieu of the place where people meet their future spouses (Miemois 1979, p.27). And Finnish occupies a very dominant position in leisure activities for young people in the Helsinki area.

These questions are of course constantly discussed in the Swedish press in Finland, and interest in matters of identity and language maintenance has been on the increase during the last ten years or so. In the summer of 1980 the discussion concentrated on the possibilities of preserving predominantly Swedish environments, from single houses or blocks in the urban areas to larger rural districts. Although nobody wants to establish isolated reserves, the importance of living in a milieu where one can use one's own language with one's neighbours is widely recognised. Another topic of discussion in the mass media in recent years has been the question of television. The two Finnish television channels devote only a few hours weekly to programmes in Swedish. Because of the enormous importance of television for our knowledge and impressions of the society around us, the language in which we obtain our information and our entertainment on television probably exercises a very strong influence on our feeling of identity – and naturally also on our linguistic habits. There is therefore a strong movement among the Swedish Finns to get a third television channel with programmes mainly in Swedish. At present it is very difficult to say whether such a channel is likely to materialise.

It is natural that the mass media play an important role in Swedish usage in Finland. There is a continuous risk that the Swedish language will be influenced by Finnish. This interference is caused by two basic factors. One is direct: people who normally use Finnish in everyday situations will be influenced in their use of Swedish, mainly with regard to vocabulary, but also at other linguistic levels. The other is indirect and therefore in a sense more dangerous. Since a considerable proportion of all texts printed in Swedish are translations from Finnish (and many of them by no means competent translations), people are constantly being exposed to usage that is artificial and sometimes not even correct. This induces a sense of uncertainty among the language users, and creates a vicious circle: if the writers of texts, including journalists, do not have a sufficient mastery of their own language, their texts cannot serve as good models, and consequently the next generation of writers will have an even poorer command of the language.

It is vital for the Swedish language in Finland that it remain Swedish, that is, that it should not deviate too far from the Swedish of Sweden and that it follow the general development of Standard Swedish. Continuous efforts are therefore being made to preserve and cultivate the language and to make sure that legal and other official texts, for instance, are translated into good

Swedish. The office where I myself work, the Swedish Language Division of the Finnish Research Centre for Domestic Languages, is a state agency responsible for Swedish language planning and cultivation and for the supervision of Swedish place-names in Finland. For this purpose we provide advice and recommendations in matters relating to Swedish usage, assist in terminological work, provide lecturers for courses on Swedish usage and keep in touch particularly with public translators. I would therefore like to conclude by stressing that the state by no means underrates the importance of the Swedish language in Finland. On the contrary, the Government has recently shown in many ways that it wishes to consolidate the position of this language.

References

Allardt, E. and Miemois, K. J. (1979) Roots both in the Centre and the Periphery: The Swedish Speaking Population in Finland. *University of Helsinki. Research Group for Comparative Sociology. Research Reports* No. 24.

Miemois, K. J. (1979) Bilingual Self-Identification. *University of Helsinki. Research Group for Comparative Sociology. Research Reports* No. 22.

— (1980) The Minority Client's View of Public Administration in a Bilingual Society. *University of Helsinki. Research Group for Comparative Sociology. Research Reports* No. 26.

Statistical Yearbook of Finland 1979 (1980) Helsinki: Central Statistical Office.

Svenskt i Finland (1978) Svenska Finlands Folkting.

Törnudd, K. (1978) *Svenska språkets ställning i Finland.* Helsingfors: Holger Schildts Förlag.

Laws

Regeringsform för Finland 17.7.1919/94.

Språklag 1.6.1922/148.

Lag angående den språkkunskap, som skall av statstjänsteman fordras 1.6.1922/149.

12. The Fight for Survival:
Danish as a Living Minority Language
South of the German Border

In Southern Schleswig (German: Landesteil Schleswig), south of the present Dano-German border which was drawn in 1920, there is a fairly large pro-Danish minority.

However, how many members it really includes is a somewhat controversial question. It is difficult to find reliable figures, because there is no official or private registration of the members.

Furthermore, the criteria which should determine whether a person belongs to the minority have never been precisely defined. In the region itself the following definition is often used: the minority consists of those who consider themselves members of the minority (cf. Sydslesvig 1979, 8). This definition is, however, both inexact and subjective. To illustrate the size of the minority by means of official figures, the election figures and the school figures are the most reliable indicators.

At the county-council election in 1978, the pro-Danish political party ssw (Südschleswigscher Wählerverband) got 24,379 votes; and at the Landtag election in 1979, 22,291 votes, which is about eight per cent of the total number of votes in Southern Schleswig. (Some of these votes were given by the so-called 'Nationale Friiske', a North Frisian association with a certain allegiance to the Danish minority (Sydslesvig 1979, 14f).)

The school figures are as follows: in 1979 the Danish private schools had 6,445 pupils and the Danish kindergartens 1,704 children (Sydslesvig 1979, 18f).

Unofficially, it is often estimated that the minority consists of about 50,000 members, but it is doubtful whether this figure is quite realistic.

Foreigners often think that the existence of such a large pro-Danish minority in Southern Schleswig means that Danish holds a strong position as a living minority language, because, traditionally, language is regarded as an important part of a minority's identity. This is not, however, the case here; and I should now like to analyse the rather complicated linguistic situation and its historical background.

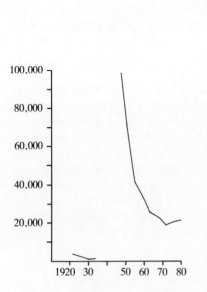

Figure 12.1. Election figures 1920-33 and 1947-80.   *Figure* 12.2. School figures 1920-80.

One important reason for the weak position of the Danish language is that the Danish minority in Schleswig-Holstein – in contrast to the German one in Denmark – is not entirely an ethnic-cultural-linguistic minority. Normally an ethnic minority will have a certain constancy of membership. This is not, however, the case with the Danish minority, as shown by the election figures before and after the Second World War, cf. Figure 12.1.

Before the war the largest number of votes gained at a local parliamentary election was in 1921 with 4,723 votes, and the lowest number was in 1933 with 1,780 votes (Jessen, Haandbog II, 510ff).

After the war the best result at a Landtag election was in 1947 with 99,500 votes, and the worst result was in 1971 with 19,720 votes (Sydslesvig 1979, 14f).

Compare these figures with the school figures (Figure 12.2). (In 1945 there were 436 pupils in the Danish schools and in 1950 13,239 (Sydslesvig 1979, 18).)

As these figures show, after the Second World War the Danish minority received an enormous influx of people – the so-called 'Neudänen' or pejoratively 'Speckdänen' – which was the result of domestic policy, primarily the chaotic situation caused by the large numbers of refugees. The increase must therefore be regarded as arising from a dislike for German rather than from a clear preference for Danish.

In the border region Danish and German had existed side by side for centuries and provided alternative points of orientation. The physical starvation and the intellectual void of Germany during and after the war drove many to look for an alternative.

As is proved by the tables above, the situation became more 'normal' after a couple of years; but during these years a great number of people had been brought into the minority who had not originally been familiar with the Danish language and culture. Some stayed, but not all of them felt any linguistic-cultural obligations.

Since the Second World War the knowledge of Standard Danish in Schleswig-Holstein has certainly increased considerably, because during the period many children have had their education in Danish private schools. However, this has not had any effect on the extension of Danish as a living minority language, as I will show later on. It only means that many people are able to understand Danish, and are also able – to a varying degree – to speak it if necessary, e.g. in communication with monolingual Danes.

However, there are other reasons besides the ones I have mentioned why the politically and ideologically Danish-minded minority do not use Danish as their daily spoken language, even if in theory some of them are able to do so.

Of importance is the old axiom, which is still valid today, that home language and national attitude do not necessarily need to be identical (see e.g. Laur 1978, 18f). German as a home language has never been in opposition to a pro-Danish attitude, nor vice versa.

We must, however, also consider an important historical aspect of the language, namely the relationship between Standard Danish (called *rigsdansk*) and the local dialect, Southern Jutish, i.e. the dialect of South Jutland. It is called *sønderjysk*. What is learnt in the Danish schools is of course Standard Danish. Historically, however, this is foreign (as a spoken language) in this region, and this reduces its potential as the natural means of communication among the local indigenous populace. Many feel that it is not local. It is too 'cultural', too 'hochsprachlich'.

The original spoken language in the whole region – apart from the western part, where North Frisian was spoken – reaching as far as the line Husum-Schleswig-Eckernförde Bucht, *without regard to national attitude*, was Southern Jutish, a dialect which differs considerably from Standard Danish and which is greatly influenced by Low German. In fact it is a separate language. This dialect is still widespread, but mainly among old people, in a small part of Central Schleswig near the border; it is generally thought that it will soon die out.

In Southern Schleswig a language shift has been taking place since the late Middle Ages: a shift from the two original spoken languages, Southern Jutish and North Frisian, via Low German, to High German. (A survey of the important change from Southern Jutish to Low German is given in Søndergaard 1980, 297ff.) Thus the area where Southern Jutish is still spoken to some extent today is only a very limited part of the region where the pro-Danish minority lives, so that there is no correlation between the two. It is characteristic of the relationship between Standard Danish and Southern Jutish that the dialect was isolated for centuries and had no support from the 'cultural language' of Standard Danish. (For example, the language used in court, in church, and later in the schools was German.)

Not until after the First Schleswigian War (1851–64) were attempts made to establish a connection between the two languages, as the authorities enforced Standard Danish as the language of the schools and partly as that of the church in the northern part of the region. One should, however, note that this provoked great resistance from the local population, even from the pro-Danish part of it.

It was felt that such an arrangement was unnatural. Standard Danish remained a foreign language in the area. The distance between it and Southern Jutish was so great that no real communication was – or is – possible.

German was the natural 'cultural language' for the greatest part of the population. During the centuries they had become accustomed to the discrepancy between the vernaculars on the one hand and the 'cultural language' on the other. This situation was felt to be quite natural.

Southern Jutish was from the beginning a nationally and politically neutral code, for which the establishment of Standard Danish in the mid-nineteenth century could offer no support.

In the course of this century, after 1920 and especially after 1945, Danish has come into Southern Schleswig first and foremost through institutions, such as the kindergartens, the schools and the church. Even in regions where Southern Jutish was still a living spoken language, there was not always enough understanding between the speakers of the two languages, and therefore the introduction of Standard Danish as an 'institutional language' – paradoxically – facilitated rather than retarded the change of language from Southern Jutish to spoken German (Wilts 1978, 156f).

Because Standard Danish, as already observed, has never been the natural spoken language of many natives in Southern Schleswig, it could have been predicted that the introduction of Standard Danish as an 'institutional language' would not noticeably influence the home language, even if the leaders of the minority have sometimes had the idea that it might do so and have agitated for it. As for the attitude towards German as the natural spoken language, there is often no difference between the members of the minority – in the ethnic sense – and the 'Neudänen'.

It is impossible to change this situation, but it is likely to be fatal to Danish as a living minority language. The language distribution in Southern Schleswig thus shows a pronounced degree of linguistic bifurcation, as this term is defined by Anastasi and Cordova (1953, 3): 'One language develops in one set of situations and the other in another set. Mastery of both languages is thus limited.' Applied to the situation in Southern Schleswig this means that German is the home language – very few homes are totally or even partially bilingual – and Danish remains the 'institutional language'. At school German is isolated in the curriculum, because it is taught as a subject only (and in practice not with a high priority at all schools), whereas Danish is both a subject and the medium of all other instruction. Danish, however, only has an 'official' status in these institutions, and is not the 'real' language; as is shown by the fact that most school children speak German to each other during lessons and breaks. It has even been reported from some schools that if the teacher speaks Danish in class some pupils answer in German, and that there is insufficient motivation to learn Danish, which is probably one of the many negative results of a strong linguistic bifurcation.

Only a few bilingual adults use Danish in their daily work, and in most Danish societies and clubs more German than Danish is spoken. Accordingly, the bilingualism of many adults is passive rather than active. Therefore Danish is not a real living minority language, because so few of the indigenous population speak it spontaneously and voluntarily in situations where they are not forced to do so for external or internal reasons. Furthermore, there are many who do not master Danish either actively or passively, for instance a great number of the parents of the children in the Danish kindergartens and schools. This – unknown in the case of German as a minority language in Denmark – reveals the low priority given to the Danish language and culture.

Such a language situation is of course unfruitful, and therefore it does not satisfy some of the leaders of the minority. Now and then there are heated public discussions, for example in the local newspapers. (One example of this is the debate on the pupils' proficiency in Danish and German in the *Flensborg Avis* in November 1979–April 1980.)

Correspondingly, various initiatives are taken to support and extend the use of Danish as a spoken language among children, adolescents and adults at home and elsewhere, but these 'speak-Danish actions' do not seem to have any long-term effects.

In the border region it is an old tradition that the population itself wants to choose its daily spoken language, and therefore it is susceptible to neither external nor internal pressures. This was proved by the so-called 'language fight' from 1851 to 1920 (Søndergaard 1980, 300f). To all appearances, the present language situation cannot be changed in the future. The hope which some leaders hold for change is ill-founded from both a historical and a synchronic point of view. The fight for Danish as a living minority language is therefore doomed to failure. This is unfortunate, but it has to be accepted.

I should like to summarise as follows. I have tried to analyse the situation of a minority which seems to be paradoxical: the existence of a relatively large pro-Danish minority in Northern Germany, combined with the fact that Danish is not a living minority language. In the analysis I have pointed out some of the most important factors: (1) The minority is not totally ethnic. (2) A full identity between home language and national political attitude has never existed. (3) Southern Jutish, the dying dialect, has never played a role in the identification of the minority. (4) It has never been connected with Standard Danish. (5) Standard Danish has never been the home language of many members of the native population. (6) In this border region there is an old tradition of discrepancy between vernacular and official languages.

References

Anastasi, A. and Cordova, F. A. (1953) Some Effects of Bilingualism upon the Intelligence Test Performance of Puerto Rican Children in New York City. *The Journal of Educational Psychology 44*, 1-19.

Jessen, F. v. (ed.) (1938) *Haandbog i det slesvigske Spørgsmaals Historie 1900-1937*, Vol. 1-3. København: Reitzel.

Laur, W. (1978) Nationale Minderheiten und Sprachgruppen im deutsch-dänischen Grenzgebiet. *Language Problems and Language Planning 2*, 17-25.

Sydslesvigsk Forening (ed.) (1979) *Sydslesvig i tekst og tal.* Kobbermølle.

Søndergaard, B. (1980) Vom Sprachenkampf zur sprachlichen Koexistenz im deutsch-dänischen Grenzraum, in *Sprachkontakt und Sprachkonflikt* (ed. P. H. Nelde). Wiesbaden: Franz Steiner Verlag.

Wilts, O. (1978) Dänisch, Nordfriesisch, Hoch- und Niederdeutsch in Schleswig-Holstein, in *Sprachkontakte im Nordseegebiet* (ed. P. S. Ureland). Tübingen: Niemeyer Verlag.

1989: In a later paper, Søndergaard (1987) has documented that the enforcing of the Standard Danish Code occurs *in informal situations* in kindergartens and schools because some teachers demand that their pupils speak Danish if the children try to speak their mother tongue.

The reason for this is that some prominent members of the minority do not want to accept the fact that Danish is limited to being the *official* language of the minority and that it only in exceptional cases is the mother tongue of the native population. Therefore they try to enforce the attitude: Always speak Danish whenever it is possible.

The author argues for abolishing this 'Partnerzwang' for the benefit of a more liberal and flexible attitude.

Finally he discusses the question: What effects does the 'Partnerzwang' have?

1. The spontaneous use of Danish is not increased.
2. It provokes negative feelings towards Danish in some young people.
3. German-speaking members suffer from a feeling of insufficiency when comparing themselves to the Danish-speaking.
4. The identity problems of young minority members are increasing.

Søndergaard, B. (1987) Om sprogtvaag i en bilingual kontekst – et psykologisk problem, in *Aspects of Multilingualism* (ed. E. Wande *et al.*). Uppsala.

JÓHAN HENDRIK W. POULSEN

13. The Faroese Language Situation

It is evident that many people abroad look upon Faroese as a minority language within the Danish Kingdom, but that is not the situation as seen from the Islands' point of view. The Faroese language is – and has always been – the sole spoken language of the Faroese people, and it is now recognised as the main language of the Faroe Islands. So, if we talk of minority languages in the Faroes, they are in fact the languages of the relatively few Danes, Inuit and other foreigners who live in the islands for shorter or longer periods of time. Nevertheless Faroese has to deal with many of the same problems as clearly defined minority languages. The language of a tiny nation is always threatened; and in our situation Faroese is still, as it has been since Reformation times, in close contact with Danish, a language which was the written language of the islands until well into this century and is still in a very strong position. The influence of Danish on Faroese is considerable, and the main task of Faroese language maintenance is to draw a line of demarcation between the two languages. We are indeed so saturated with Danish that it is not unusual, when writing a Faroese text on a subject outside the scope of traditional everyday life, to find that it is the Danish words which first spring to mind. One of the most valuable aids in Faroese language cultivation, therefore, is the Danish-Faroese dictionary by Jóhannes av Skarði.

However, there are also ancient cultural and linguistic links with other countries. Before the Norse settlers occupied our islands early in the ninth century, bringing with them the language from which Faroese has developed, Irish monks had lived there for a century or so according to the famous account of Dicuil the monk. But recent investigations based on pollen analysis have revealed that people lived in the islands around the year 600 A.D. The Norse settlers – or at least some of them – certainly came from North British areas, where they had been in contact with Celtic-speaking people. There are quite a few words and place-names in Faroese which are of Celtic origin.

Another connection with the south is the fate of the Norn languages of Shetland and Orkney, sister languages of Faroese and Icelandic. The Faroese scholar Jakob Jakobsen (1864–1918) travelled in Shetland in the last decade of the nineteenth century, and collected the remnants of a dying language very similar to our own. The main results of his investigations were his doctoral thesis on the Shetland Norn and his impressive etymological dictionary of the language. We deeply miss these languages in the tiny Norse family, and cannot but think of how near our language might have been to suffering the same fate.

The actual position of Faroese as the main language of the Faroe Islands is in no way the result of a quiet and 'natural' development, but rather the consequence of a conscious language policy.

There are no reliable statistics available of the national distribution of the approximately 43,000 inhabitants of the Faroe Islands, i.e. how many are born and bred in the islands, with Faroese as their mother tongue, and how many are foreigners, mainly Danes; but roughly estimated the latter hardly exceed 3,000. Neither do we know exactly how many Faroese live in other countries – mainly Denmark – but their number is usually estimated at about 10,000. Thus the total number of Faroese speakers should be roughly 50,000.

The Home Rule Act of 1948 makes provision for the legal position and rights of the Faroese language. Faroese is recognised as the principal language of the country, but Danish is to be taught well and thoroughly, and may continue in use for all official purposes on an equal footing with Faroese. It may not be usual to decree in a constitutional law which foreign languages should be taught in school. However, the background for this was the dominant position of Danish in the church, in the schools, and in administration, dating back to the Reformation. In 1912, when the movement for the rights of Faroese was more than twenty years old, the Education Act was amended to make Danish the principal language of instruction, and lessons in Faroese were limited to one hour a week in reading – not writing.

In spite of adverse conditions for the official status of the Faroese language, it never came to the point of Danish replacing Faroese as a spoken language, apart from narrow, half-Danish circles in the capital Tórshavn. With only a few exceptions Danes living in the Faroes did not take the trouble to learn Faroese, as everybody was supposed to understand Danish. Officials, practically all of whom were Danish, took it for granted that Danish was understood by everybody, and consequently all communication between them and the Faroese was in that language. Danish was also the language of divine service, even Faroese ministers being obliged to use Danish in church. Even today it is not common for Danes living in the Faroes to master the Faroese language, but in recent years it has become quite natural, especially for the younger generation, to use Faroese in conversation with Danes, who are supposed to understand the language.

The contact between Danish and Faroese in the Faroes is a most interesting phenomenon, which as yet has not been seriously studied. On the one hand there is the immense influence that Danish has had and still has on the Faroese language; on the other, the strongly Faroese-coloured pronunciation of Danish, which has proved an excellent auxiliary language in communication with other Scandinavians. Swedish and Norwegians understand this form of Danish better than the form used in Denmark itself.

For a long time some Danes were reluctant to concede that Faroese was a language in itself. They wanted it to be classed as a dialect of Danish. Thus a headmaster of a Danish teachers' training college returned from a visit to the Faroes in 1920 declaring that Faroese was no more distant from Standard Danish than for example Jutlandish, the dialect of Jutland, because he understood most of what the natives spoke to him. However, he had not realised that the Faroese had been trying to speak Danish to him in their own way!

As I said before, Faroese is spoken by all Faroemen and has gradually become the written language of most of them, as those who were not taught to write Faroese in school pass away. Written Faroese was not taught in school until 1920. There are however many people over seventy who can write Faroese. They may have learnt it on their own initiative, for interest, or they may have had a teacher who in spite of the regulations gave instruction in written Faroese.

The diversity of dialects is considerable, but they are all mutually intelligible. The dialectal differences are particularly noticeable in the phonetic system; less so in morphology and lexical forms. The modern orthography created by V.U.Hammershaimb (1819–1909) in 1846 is based on etymological principles with Icelandic or Old Norse orthography as a model, but with due consideration to important changes in modern Faroese. Hammershaimb chose the oldest traits of the various dialects, irrespective of the number of speakers. In this way no dialect has in principle preference over another.

With the Home Rule Act the Løgting, the ancient parliament, regained legislative power in internal Faroese matters. The government, Landsstýrið, administers and executes the laws passed by the Løgting. Affairs still under Danish jurisdiction are administered by the representative of the Danish government in the Faroes, the Ríkisumboðsmaður. The Faroese administration uses Faroese all the time. Laws are drafted in Faroese, but are published with a parallel Danish translation. The Ríkisumboðsmaður uses Danish when addressing the Faroese public, which he is entitled to do according to the Home Rule Act.

The postal services became a Faroese responsibility in 1975, and since then all forms, boards, etc. which were formerly in Danish are now in Faroese. Last year the administration of educational affairs was taken over, and the language in this area is now Faroese.

In the church Faroese has finally won out. The creator of Faroese liturgical language was the dean Jákup Dahl (1874–1944), who translated the ritual, the book of service and part of the Bible into dignified language. (The translation was completed by the pastor K. O. Viderø.) The book of service was authorised in 1930. The New Testament appeared in 1937, and the complete translation of the Bible in 1961. The hymn book was published in 1960; and now the entire church service is conducted in Faroese.

It should be mentioned that Faroese had come into use earlier in the independent churches: especially that of the Plymouth Brethren, the most important free church in the Faroes, founded in the last century by the Scottish preacher William Sloan. Their leader Victor Danielsen (1894–1961) translated the New Testament, which appeared in the same year as the translation by J. Dahl, but is closer to everyday language. His translation of the complete Bible appeared in 1948. Successive editions have been tending towards the more elevated style of J. Dahl's translation.

It took a long and hard struggle on two fronts to introduce Faroese into the church. One obstacle was the conservatism of the people, who for centuries had been accustomed to associate the Danish language with solemn occasions and considered Faroese too plain for church services. Most people took a negative attitude to J. H. Schrøter's translation of the Gospel According to St Matthew (1823), to V. U. Hammershaimb's attempts to use Faroese in the church in the 1850s, and to the efforts of Føringafelag, the national society founded in 1889. On another front certain Danish state officials were opposed to the promotion of Faroese to the status of a church language.

In the schools the language of instruction is now Faroese. However, there are several Danish teachers in the secondary schools who are not able to use Faroese. In 1930 a regulation was passed by the Løgting to the effect that teachers in primary schools who had received their training abroad would need to pass a special examination in Faroese. The ill-fated Paragraph Seven of the ordinance for Faroese school affairs of 1912 was not repealed until 1938, when Faroese teachers became free to choose the language of instruction. Now Faroese only is taught during the first two years at school, i.e. from the children's seventh to ninth years, after which Danish is introduced.

Already at the turn of the century some textbooks were written in Faroese, the first ones being for the subjects of Faroese and religion. The number of schoolbooks in Faroese has increased considerably since then, but is still far from sufficient. Especially in the higher classes the need is considerable. The shortage of Faroese school-books inevitably has a negative effect on the children's command of the language. The only available dictionaries are Faroese-Danish and Danish-Faroese. An English-Faroese dictionary is in preparation.

There are seven newspapers, published in the islands, all written in Faroese with the exception of the old-established *Dimmalætting*, which is partly in Danish. This paper is the organ of Sambandsflokkurin, the Unionist Party. However, the Faroese share of this paper has increased over the past years and is now by far the larger.

In 1957 the Faroese broadcasting service, Útvarp Føroya, was founded. The radio has had great influence on the spoken language. Many new coinages have found their way into the spoken language. Even earlier, since 1950, there had been a weekly programme in Faroese from the Danish broadcasting system in Copenhagen, conducted by Faroese students under the supervision of Chr. Matras, then professor of Faroese at the University of Copenhagen, when Faroese was employed for the first time as a broad-casting language. This tradition was transferred to the Útvarp Føroya by its first leader, Axel Tórgarð, who had been one of the pioneers of the Copen-hagen programmes. The language of Faroese radio is exclusively Faroese, but talks by and interviews with Scandinavians are generally not translated, as most Faroese understand the Scandinavian languages sufficiently well. In this connection I wish to point out the influence on Faroese language and cultural life exerted by Faroese students and intellectuals in Copenhagen. There they first came in contact with Icelanders, from whom they learned the means and methods of language cultivation. Much of our best poetry and prose literature has been written in Copenhagen. Especially during World War II, when connections with the Faroes were severed, there was a lively interest in the language among Faroese in Copenhagen, reflected in their paper *Búgvin* and other publications. In due course this activity had great influence on the language development at home.

In the short time that has elapsed since Faroese became a written and literary language, a considerable amount of printed literature has appeared, especially in recent years, though far from enough to fulfil the needs of the average reader. In the last few years, about one hundred titles have been published annually. It has been pointed out – I think rightly – that serious and informative genres have been given a higher priority than popular light reading. The most popular and widespread reading matter, therefore, is nearly all in Danish, such as popular weekly magazines, illustrated papers, etc. This does not strengthen the position of the Faroese language.

Another severe threat to the language is a recently-established private television service. It is merely a re-broadcasting of Danish programmes without Faroese sub-titles or dubbing. It is to be hoped that a planned Faroese television will soon be established.

It is also worth mentioning that in Tórshavn there is a semi-professional theatre staging both original and translated plays, and amateur dramatic groups are active in many places. The plays are all in Faroese.

Foreign films are not supplied with Faroese subtitles but appear with the Danish ones, the only exception being an Icelandic film which was shown in the summer of 1980.

Place-names were previously written in Danicised forms, and often gro-tesquely maltreated. Older maps of the Faroes have the names in their Danish versions. This is now completely changed, all official maps being printed with purely Faroese names.

As the language of church and administration was formerly Danish, personal names were Danicised in the parish registers and other writing. Orally, the genuine Faroese forms of the names prevailed. With the restoration of Faroese as a written language this situation has changed, but many people still stick to the Danish form when writing their names. In the time of Danish language supremacy the stock of personal names had shrunk to a small number, particularly those of Biblical provenance. In recent times there has been a revival of Faroese and Norse names, and consequently an enormous expansion of the name stock, some of it from international sources. As to surnames, the patronymic system was abolished at the same time as in Denmark following a royal ordinance of 1828. The result was that we got surnames mostly in Danish form, ending in *-sen*. Since then, many have adopted surnames of Faroese form, generally derived from place-names. There is a widespread interest in re-establishing the patronymic surname system, but this would require a change in the constitutional law: this area, strange to say, belongs to the affairs which are exclusively under Danish jurisdiction.

Faroese had no written literature to build on after the Reformation. We do not know what had existed before, but there are a few documents preserved in the vernacular, all of a legal nature. The reading of the people was entirely in Danish: the Bible, hymns, sermons, etc.; and so it has been until this century. By contrast, the New Testament was translated into Icelandic as early as 1540 and the complete Bible in 1584, and the rich literary tradition of Icelandic was never interrupted.

Why then was Faroese not entirely impoverished in its vocabulary beyond words of everyday use? This fact may be the effect of the rich oral tradition, particularly of the epic ballads, the oldest dating from mediaeval times. These were sung to accompany the old chain dance, which has survived only in the Faroe Islands and is still vigorous. There was also a tradition of composing satirical ballads, as well as folk tales, proverbs, riddles and the like that have been handed down in a traditional language.

V. U. Hammershaimb formed his orthography of 1846 in such a way that ballads, tales and other folklore texts would be accessible to foreign scholars familiar with Old Norse. The prose texts on folk life which he composed himself appear in a language purified of the Danicisms common in the everyday spoken language. It is obvious that Hammershaimb's orthography, so like the Icelandic and Old Norse, dictated a puristic course similar to that chosen by the Icelanders a long time before, a course which so far has been maintained by most writers.

In the 1870s there was an awakening of interest in the language and national values among Faroese students in Copenhagen. They composed songs in praise of the Faroese language. One of these was Fríðrikur Petersen (1853–1917), who had attended school in Reykjavík in Iceland, where he had been influenced by the Icelandic independence movement. The national revival was transferred to the Faroes in the late 1880s with the formation of the Føringafelag (Faroese National Union), which aimed at restoring the status of the Faroese language and working for the progress and self-sufficiency of the Faroese people in all respects. Among the leading figures were the agricultural consultant and poet Rasmus Effersøe (1857–1916), of Icelandic descent, and the young farmer and poet Jóannes Patursson (1866–1946), who had attended an agricultural school in Norway and was obviously inspired by the Norwegian language movement (målstrev). Not least important as an influence were the ideals of the Danish folk high schools. In 1899 a Faroese folk high school was founded by Símun av Skarði (1872–1942) and Rasmus Rasmussen (1871–1962). For many years this was the only school to use Faroese as a medium of instruction. The Føringafelag published a small monthly (later fortnightly) newspaper, Føringatíðindi (1890–1906), written exclusively in Faroese. In this paper the Faroese people in general were first confronted with their own language in print.

The national revival was followed by a release of energy which for a long time had lain dormant. Almost as if by magic a number of excellent poets and writers came to the fore using a completely new medium, their mother tongue, hitherto proscribed by convention except for the traditional oral literature.

The task of developing the language to meet the demands of modern life was by no means easy. In some fields, such as nature, everyday life and traditional work, there was a rich vocabulary, but the language lacked abstract, religious, philosophical and modern technical terms. Already at the beginning of the language movement it was decided to supplement the vocabulary by coinages from internal sources with loans from Old Norse or Icelandic as an alternative. The philologist Jakob Jakobsen was a pioneer creator of Faroese essay style, and one of his most eminent followers is Chr.Matras (b.1900), who combines a profound philological knowledge with good taste and artistic sense.

I shall mention a few others of the best innovators. The pastor A.C.Evensen (1874–1917) was the author of some Faroese readers for schools. He began a Faroese dictionary published in instalments, but it was never completed. Rasmus Rasmussen, one of the founders of the folk high school, composed a complete botanic terminology. Jákup Dahl, who created the liturgical language, was the first to use Faroese grammatical terms in his grammar of 1908. Perhaps the most ambitious innovator is Hans Debes Joensen, MD, who has written a physics textbook of more than six hundred pages. In this book he has launched an impressive number of Faroese scientific terms. He has also compiled a list of anatomical terms.

Various periodicals are published in Faroese, the most important being the literary magazine Varðin, which first appeared in 1921.

I should also mention Fróðskaparrit, the annual of Føroya Fróðskaparfelag, the Faroese Society of Sciences, which was founded in 1952. This annual has been an important factor in shaping Faroese as a medium for scientific and scholarly exposition. In 1959 the Fróðskaparfelag established the Málstovnur, an institution for the purpose of developing new terminology. It publishes lists of words in various fields. Recently it has opened an office to advise on questions of language. The society also took the initiative in the founding of Fróðskaparsetur Føroya (Academia Faeroensis) in 1965, in which the Department of Faroese Language and Literature has a central position. Among its purposes is the teaching of Faroese language and literature at university level, and conducting research. Today Faroese students can satisfy two years of Scandinavian university requirements in Tórshavn. Our collections include the extensive archive for a Faroese dictionary founded by Chr. Matras, who was the first head of the Department of Faroese. The recording of lexical material still continues and is far from complete. We have successfully used the radio to gather information on words and phrases of which we had insufficient knowledge. I should also mention that there is a place-name archive and a collection of tape-recordings of ballads and dialect material.

Although there are people who are opposed to puristic language cultivation, it has nevertheless been the prevailing tendency. There are of course many problems connected with the upholding of this principle, considering the constant bombardment with foreign lexical material by mass media and literature. In spite of all difficulties, of which we are fully aware, the fact remains that by active guidance we have succeeded in developing Faroese, for many centuries a language without a written form, into a medium well fitted to meet the requirements of modern life.

Two hundred years ago J. C. Svabo (1746–1824), the first to record ballads and word-material, had little hope for the future of the Faroese language. In 1783 he wrote in his *Indberetninger fra en Reise i Færøe 1781 og 1782* (Copenhagen 1959): 'Considering any improvements of the Faroese language, corrupt as it is today, there are, in my opinion, two ways to go. Either (1) to bring it back to its original purity, reintroduce the missing Old Norse words, expel the new and corrupt words, and give the language, if not a new pronunciation, at any rate a new orthography. But imagine all the travels to be made through the old Icelandic manuscripts, which are the only sources for improvement. This undertaking would meet with immense, if not insurmountable obstacles. Or (2), as I consider more reasonable, to introduce the Danish language in the purity which it has recently obtained, and which it will obtain in the future.'

The solution chosen a hundred years later approximated J. C. Svabo's first suggestion: an active intervention in the development of the language, which today would be referred to as 'language planning'. I would say that we have, in spite of all problems, reason to be more confident than Svabo was that the Faroese language will survive.

14. The Status of the Sámi Language

The term 'Sámi' is the genitive case of 'Sápmi', which denotes the land and the people. This is increasingly preferred in international use as a substitute for the perhaps more widely known word 'Lappish'. There is a scientific and partly official consensus that the Sámis are the indigenous population of the northern corner of Europe, at least in historic times. The Sámi habitat has in the past been considerably wider than its present extent, up to the late mediaeval period, comprising most of modern Finland. Further, this historical indigenousness does not contradict the hypothesis that the Sámi are descended from the earliest stone-age population along the Arctic coastline. There is no historical evidence of a centrally organised Sámi state or superstructure. However, local organisations called 'siida' regulated land use, administered the laws internally, and conducted negotiations externally. There is evidence of joint political initiatives by large groups of siidas, and Sámi customary law was to a certain extent recognised by the Danish and Swedish kings, and by the courts even well into the eighteenth century (Vorren and Manker 1962, Hyvärinen 1979).

In recent decades, there has been a vigorous organisational movement towards ethnic unification in its specific sense (Eidheim 1971). It is important to note that there is a permanent organisational network across the state borders of Finland, Norway and Sweden. The Sámi organisations in these three countries have adopted joint strategies for land rights, cultural development, language planning, and education (Nesheim, Nickul and Ruong 1957, Davviriikaid Sámiráddi 1974, Sámiráddi 1980). Also important is the fact that the Nordic governments have recognised these efforts as realistic through several recommendations and concrete projects in the Nordic Council. The Sámi organisations participated actively in the formation of the World Council of Indigenous Peoples (wcip), which has gained consultative status with the un Economic and Social Council.

The Sámi language is a very important ethnic criterion, and possibly surpasses any other single cultural trait as a unifying force. Sámi language policy and planning must be understood in the light of the fact that the viability and continuity of the language is almost a necessary condition for the continuity of the ethnic group as such.

Demography

The area of Sápmi is divided among four states. Consequently, different methods and criteria have been used to establish demographic and linguistic data. *Finland* is the only state where an official definition of a Sámi person is employed. This is done in connection with elections to the Sámi 'delegation', which has advisory status with the government. The Sámi population in Finland is close to 5,000, and in the last decade has shown a definite tendency to increase. Registration for election can be claimed by a person who has Sámi as first language, or at least one of whose parents or grandparents has or had Sámi as first language. Conversely, the electoral census itself functions as a criterion by descent. It is worth noting that first language ascription seems to function well as a complete definition of ethnicity, so that complicated and less practicable theoretical approaches are avoided (Nickul 1977).

In *Sweden* somewhat different criteria have been used. In 1975 a governmental committee published material indicating a Sámi population of about 17,000 in Sweden (SOU 1975, 99). The basis for this count was the reindeer breeding population and up to third generation affiliation with it, supplemented with data on migration and kinship. Possibly a registration in Sweden based on the same criteria as in Finland would give a somewhat higher total.

In *Norway*, censuses from 1920 and 1930 show a Sámi population of about 20,000. The national census of 1970 contained special inquiries for most communes in the northern part of the country. The results are extremely uncertain, for reasons which will be commented on later. About 27,000 persons were registered as having 'some Lappish affinity'. In his summary of the census, Professor V. Aubert comments that: 'There are in Norway probably some 40,000 persons whose life is in one way or another affected by their Lappish ancestry. But how many Lapps there are in Norway, poses a problem no census can decide' (Aubert 1978).

As for the USSR, various sources suggest a tentative estimate of 2,000 Sámi.

On the background of these highly diverse approaches, a very modest and reasonable estimate of the total Sámi population with a *self-ascriptive* ethnic identity would number approximately 40,000. The number of people with active competence in the Sámi language would be considerably lower, however, and closely comparable to other linguistic minorities within Nordic jurisdiction, such as Faroese and Greenlandic. Even if Sámi lacks the natural protection that island languages have, the demographic background seems to be well above a hypothetical threshold for viability, especially in the Nordic countries, where language politics and planning is a frequent topic of general debate.

Linguistic Variations

The Sámi language belongs to the family of Uralic languages, which besides the Finno-Ugric tongues (Finnish, Sámi, Mordvinian, Mari, Komi, Udmurt, Mansi, Hanti and Hungarian) also contains the Samojedic languages. Closeness to Finnish is often emphasised, but much of this kinship is probably caused by historical contacts. One should perhaps state merely that Sámi is a western Finno-Ugric language.

There are approximately fifty local varieties of the Sámi language. Traditionally, linguistic research has grouped these varieties into the following dialects:

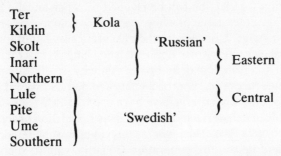

Dialect grouping has been partly confused in popular usage because of differing linguistic terminology in the countries concerned. The terms 'Russian' and 'Swedish' are more geographical than linguistic; and the scale 'eastern', 'central', and 'southern' refers especially to linguistic usage in Sweden.

There are varieties within each group. The northern dialect, which is spoken by roughly seventy-five per cent of all Sámi speakers, can be divided into coast and inland varieties, as well as into varieties in the east-west direction. (See further, on dialects, Bergsland 1967.)

Even though the Sámi population is spread over a huge area, the Sámi language spectrum is continuous in the sense that neighbouring dialects almost everywhere are mutually intelligible, and there is no absolute linguistic border. Migrations, too, have caused some inter-dialectal influence. Significant differences – which have led some scholars to distinguish between Sámi *languages* instead of dialects – are visible if one compares dialects which are widely separated. The northern and southern dialects, for instance, are not mutually intelligible without considerable practice.

Orthography and Norms

The Sámi language has never had a common writing norm for all dialects. A main obstacle has of course been that the area was divided among different administrations during the period in which a common norm could have been achieved. Today purely linguistic variations make a common norm virtually impossible. Morphological variations within the area (such as the number of cases and verb suffixes) could have been overcome, but systematically important phonemic differences, such as varying numbers of vowels and consonants – which even show different alternations – are difficult to reconcile in a comprehensive writing system. In addition to purely technical complications, we get variations within vocabulary (differing forms for the same content, differing contents of 'identical' forms).

The oldest written Sámi material is a small dictionary from Kola written down by an English sea-captain in 1557. The first printed work was a tiny A B C-book in a deplorable mixture of Sámi and Finnish printed in Stockholm in 1619. The first real work in the Sámi language was Johannes J. Tornaeus's *Manuale Lapponicum*, 1648, based on the Torne tongue (a variety of the northern dialect) with data from other areas. Tornaeus wished to create a common orthography, a 'dialectus maxime communis' as he expressed it. In the 1600s, the *sydlapska bokspråket* (South Lappish book language) was created, based on the Ume dialect, culminating in the first complete Bible translation in Sámi (*Tat Ailes Tjalog*, Haernoesand 1811). With Lars Levi Laestadius's works and translations (sermons, Bible history, catechisms) the foundation of the written language was again moved northwards – to the Lule dialect. In Norway attempts to establish an orthography have mainly stressed the northern dialect. The first work was Morten Lund's translation of Luther's minor catechisms, which established a lasting foundation. Nils Vibe Stockfleth's translations of religious books and pamphlets brought the written language into the hands of the people themselves from 1837 and onwards. Stockfleth introduced the 'Sámi' characters, which of course are international, but today have strong emotional meaning to many people. A complete translation of the Bible into the northern dialect was issued in 1885 with J. A. Friis's orthography, which created a tradition still living today. Professor Konrad Nielsen with his standard works (grammar 1926 and 1929, dictionary 1932 and 1962) laid the foundation for an orthography (different from Friis's) which in Sweden and Norway became the educational norm in 1950, whereas in Finland a 'Finnish' orthography was used, undergoing slight revisions. K. B. Wiklund created a 'book language' for the Lule dialect (from 1899), but its use has not been widespread. Knut Bergsland and Gustav Hasselbrinck in 1957 issued a small southern Sámi textbook, which with some revisions has subsequently become normative for southern Sámi.

The Sámi Language Board or Committee was established in 1971 by the joint Sámi Conference, and is now a permanent institution with its secretariat at the Nordic Sámi Institute. It is also recognised by the governments, in that it participates formally in the Nordic Language Secretariat, and is recognised as normative by the educational authorities in the three countries concerned.

The division of the Sámi area by state frontiers and dialect boundaries is in itself a complicating factor in Sámi language planning and policy. The Sámi Language Committee has, however, established working procedures which make it possible to achieve practical results. A common orthography has recently (1979) been established for the northern dialect, which is the only one spoken in three states. Border-crossing orthography for the southern dialect is also confirmed, and a norm for the Lule dialect in Norway and Sweden is being developed. Besides this, there are functioning orthographies for the Skolt, Inari and Lule dialects in use within the countries concerned.

One can now say that questions of orthography are both formally solved and well on the way to a pedagogical breakthrough. The northern dialect in particular (which is spoken by three-quarters of the Sámi population) seems now to stand on a firm base in education, the press and literature.

Codification and Recognition

In the Nordic countries, codification of language education and official use is an important part of legal history and public debate. It is sufficient to point to the codification of *two* official forms of the Norwegian language, to the official status of Swedish in Finland, and to the Danish recognition of Faroese and Greenlandic. From a Sámi point of view it is then a matter for wonder that such a recognition of the Sámi language has been, and still is, a very difficult aim to achieve. In Finland some preliminary attempts have been made at sketching a language law for the Sámi language with certain parallels to the status of Swedish. The Sámi language is recognised as one of three indigenous languages of Finland through participation in the research centre for such languages, but there still seem to be considerable obstacles to formal codification. In Norway, the government promised in 1980 to appoint a special board to clarify Sámi cultural conditions, including the feasibility of a language law. In Sweden concrete plans are still pending. The joint Sámi conference (1980) demanded a definite codification of language use in all three countries, and the Sámi member of the Nordic Language Secretariat has raised the question as a common Nordic responsibility.

Despite the lack of legal codification, there are nevertheless comprehensive *ad hoc* measures officially taken (as a result of Sámi organisational pressure and propaganda) to ensure its use and support in education. It is now possible to demand primary education both about and through the medium of the Sámi language, at least for the three first years of primary school, in special schools outside the core area, and as an ordinary part of the school system within this area. Beyond that stage Sámi is taught as a subject through primary and secondary school in the core area. University education is given at six universities (Helsinki, Oulu, Uppsala, Umeå, Oslo and Tromsø). Three teachers' colleges give linguistic and pedagogical training for the Sámi school system.

There are regular radio broadcasts in northern Sámi in all three countries, and some radio service for other dialects. There are, however, no regular television broadcasts; though there are occasional programmes in Sámi or with Sámi subtitles. There are several Sámi organisational periodicals, but only one weekly newspaper wholly in the Sámi language. Sámi literature has grown considerably in the last few years, as a result of growing active literacy in the language and various forms of financial support, especially in Norway.

Even if these developments give some reason for optimism, it is a definite Sámi opinion that in the long run legal definition of Sámi language rights is necessary. The need for legal protection is of course to be sought in observable trends in the society where the language is spoken, and where it has its social base. A contemporary flowering of the language must not be taken as a reason for complacency, when fundamental changes may confront the society which is the soil of this growth.

Degrees of Social Function

Besides the classification into dialect areas, it is possible to discern three characteristic areas based on the degree and mode of function of the Sámi language in society.

The reindeer-herding area comprises most of the traditional Sámi habitat (from Lake Femund northwards). The language situation in this area is probably best labelled by the term 'modernisation' in a negative sense. The Sámi population has traditionally been spread out in small kinship societies with limited mutual contact, or as islands in the rural population. This has led to privatisation of Sámi language events. Colonising and industrialising activity in the area have forced the small Sámi societies out of isolation without the compensation of effective schooling in Sámi. The Sámi language came to be replaced by the majority languages even in situations where one would expect the use of Sámi. The strong organisational movement among the Sámis in the south in the nineteenth century may have led to a loss of Sámi as a language of communication. This tendency is clearer the further south one looks. The result is that in the south the Sámi language is mastered only by some members of the older generations. But the Sámi *identity* is not stigmatised or kept hidden, and the will to language competence and language planning is strong. Nevertheless language work here faces severe problems, not least because of the lack of personnel resources (teachers, media workers, etc.).

The coastal area comprises the fjord districts in the northernmost part of Norway. Areas which we definitely know to have been Sámi-speaking in the past (Friis's ethnographical maps) have with a few exceptions been almost wholly Norwegianised in language. The anthropologist Harald Eidheim concludes that strong pressure towards Norwegianisation and oppressive behaviour from the Norwegian part of the population have led to the stigmatising and concealment of Sámi identity. The language disappeared from the official scene, and the lack of other ethnic symbols and organisational potential led to a creeping assimilation, at least on the surface. In some areas with Finnish immigration, there has been a tendency to adopt a partially fictitious Finnish ancestry, or at least to stress this heritage over Sámi identity. There is little or no passing on of the language to children. In contrast to the reindeer-herding area, the interest in language policy seems rudimentary. This is not however the whole picture. A couple of the fjord communities must be reckoned as optimal language areas. There is also in the coastal zone a general passive, but enduring, language competence in Sámi.

The core area for Sámi language broadly functioning in society is constituted by five or six administrative communities ('Boroughs') in Finnmark County in Norway, two communities in Finland, and some villages in the northernmost communities of Sweden. Because of a continuous concentration of eighty to ninety per cent Sámi population, the language is employed in all types of daily contacts, commerce and communications, and partly in administration and education. One also encounters here tendencies to a growing 'physical' Sámi language milieu in the form of geographical names in post, tele- and other communications, road marking, street names and official and private advertising.

There are tendencies to a local language policy outside the school, for instance in connection with the new communal general planning. Besides having strong ethnic reference, the language is also learned by parts of the non-Sámi population. The core area must be considered as an optimal locality for Sámi language policy. First, one cannot expect positive tendencies to be traceable in a global perspective, if they do not gain momentum in the core area. Secondly, the normative development of the language system depends on what happens in the core area, because of linguistic innovations in different sectors of society. Acceptance of normative work, lexical development processes and official codification of language status is hardly conceivable without the high frequency and the concrete use of language in the core area. From the point of view of general cultural policy, it is significant that language is the most comprehensive ethnic criterion in the core area. This makes possible a Sámi cultural policy which is not 'conversely' discriminatory, because one can point to generally accepted principles of language rights and language obligations.

Critical Factors

We shall concentrate on the language situation in the core area as a threshold or minimal factor for Sámi language planning. We shall try to assess the situation according to four critical factors for the viability of the language: the social frequency of the language; language learning in society; linguistic and social competence; and the private and official status of the language.

By *social frequency* we understand the use of the language in the events of daily life, viewed in relation to the use of a complementary language. If we take a closer look at the Kautokeino community (κ) in the core area, and regard it as typical, we get the following picture. Out of a population of about 2,800 persons in κ, eighty per cent have Sámi as their mother tongue and first language, and the other twenty per cent Norwegian. As almost all Sámis master Norwegian, many perfectly, and only a few Norwegians (because of a widespread migratory tendency, etc.) master Sámi (we can here disregard stigmatisation phenomena) we get a typical asymmetrical relationship between majority and minority languages. The result is that the Sámi language, even though it is the mother tongue of an overwhelming part of the population in κ, is grossly under-represented in the total number of language events. To borrow a term from genetics, one could say that in most language events Norwegian functions as a dominant gene and occupies the language event. We can make an approximative graphic picture (Figure 14.1). The fact that the percentage for Sámi increases and stabilises with increasing numbers of participants is often interpreted as being caused by 'officiality' in many situations and increasing use of translation and interpretation.

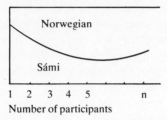

Figure 14.1.

Still more strikingly than in oral use, the written language use shows a clear under-representation of Sámi in κ. This refers for instance to road signs, tele- and postal communications, administrative documents: in short, official written use of the language. On the private commercial sector the lack of written use contrasts with the fact that many undertakings internally use Sámi as oral language in administration. 'No smoking' and 'Dogs not allowed' are the only common official placards with Sámi texts.

Except for an increasing use of Sámi on road and street signs, there is little in the written language use in κ which reflects the real proportions of language use. This under-representation of Sámi in society affects the intuitive picture each individual, consciously or unconsciously, gets of the language and opportunities for its use in society, and therefore indirectly shapes individual attitudes to language status and use of language.

By *social language learning* we understand *not* the immediate learning of the mother tongue which generally occurs in the intimate family circle. One can also mean the *learning* of language usage in society, primarily the learning of *attitudes* to the use of the language/languages and the learning of *terminology* associated with the social functions of the language in the broadest sense.

It seems clear that the relatively low frequency of Sámi in wider social settings has negative consequences for the language user's *sureness* and *immediacy* in choice of communicative language. As the population of κ (especially the Sámi part) grows rapidly, with depersonification and anonymity of language events as a result, the society in κ has in fact become an urban society in the sense that far from all people know each other personally or by sight. This leads many language users to follow the line of least resistance, and use Norwegian in speaking to persons whom one cannot place linguistically. This insecurity is especially conspicuous among persons who are separated by age by more than a school period (nine or ten years), and so do not necessarily know each other. This reluctant attitude, reflected in language events, in itself contributes to the reduction of Sámi frequency, in addition to asymmetrical language competence, possible stigma, etc.

A part of one's vocabulary has even wider social functions. In Sámi circumstances this is especially clear for *kinship terminology* which is very comprehensive and goes far beyond the core family; and *economic terminology*, especially concerning reindeer-breeding, hunting, and fishing, which are all traditionally built on extensive co-operation and social participation. The same can be said for *topographic terminology*. These parts of language must be learnt through social practice, and are in many ways cornerstones in the structure of the language. When the social frequency of their use is diminished, the possibility for systematic mastery diminishes for those parts of language that must be learnt outside the home. Clearly, this may again negatively influence the non-linguistic social structure such as the kinship system and economic activities, and so have a destructive effect on the culture itself.

For those who do not have Sámi as their mother tongue, it seems to grow increasingly difficult to learn the subtler distinctions of the language. There is considerable evidence favouring the hypothesis that at least half the people of a given society must be minority-language speakers to give a frequency sufficient to ensure the opportunity for others to acquire the language in daily communication. One could say that the linguistic core area is constituted precisely by a frequency threshold that is critical for social language learning. Sámi language planning must also pay heed to the fact that we are working with discontinuous processes, which may suddenly change the language situation within the area in a negative or a positive direction. I would personally state strongly that the Sámi language today is absolutely dependent on the large local Sámi societies, and that these are linguistically stable.

By *linguistic and social competence* one can roughly understand the totality of learning processes in society. The opportunity of learning the language includes the opportunity of being assimilated into the society generally. In the Sámi core area, it is clear that language competence is not only a direct condition for full participation in society. There is also a certain relation between language competence and ability to understand or appreciate the problems encountered by the Sámis as an ethnic minority in a wider context. The claim to communicative competence is closely tied to the possibility of official language reforms, that is, to ensure that reforms are understood and accepted by the population. Language competence also creates respect for the language. When the individual has learnt that the Norwegian language has some sort of dominant prerogative in unofficial social circumstances also, it can easily lead to a belief that this dominance is natural and normative – or conversely to a latent intolerance towards the Norwegian language. The result is often a polarisation in attitudes to language which may disrupt reasonable discussion and attempts at reform. We are here speaking both about formulated political attitudes and typical reaction patterns in social events. It is a part of the phenomenon that language-political attitude and social reaction patterns need not coincide for each particular individual.

Each language has structures that are more or less accessible seen from the previous competence of the language learner. Difficult parts may mean critical thresholds for the person learning the language, especially for adult learners. For instance: as compared to Norwegian, Sámi language phenomena such as verbal suffixes, the dual, etc., are especially difficult to learn. One can reckon that an adult will not try to say anything in Sámi if he does not master the dual forms. This shows that there are leaps, not smooth curves, in the process of achieving language competence. It should be a task for linguistics to chart such 'quanta' for each particular language. Certainly they are relevant for the processes to which minority languages are exposed.

The private and social status of language is a key issue. In κ, the status of the Sámi language is ambiguous with regard to its social under-representation. Most language users will find it incomprehensible that the language, which is held as a supreme value by an overwhelming majority of its speakers, nevertheless does not have a corresponding place in the official picture. This readily leads to resignation and passivity in concrete situations of choice, in daily life and in the political field. Only a determined language policy can in the long run save the Sámi language from being 'privatised' even in the core area.

In the debate on human rights as they affect language, the *right* to language is often mentioned, but it seems that for minority languages a *language obligation* must be formulated. (Such obligations are commonplace for dominant languages.) In my view, one cannot obtain a just status for the Sámi language, unless it receives equal status in administration, education, and the media. This can happen only through legal reforms. Tragically, it is difficult to create a consensus for this without a prerecognised status, and such a status presupposes to a high degree a generally positive attitude in the population, which can only be created through communicative competence.

The sketch in Figure 14.2 might illustrate the problem of Sámi language maintenance and planning. In Norway, for instance, one has lived with both a language *right* and a language *obligation*. This double obligation towards the *Norwegian* language has until now applied to all Sámis in Norway as well. Only recently has it become possible for Sámi pupils to replace one of the two Norwegian language forms by Sámi as an alternative language. The time seems ripe for beginning to discuss, not only a complete Sámi language *right*, but also a Sámi language *obligation*, at least in the core area. Such an

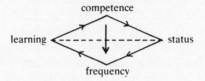

Figure 14.2.

obligation is in itself not an extreme claim. In the Nordic countries there are several examples of such obligations. The closest instances are Åland, the Faroes, Greenland, Swedish in Finland, and of course the double language obligation in Norway. Such a Sámi language obligation must in the long run include administration and education, the media, and commerce.

Acknowledgement
The writing of this article has been greatly eased by access to unpublished material compiled by Mr Ole Henrik Magga at the Nordic Sámi Institute, Kautokeino, Norway. This refers especially to facts on demography, dialects and orthographies.

References
Aubert, V. (1978) Den samiske befolkning i Nord-Norge (Summary in English), in *Statistisk Sentralbyrå, artikler nr 107.* Oslo: Statistisk Sentralbyrå.
Bergsland, K. (1967) Lapp Dialectal Groups and Problems of History, in *Lapps and Norsemen in Olden Times.* Oslo: Universitetsforlaget.
Davviriikaid Sámiráđđi (1974) *Sámiid Kulturpolitiikalaš Prográmma.* Helsinki.
Eidheim, H. (1971) *Aspects of the Lappish Minority Situation.* Oslo: Universitetsforlaget.
Hyvärinen, H. (1979) Saamelainen Kiinteistö Oikeudessamme, in *Saamelaisvaltuuskunnan Julkaisuja No 1.* Helsinki: Komiteanmietintö 1979: 30.
Nesheim, A., Nickul, K. and Ruong, I. (1957) Föredrag vid Den nordiska samekonferensen Jokkmokk 1953, in *Sámiid Dilit.* Oslo: Universitetsforlaget.
Nickul, K. (1977) *The Lappish Nation.* Indiana University Publications, Altaic Series, Volume 122.
Sámiráđđi (1980) *Sámepolitihkalaš Prográmma.* Ohcejohka.
SOU 1975: 99 (1975) *Samerna i Sverige.* Stockholm: SOU.
Vorren, Ø. and Manker, E. (1962) *Lapp Life and Customs.* London: Oxford University Press.

15. Why and How
do the Frisian Language
and Identity Continue?

I distinguish three factors which influence the survival or disappearance of a vernacular.

First, the question whether it is a matter of course that the vernacular is the home language in certain social groups in the region; secondly, the ideological justification of the language and the language group; thirdly, the socio-economic and political position of the speakers of the vernacular themselves, and the position of their language at school, in the administration, etc. I will discuss principally the first two factors.

Frisian and Urban Frisian as Home Languages
It is presumed that in Friesland during the Middle Ages Frisian was generally used as a home language. The decline of written Frisian and the increased use of Dutch during the fifteenth century could be an indication that spoken Frisian was declining in certain social groups as well. In such cases of language contact in areas of less socio-economic importance, the normal development is that the more influential foreign language, which represents more modern cultural tendencies, is accepted first by the higher circles in the towns; and that the old indigenous language is maintained longest by the lower classes in the towns and especially by the people in the country. We may assume that the development in Friesland took place in the same way and sequence.

We do not know at what precise time the upper classes in the larger Frisian towns as a whole had adopted the new spoken language as their home language. This was the so-called Urban Frisian: a form of Dutch, influenced by Frisian, but stripped of (partly new) characteristic Frisian elements, and thus in a way a more or less 'neutralised' variety of Frisian. Nor do we know at what time the lower classes in the larger Frisian towns gave up the Frisian language and commonly began to use *their* form of Urban Frisian: a language more influenced by Frisian, but, like the upper-class language, a 'neutralised' variety of Frisian, stripped of several striking Frisian elements.

We do not know when that situation stabilised, and the urban languages concerned developed a phonology, morphology, syntax and vocabulary of their own, with special variations for each town. Frisian urban languages are considered as separate languages, and not as continuing attempts to speak the 'higher' Dutch language; although the influence of Dutch has always been considerable. In our time Urban Frisian is losing many of its Frisian peculiarities. It is becoming virtually Dutch with a Frisian accent. At first the difference between Dutch and upper-class Urban Frisian was probably not considered to be very important. Regional variation in Dutch in the Netherlands was probably accepted without problems, and the same written text could be pronounced very differently in the different provinces of the Netherlands. We know that interprovincial discussions about a uniform standard for Dutch were held in the eighteenth century; and after 1800 the question of one standard Dutch language became more and more important. The Frisian variety of Dutch therefore became less acceptable; and nowadays Urban Frisian has no longer its former prestige, and only functions as an informal spoken language.

So, in Friesland, roughly from 1500 until 1900, three different languages were used as home languages: Frisian by the country-people; Urban Frisian by upper- and lower-class townspeople; and later on, probably in the course of the nineteenth century, under the influence of the unifying tendencies of the central administration and school education, also the Dutch of Holland by some (or many) families in Frisian and non-Frisian higher circles.

During those centuries the home language of a family in Friesland was to a very large extent a matter of course: it depended upon the social class to which the family belonged and the place (town or country) where they lived. The home language of a family was not a question of more or less ideological choice but was predetermined; and immigrants, as a rule, assimilated, and adopted the Frisian linguistic habits. Likewise, the use of Dutch (with Urban Frisian pronunciation, vocabulary, etc.) in administration was not a controversial matter. As a rule Dutch was also the language of the church and the language to be learnt at school. The Reformation generally introduced the language of the state, not the vernacular as such, into the church. The written language was always Dutch, except for some few literary products. The ideological value of those Frisian literary texts, especially those of the famous seventeenth-century poet Gysbert Japicx, was probably more important for a long time than its impact on language use. We may conclude that a stable diglossia existed in the rural districts in Friesland. We infer this principally from the language situation in the present century. We may corroborate and differentiate that conclusion by the written statements which have come down to us.

In any case before 1800 we know of sentences in Frisian, cited in depositions at law-courts, generally more or less insulting expressions which the defendant had uttered and which were part of the charge against him. Isolated Frisian utterances in more official circumstances, for instance in church or in assemblies, functioned as a means of drawing attention or provoking people. Frisian was not a subject of instruction at school, but teachers and pupils must have spoken Frisian together at several elementary schools in the countryside before 1800. Also several Mennonite lay preachers must have preached in Frisian, some of them even after 1800. But by that date not only were the sermons nearly all in Dutch but the religious language of the people seems to have become more and more Dutch as well, and it seems not to have been common for ministers to speak Frisian even in informal social intercourse.

Qualitative Decay before 1800

Regarding the decay of Frisian in the course of history, complaints have come down to us from the seventeenth century onwards. About the quality of the spoken language in the countryside, one source of information is the Frisian historian Foeke Sjoerds, who observed (1765, 314–15) a qualitative decay in spoken Frisian in the past forty years (Foeke Sjoerds was fifty-two years old in 1765, and was thus complaining of a decay in Frisian during his own lifetime) and expressed the fear that Frisian would pass away at some time in the future.

In 1793 E. Epkema, a Frisian philologist and editor of Gysbert Japicx's works, mentioned some cases of language use by his grandmother, who wished to speak nothing but Frisian (Epkema 1793). Epkema's grandmother, born before 1700, seems to have used words and idioms which Epkema only remembered from her and which were no longer current.

From such statements one may conclude that the vernacular spoken in the country was approaching the Dutch language through interference and was losing old words. Undoubtedly there were others like Epkema's grandmother who wanted to speak no other language than Frisian. Apart from some notables, the Frisian villages were linguistically homogeneous as regards the spoken language in informal social intercourse. Joast Halbertsma (1867) claimed that he had never spoken a language other than Frisian before the age of twelve (1801).

The Frisian author Eelke Meinderts (1777) also remarked that the old Frisian language had many words that were unknown to him and his contemporaries. But the language referred to here is probably the literary language of Gysbert Japicx, and not – or perhaps only partly – the spoken language of older people. And Japicx's literary language probably also differed more or less from the spoken Frisian of his own time, the seventeenth century, at least in some lexical aspects. Japicx undoubtedly used purisms and neologisms, and was influenced by the Dutch literary language.

The Nineteenth Century

On the other hand, Japicx must also have used several words and idioms which were current in seventeenth-century spoken Frisian but which have disappeared or at least lost ground in later centuries. J. H. Halbertsma

(1851) stated that he found almost the entire vocabulary of Japicx in the various contemporary Frisian dialects.

Joast Halbertsma and his brother Eeltsje were the authors of the famous *Lapekoer fen Gabe Skroor* ('The ragbag of Gabe the tailor') (E. and J. Halbertsma 1822). This book became very popular and formed the starting-point of the Frisian 'classic' *Rimen en Teltsjes*, a collection of poems, songs and narrative prose. For Joast Halbertsma the promotion of the Frisian language seems to have been the most important reason for his activities in this field. He explained the situation of Frisian as a spoken vernacular in the context of the bilingual situation in Friesland (J. H. Halbertsma 1829): 'The Frisian language has lived as a sort of creature in the air, flying from tongue to ear'. The reading of Dutch, and the use of Dutch in religious education and in administration, should normally have destroyed the Frisian language, but the illiterate Frisian people remained bilingual. But, he said, since they began to read more, Dutch words were coming in, instead of Frisian forms. Halbertsma's aim was now to try to preserve the Frisian language for longer and in a purer form by writing it, for the Dutch language threatening Frisian was also a written language. In a written language one can more readily preserve older words.

Halbertsma considered the Dutch interferences in Frisian as a new development: in his opinion the Frisian language was threatened by new dangers. He wished to save obsolescent and less current words. Some of those were found only in certain specific Frisian dialects, and Halbertsma liked to use such local words which perhaps had been used in a much larger area of Friesland in the past (and in some cases in the works of Gysbert Japicx too). For most contemporary readers of Halbertsma's works, such words no longer belonged to their own Frisian vocabulary.

In the beginning of the nineteenth century (Halbertsma's time), school education in the Netherlands was improved and centralised. One of the consequences was that spoken Frisian as a medium was in fact banished from the elementary school. In a school almanac (Almanak 1816) the teachers were urgently advised not to allow the children to speak Frisian nor to speak Frisian to them themselves. To that advice was added a rough description of the situation of Frisian in the country which I briefly paraphrase here. The children were said to know their mother tongue, Frisian, when they came to school, and to continue to speak that language in informal social intercourse, even when they were not taught in it. Besides, there were no books or teachers for the teaching of Frisian. And to get by in their profession as a merchant, an artisan, a bargeman or something like it they had to learn Dutch.

As to the actual knowledge of Frisian in the beginning of the nineteenth century, this description seems to be realistic. But not everybody was so optimistic regarding the chances of survival of the Frisian language under the new system of school education. J. H. Halbertsma (c. 1840), for instance, stated: 'In the last fifty years Frisian has deteriorated more than it might have in two hundred years'. (Halbertsma was about fifty years old when he wrote this, and was thus complaining, like Foeke Sjoerds seventy-five years before, of the decay of Frisian during his lifetime.) Halbertsma argued that the schools were more dangerous for Frisian than they used to be, pointing out that there were more people who learned to read and write Dutch, and at many schools it was now forbidden to speak Frisian.

Some Frisians wanted their language to be taught in the school, and others practised education in Frisian outside the school. For instance Johanna Frederike Rutgers, who conducted her Sunday-school classes in a Frisian village in Frisian (c.1875), advocated a cheap edition of the Frisian translation of the Gospel of St Matthew, for, as she said (J.T.Eekhoff 1883): 'The Kingdom of Heaven will not descend in Friesland before the Gospel comes to the people in their mother tongue'.

It was noticed (R.van Zinderen Bakker 1893, 47) that most Frisian labourers were only able to express themselves properly in Frisian, in the 'folk speech'. They could express themselves efficiently and pregnantly in Frisian, but had not a word to say in a discussion with a socialist from Holland.

Similar facts were reported in accounts of some law-court sessions in Friesland in 1902 (J.J.Hof 1940, 180–3). The witnesses at one of those sessions were obviously unable to express themselves in Dutch and continued to speak Frisian in spite of repeated requests by the president to speak Dutch.

The publisher and bookseller J.T.Eekhoff (1883) considered that in the future the need for Frisian Bible translations (if the religious need really existed) would diminish through improved education, so that a Dutch Bible translation would serve equally well, and then a Frisian translation would be needed only for its literary qualities. Eekhoff did not seem to regret the decline of the Frisian language and paid attention only to the development of (Dutch) education.

The popular nineteenth-century author Waling Dykstra explained both sides of the situation (the actual knowledge of Frisian and the negative expectations concerning its future) in a speech in 1894. Dykstra mentioned the Dutch influence in the school and the church. Almost all Frisians, he claimed, could read and understand Dutch to a greater or lesser extent, but found it difficult to speak Dutch. Dutch was still a foreign language, but the Frisians had more contact with it than with other foreign languages. If one wished to speak to Frisians heart-to-heart, one should speak Frisian. That held true also for public speaking and for writing. Eventually the time would come when the Frisian language would vanish. The Dutch language was interfering with it continually. Dykstra mentioned as factors undermining the position of Frisian: the church, municipal administration, national education, Dutch books and newspapers, politics and trade, conscription, drama societies of the *rederijkers*, and especially as a new factor sporting terminology. Many Dutch words were imperceptibly entering via those channels into everyday Frisian. Besides, several Frisians were making a point of being un-Frisian both in speaking and behaviour. (Here we observe that the stable diglossia is being encroached upon through the higher status of Dutch.)

In an article on the same subject, W. Dykstra (1884) also mentioned the influence of the law-courts, of the Urban-Frisian-speaking townspeople, and of the non-Frisian (and Frisian) officials in the countryside. Many teachers, too, were opposed to the Frisian language, even if they had been born and bred in the Frisian country. In the future, when the Frisian language would not exist any more, it would still be possible to regard the Frisian literature 'as a lasting monument to the honour of our cherished vernacular, when once it has passed away for ever'.

The different sources about the situation of Frisian in the nineteenth century corroborate each other.

The Twentieth Century
Until the middle of the twentieth century spoken Frisian remained the home language and the language of informal social intercourse for ordinary people in the countryside (lower and middle class). The language was drawing closer to Dutch through loss of Frisian words and interference from Dutch. That process was already going on before 1800, and probably started very early. Probably the Frisian language in the period of Frisian independence before 1500 was not pure either. The improvement of school education and the centralisation of the administration after 1800 no doubt reinforced the Dutch influence on the spoken language.

An altogether new situation was created by the strong immigration of non-Frisian speaking people (and the rise of television) after the Second World War, especially from the sixties onwards. The use of Dutch in Friesland is now no longer restricted to the upper class, formal social intercourse and foreign immigrants, and Dutch is now heard in Friesland in its colloquial, informal variant. Dutch is penetrating into the area where Frisian has had the absolute monopoly for centuries. The homogeneous Frisian-speaking village does not exist any more. Immigrants no longer assimilate, the language of informal social intercourse in the country districts for both children and adults is no longer always and as a matter of course Frisian, and the Dutch influences on the language are rapidly increasing. Hence, the emphasis in the arguments for school education in Frisian has in the last twenty years been moving from the interests of the child (who was much more familiar with Frisian than with Dutch) to the maintenance of the Frisian cultural heritage.

That development of the language situation will probably bring about a total change in the way Frisians feel towards their own language. For the present generations of adults it is the mother tongue to which they are attached through the experiences of their childhood. In that respect Frisian generally has no rival. It is the only language allowed in the circle of close relatives, and its speakers are familiar with all its affective connotations, still more by contrast with the 'higher' Dutch language in which they are less familiar with the affective connotations in the informal sphere.

Those affective ties with the language give special opportunities for both cabaret jokes and poetry. They give the Frisian language-movement a special strength, and are part of its ideological motivation. The future will show if generations who have grown up in linguistically mixed surroundings, with much less opportunity of resorting to a homogeneous Frisian community, will have as strong a motivation to defend the Frisian language as the generations before them who had both a Frisian community and the contrast with Dutch.

Frisian Ideology and Literature

It is striking that precisely in this very unfavourable period for the Frisian language the 'Frisian ideology' has or seems to have so many partisans. I will try to determine the role of this 'Frisian ideology' in the course of history, especially with regard to the position of the Frisian language.

The old medieval Frisian freedom was an important tradition which was constantly renewed and adapted to new circumstances, for instance in the struggle for freedom with the other Dutch provinces against Spain. The Frisian sovereign province (one of the Seven United Provinces of the Netherlands) was jealous of its independence. The existence of a separate Frisian language supported the historical rights of the Frisians. Moreover, Frisian was a written language in the Middle Ages, and this fact contributed to its glory. Those ideological factors created the possibility of a modern Frisian literature during the Renaissance. And that Frisian Renaissance literature was in fact one great poet, Gysbert Japicx (1603–66). It was the time of the promotion and cultivation of the great European vernaculars. For the vernaculars which for political and economic reasons had been relegated to the background but which nevertheless had preserved a relatively strong sense of identity, a literature of their own became possible in conformity with that modern trend. And this was the case in Friesland with Gysbert Japicx. Friesland was no longer an important region. The economic centre of the Netherlands was in Holland. But the Frisian ideology and sense of identity were not lost, the Court of the Frisian stadtholders maintained a cultural climate in Friesland, and the Frisian-speaking farmers were prosperous in the first half of the seventeenth century. All those factors contributed to the climate which could give rise to a modern Frisian poetry.

Gysbert Japicx's poetry was read by the Frisian nobility and other members of the higher circles, and was considered a suitable present also for non-Frisian friends. Japicx, in his turn, became part of the Frisian ideology. The Frisians could now prove that they had their own modern literature, and this contributed greatly to the prestige of the Frisian language. Japicx had created an upper-class literature in Friesland; he wished to prove that Frisian was capable of the same things as other languages.

In the seventeenth and eighteenth centuries there was also a popular

Frisian literature, such as Frisian almanacs, but it is difficult to say if the readers of that literature were indeed ordinary Frisians or mainly Frisian ideologues. One is tempted to believe that the relatively large number of Frisian booklets produced in the 1770s coincides with a greater interest in Frisian popular literature, not only among the educated classes, but also among ordinary country people. It was mainly popular almanac-literature; and in the advertisements for it, the fact that the books were written in Frisian seems to have been an important factor in the publicity.

The problem is illustrated by Eelke Meinderts in his foreword to a poem in honour of Prince William v (Meinderts 1777). He wrote his rhymed welcome in an orthography as simple as possible, for simple peasants, and used the actual spoken language. But he found that many of them were not yet able to read his poem. Many notables, on the contrary, read it with pleasure. We may conclude from Meinderts's words that there were peasants who read his poem, but that the notables ('Frisian ideologues') were his most important public. Presumably the same holds true for many popular texts in Frisian in the seventeenth and eighteenth centuries. There must have been great differences in education among the Frisian-speaking country people. One wonders if in a village some people might have read aloud for others, so that those who were unable to read could also be informed.

Romanticism and Frisian Ideology

Something quite new happened in the beginning of the nineteenth century. The ideas of the Romantic movement about the value of the past, the people, the national characteristics, the spoken vernacular, came to form a new ideological background for the cultivation of Frisian language and literature. Now, it was no longer the rules of official literature which were to be followed: the authentic spoken vernacular became the norm, and it was the 'new' popular genres (ballad, romance, popular tradition and tale) that now became fashionable in the Frisian literature of that period, in conformity with the European dialect literature before and during the Romantic period. It was first of all the 'little' Romanticism, the national-popular aspect of the movement, which Frisian authors adhered to, and it was that aspect of the Romantic movement that gave the developing Frisian language movement the necessary ideological support from without and gave a new impulse to Frisian literature.

Joast Halbertsma was now able to glorify the authentic Frisian spoken vernacular as the democratic property of the whole people, with no gap between upper and lower class or between written and spoken language, a vernacular not dominated and corrupted by the rules which orthography, grammar and literary culture had imposed upon other languages. In all those respects, he argued, Frisian was clearly superior to Dutch (J.H. Halbertsma 1865).

For the minority languages Romanticism was a rather revolutionary, democratic movement. Later, Frisian literature became largely a realistic

Heimat-literature, with many, more or less romantic, ideas about the excellence of the Frisian people, the Frisian peasant, the Frisian past, and the Frisian language: a somewhat impoverished heritage of the romantic 'revolution' of the first half of the nineteenth century.

In the writings of Harmen Sytstra, Romanticism resulted in truly Frisian national ideas. He tried to work out the pretensions of Frisian Romanticism in a practical programme, in which the Frisian language would be promoted and the possibilities of its use increased, and in a new archaic orthography and grammar. In 1848 he proclaimed his fundamental position: the Frisian nation is the first community to which the Frisians belong, prior to (but not outside) the Netherlands.

The Frisian national idea in the explicit form of Harmen Sytstra ceased to play an important role after his death in 1862, but was taken up again by the Young Frisian movement of 1915, which was very radical in proclaiming a totally new (and modern) Frisian literature as a reaction against the nineteenth-century popular literature, and in proclaiming at the same time Frisian nationalism more or less as a continuation of the national ideas of Sytstra.

Eeltsje Halbertsma and Dialect Literature

There is, however, another trend in Frisian Romanticism to which we have to pay attention. In 1818 Joast Halbertsma's brother, Eeltsje Halbertsma, studied for about six months in Heidelberg, where the German national romanticism had had its centre some years before (from about 1805 onwards). Eeltsje Halbertsma took part in Heidelberg student life, and Romanticism must have influenced him during his stay in Heidelberg. In *Lapekoer fen Gabe Skroor*, the booklet that Joast and Eeltsje Halbertsma published in 1822 (four years later), there were adaptations by Eeltsje Halbertsma of poems of J. P. Hebel and Ludwig Hölty.

The influence of Hebel (who is not regarded as a romantic) is particularly interesting, because Hebel was the author of *Allemannische Gedichte* (1803a), one of the greatest achievements in German dialect-literature. The climate for Hebel's poetry in Allemannic was favourable, because of the prestige of Allemannic and its past in Hebel's time, because there had been forerunners in German dialect poetry, and because of the classic example of the Greek poet Theocritus. Hebel influenced both Eeltsje Halbertsma and for instance the Low German poet Klaus Groth.

Hebel's influence on Halbertsma is not accidental. Halbertsma himself was aware of the similarity of his own work to that of the German dialect poets. Poetry in a spoken vernacular had for him its special natural charms, and seemed to him to be uncorrupted and authentic. The Nuremberg dialect of the German poet Grübel was, according to Halbertsma (1831), alive and uncorrupted in the speech of middle-class people, and did not allow nonsense or corrupted taste. He described Groth's verses as lovely poems in the same spirit as his own first poems in *Lapekoer*: lovely, natural and truly poetic (E. Halbertsma 1856 and 1857).

A quotation from a letter of J. P. Hebel (1803b) clearly expresses how he regarded the artistic qualities of his dialect. He states: 'Only the fortunate idea of writing a refined poetry in this unusual way is my own. Most of the other merits of my poetry should be ascribed to the dialect: the simple, poor and neglected, but in itself not unpoetical dialect, which possessed those charming and agreeably surprising qualities, a dialect which through constant practice was to me almost more natural than High German. With some selection and flexibility one can represent things as the Oberländer sees and feels them, so that it sounds naive and original.'

For Hebel his *Allemannische Gedichte* were in the first place poetry; the dialect was not unimportant, but Hebel was not first of all a promoter of the Allemannic dialect. The authenticity of the spoken vernacular was for Hebel rather a favourable factor for his poetry. For the Halbertsmas it was at the same time, and perhaps in the first place, an ideological principle, expressed with romantic emphasis.

Another difference: the Halbertsmas did not add a glossary for the non-Frisian readers of their works, as Hebel did. Obviously they wrote for people who knew the Frisian language well enough to understand the Frisian text. Allemannic seems to have been regarded more as a dialect. The editions of *Lapekoer*, mainly intended for the Frisian public, are indeed much smaller than those of *Allemannische Gedichte*, sold throughout Germany and the German-speaking world.

The works of Hebel and of the Halbertsmas were clearly intended for both educated and ordinary people. In the foreword of *Allemannische Gedichte (Für Freunde ländlicher Natur und Sitten)* (1803a) Hebel explained the aim of the book in this way: 'It is written for friends of the nature, manners and customs of the countryside. When readers of higher education do not lay them aside wholly unsatisfied, and when truth, goodness and beauty enter into the common people's souls in a more lively and effective way through the familiar images of the countryside, then the author's wish is fulfilled.'

The Halbertsmas, too, wrote their poetry and prose for both the educated and the common people (J. H. Halbertsma 1829): 'The greatest difficulty was to find pieces in which the simplicity of view and expression was mixed with so many grains of salt, that they, understood by illiterates, would not at the same time be insipid at the tongue of more educated people.'

Both Hebel and the Halbertsmas knew country life from their childhood and were at home in the great world of culture. The confrontation between these worlds must have been an important source of inspiration for their works in their own vernacular. The Romantic (and pre-Romantic) view of the spoken vernacular made the appearance and the success of their works possible.

Hebel's *Allemannische Gedichte* had great success with the reading public (both educated and illiterate people). The same seems to have been true of the Frisian *Lapekoer*. The first edition in 1822 was published in 200 copies which were sent to friends of the Halbertsmas, i.e. generally to educated people, Frisians and non-Frisians. It is a little book of thirty-six pages with poems and short prose-texts in the Romantic and rustic style, just the Romantic booklet in the Frisian vernacular which could please the educated people it was intended for. Nevertheless this first edition was also read by peasants.

The second, enlarged, edition of 1829 appeared in 400 copies. W. Eekhoff (1858) gives an enthusiastic description of the success the *Lapekoer* had in Friesland: 'The second edition was out of print within three months. People who had been opposed to the Frisian language became supporters of it. The book was used at home, at parties and in choral societies; and roused a general enthusiasm, a Frisian revival and a love for the old vernacular which were hitherto unknown. Frisian became something to be savoured, a language of delight for all classes, both for the nobility and the townspeople, and the countrypeople. The *Lapekoer* had won a victory over ignorance, prejudice and bad taste. And the demand for the book continues. The book had a lasting success.'

Hebel had not only an artistic but also an educational aim with his works. The moralism of the Halbertsmas is equally obvious. The Enlightenment did not disappear in the Romantic period: the fight against superstition, for instance, is an important characteristic of nineteenth-century Frisian literature. The special, naive and educational task of the vernacular in Romantic literature confines its domain more or less to tales, idylls, regional literature and the like. Because of the old literary tradition in Friesland, which existed before the Romantic period, Frisian literature covers a larger field; but even today the expectations concerning Frisian books are restricted, and in fact exclude the modern 'immoral' elite-literature and the lowest popular literature, the crude, lewd kind (the *Schund*). Modern trends in Frisian literature often meet with serious difficulties and are not easily accepted by the general reading public, whereas some of these readers are ready to accept the same things, such as descriptions of sex, in Dutch literature. This situation has, I think, historical ideological rather than economic causes.

Frisian Literature and Ideology in the Nineteenth Century

As to the other Frisian books which appear in the course of the nineteenth century, their copies often seem to number about 500. We do not know very much about the sale of these books. Perhaps there was a group of regular customers consisting of the members of the two existing Frisian organisations. For very popular editions like the books of the Halbertsmas and Waling Dykstra there must have been a broader group of buyers. Perhaps the group of regular customers made it possible to publish Frisian books, and some of those books played a great role in spreading the reading of Frisian among the common Frisian-speakers.

Both the Halbertsmas and Waling Dykstra wrote Frisian songs. The new Frisian songs were also meant to be educational. They were intended to replace the old, rude street-songs and thus to educate the people to sing something better. They became very popular.

In the second half of the nineteenth century the Frisian (amateur) theatre began to play an important role. The theatre enjoyed the active support of the Frisians themselves, and provided Frisian entertainment in the villages (and in towns too).

Frisian literature, song and theatre were all important factors in promoting the Frisian language, as Joast Halbertsma had already stated. Important, too, was the Frisian ideology which they expressed: the positive value of being Frisian – and hence free, loyal, sincere, diligent, simple – with an idyllic view of childhood, youth, life of the people and nature, and opposing the morals of town life and what is foreign. That the same values were advocated in other languages as well does not affect the matter either way for the Frisians.

Development of Frisian Ideology

It is probable that the Frisian ideology before 1800 was mainly to be found among the upper classes. Anyway, in the nineteenth century the Frisian ideology was or became the property of the common people too. Maintained for a long time by the upper class as a remnant of the old Frisian glory and as a weapon to defend the actual Frisian independence, sovereignty or autonomy, it was incorporated in different political and cultural movements, and also in the Romanticism at the beginning of the nineteenth century. The Frisian ideology was at the same time a sort of escape and compensation in the new political situation where the centralised Dutch state had eliminated nearly all vestiges of the old Frisian independence and hence diminished the influence of the Frisian notables. The emancipation of the middle class, the awakening of the peasantry, of those in the country who spoke Frisian, caused a sort of democratisation of the Frisian ideology. The Frisian language was important as part of that ideology but also as a means of spreading it. Hence the Frisian language had a highly symbolic function beside the communicative function in informal social intercourse. So, when we describe the language situation in nineteenth-century Friesland as a diglossia, we should add the qualification that the symbolic value and hence the prestige of the Frisian language was much higher than usual for the 'low' language in diglossic situations. It was only because of this high symbolic value that Gysbert Japicx was possible at all, and that he in fact *was*, all by himself, the institution of Frisian literature for nearly two centuries of minimal literary production. And only because of this high symbolic value could the Halbertsmas translate Romanticism into such an emphatic Frisian ideology with such literary success.

The nineteenth-century Frisian movement is both conservative and democratic, often in the same person. It was the old conservative ideology which made possible the self-confidence of the whole Frisian people as such and the emancipation of the native speakers of Frisian with regard to their language. And this again can be and has been a stimulus to (and a part of) the social and cultural emancipation. Romanticism and Enlightenment went together very well in Frisian literature, and later on in the nineteenth century the Enlightenment and the didactic, educational aims prevailed. Frisian literature and ideology were bound up with social and cultural progress, first for the middle class, especially the farmers, and afterwards also for the labourers. That democratic and social trend corresponded with the Frisian non-feudal tradition of freedom, which originated in the 'democratic' medieval organisation of the Frisian community. That social trend in part of the Frisian literature and the Frisian movement has culminated in the recent more or less Marxist theories of 'small is beautiful'. It is a movement against the old status, prestige, ideology, and standard language, against capitalism and environmental pollution. The repression of the Frisian language is regarded as a form of repression of the social underdog. Frisian is considered as the language of the lower classes. The paradox is that, without the old, conservative Frisian ideology, this new Frisian ideology would not have been possible. For the idea of a Frisian identity is based upon good old Frisian ideology.

And another paradox: it is only after the Second World War that the Frisian movement has won any real influence at all in the administration and government of the province of Friesland. That would not have been possible without the actions, so often seemingly impotent, of the Frisian movement in the years before. But right now the regression and corruption of the Frisian language assume enormous proportions. Frisian ideology has acquired real influence in political life, while on the other hand the base of the Frisian language seems to be fading away.

References
Almanak (1816) Almanak voor het Lager Onderwys en de Opvoeding, vooral in Vriesland, voor het jaar 1816. Sneek F. W. v. B. Smallenburg (Eenige raadgevingen aan onderwijzers).
Dykstra, Waling (1884) Iets over de Friesche taal. *Nederlandsche Dicht-en Kunsthalle* 7e jg. 4e Afl. Sept. Antwerpen, 1-8.
— (1894) Feestrede útspritsen to Ljouwert by 't oantinken fen 't fyftichjierrich bistean fen 't Selskip for fryske tael- en skriftenkennisse. Ljouwert R. van der Velde.
Eekhoff, J. T. (1883) Friesche Bijbelvertaling. *Nieuwsblad voor de Boekhandel*, no.21, 1-4.
Eekhoff, W. (1858) Levensbeschouwing van Dr. Eeltje Halbertsma. *Eeltje Halbertsma, De Jonkerboer of Krystyd in Sint Steffen yn Ald Frieslân.* Ljouwerd W. Eekhoff, 5-27.
Epkema, E. (1793) Animadversa in specimen Philolog. Patr. Academi-cum (ms. Brieven aan E. Wassenbergh 46 Prov. Bibl. Leeuwarden) (edited in A. Feitsma en R. Bosma, *Frysk út de 18de ieu IV.* Estrikken xxiii. Grins 1962, 114-15).
Feitsma, A. (1980) The Frisian native speaker between Frisian and Dutch. D. J. van Alkemade et al. (eds) *Linguistic Studies offered to Berthe Siertsema.* Amsterdam Huis aan de drie Grachten, 335-9.
Halbertsma, E. (1831) [Letter to J. H. Halbertsma of 20.1.1831] (ms. hs. 1169 Prov. Bibl. Leeuwarden).

A.FEITSMA

Halbertsma, E. (1856) [Letter to J. H. Halbertsma of 20.10.1856]
(ms. FLMD Leeuwarden Halbertsma brieveboek I).
— (1857) De Quickborn. Liouwerd E. Hosbach J. Cz. (Voorberigt).
Halbertsma, Eeltsje and Joast (1822) De Lape Koer fen Gabe Skroor.
Dimter: J. de Lange.
Halbertsma, J. H. (1829) *Het geslacht der Van Haren's.* Deventer:
J. de Lange (Voorbericht).
— (c.1840) De Stûke (ms. Prov. Bibl. Leeuwarden) (edited in: J. J.
Kalma en Y. Poortinga, *Fluit en doedelsek.* Drachten 1971, 36-59).
— (1851) *Aanteekeningen op het vierde deel van den Spiegel Historiael
van Jacop van Maerlant.* Deventer: J. de Lange (Inleiding).
— (1865) De vertaling des euangeliums van Mattheus in het Land-
Friesch, *De Vrije Fries, 10,* 1-78.
— (1867) Over de uitspraak van het Landfriesch, *De Taalgids 9,* 1-52.
Hebel, J. P. (1803a) *Allemannische Gedichte. Für Freunde ländlicher
Natur und Sitten.* Carlsruhe: Macklots Hofbuchhandlung.
— (1803b) [Letter to Wild 27-2-1803] (ms.) (edited in: Eberhard
Meckel, *Johann Peter Hebel Werke II.* Frankfurt am Main Insel
Verlag, 258-60).
Hof, J. J. (1940) *Fjirtich jier taelstriid,* I. Dokkum: J. Kamminga.
Meinderts, Eelke (1777) *Folle gelok in wolkomst winsk* (second edition)
(Ien wirttje oon de lezzer). Dockum: H. Groenje.
Position (1973) The position of the old, relatively less influential
vernaculars in Europe in the 16th and 17th centuries. Ljouwert
Ynteruniversitaire Stúdzjerie Frysk.
Sjoerds, Foeke (1765) *Algemene Beschryvinge van Oud en Nieuw
Friesland.* Leeuwarden: Pieter Koumans.
van Zinderen Bakker, R. (1893) Wenken en wenschen ter bevordering
der propaganda voor de arbeidersbeweging. Wolvega.

16. Some Recent Developments in Official Language Planning in Friesland

Professor Feitsma ends her chapter, 'The Frisian ideology has acquired real influence in political life, while on the other hand the base of the Frisian language seems to be fading away'. This chapter concentrates on that political life.

Governmental Support
The Netherlands is a centralist state – most power is exerted on a national level, in the Hague, and the provincial governments have only limited powers. Final decisions on Frisian issues, therefore, will not be taken in Ljouwert, but in the Hague. It is only since the Second World War that the provincial administration has taken a somewhat more positive attitude towards the language within its administrative boundaries. Before the war the unwritten rule was that in a Dutch governmental body the language one should speak, let alone write, was Dutch as a matter of course.

In 1952 the Provincial Council made its first pro-Frisian statement: (translated quote) 'in principle the right to use Frisian in administrative and legal matters is acknowledged' (Gorter 1979). But after this small tribute to the principle of linguistic rights, things remained as they were for several years. Likewise in 1953 a national cabinet standpoint was announced on the use of Frisian in formal administrative affairs; and in 1956 a law was approved providing for the use of Frisian as a spoken language in the law courts. The intention of both measures was more to limit the use of Frisian as much as possible than to allow it. Both are formally still valid today, though not in practice. It was not until 1969, in response to an initiative of the Council of the Frisian Movement, that the Commission on Frisian Language Politics was installed by the national government. Its purpose was to study the language use, the consequences of bilingualism, and the wishes of the Frisian movement and the provincial council (Report 1970).

It must be admitted that this Commission did a number of positive things in support of Frisian. But in general it assembled evidence and did not substantially change things for the language. Some of the ideas in its report would seem decidedly uninformed to language specialists. The Commission states that, because every Frisian-speaker is obliged to learn Dutch as well, the Frisians have two mother-tongues. Another example is that the Commission admits to recognising Friesland as a bilingual province, but denies that this means that the Netherlands is a bilingual nation. Bilingualism is thus a provincial problem and needs no special national care.

One of the most positive results of the Commission's report has been that Frisian is now required in the curriculum of all primary schools. The mandatory aspect came only after parliament made the decision: the Commission itself, and with it the government, thought that Frisian in schools on a voluntary basis would be enough.

The Commission did not deem it necessary to review the 1956 law on language use in the courts; nor to accept written Frisian in legal documents. On this last point there is a nice illustration of how data on the position of a linguistic minority can either be used to argue in favour of the threatened language or against it. In his reply the Secretary of Justice argued that: 'About four per cent of the inhabitants of the Netherlands live in Friesland, and only eleven per cent of them are able to write Frisian well. Add to this the fact that only one in every thousand citizens goes to law in his lifetime, and the whole issue of Frisian legal documents would be organised for one and a half persons and a horse's head' (Report 1970).

After the report of the Commission and the official recognition for Frisian that came with it, everybody seemed quite satisfied for some time – and nothing further happened. Some students at the University of Groningen, however, were less satisfied and took action. All of a sudden Friesland had its 'Frisian Organisation for Cultural Autonomy' (FOKA). A number of place-name signs were painted white, and everybody was up in arms. FOKA proclaimed that they were not only struggling to conserve the language itself, but fighting for the Frisian-speaking people. This action had at least one consequence, mediated by a petition from the Council of the Frisian Movement: the installation of an important provincial workgroup in 1975, the Workgroup on Frisian in Public Administration. In 1978 it published its first interim report.

In this, for the first time in an official governmental report, the linguistic composition of Frisian society was thoroughly analysed. On the basis of that analysis goals were formulated and a policy set out for the province to follow. Two broad policy goals were:

> First, to clear away obstacles to the use of the Frisian language in communication between citizens and government and in legal matters; Second, to stimulate and/or bring about rulings that will lead to an active and frequent use of the Frisian language by governmental bodies and persons in legal transactions, spoken as well as written, on a basis of equal status and equal rights with the Dutch language.
> (Interim report, 1978)

The report was well received by the Provincial Council, and unanimously accepted by all political parties. Most of the speeches delivered were mainly rhetoric showing the prevailing good will and concern for the language. A good illustration of the atmosphere and the manner in which provincial representatives pay tribute to the language rather than really accepting the consequences is the discussion over the wording of a motion forwarded by the Frisian Nationalist Party. The original words of the motion are as follows: 'The Provincial Council of Friesland, assembled on 15 November 1978, holds the opinion that Frisian should be promoted as much as possible, with special regard to spoken communication. Therefore it is necessary to develop a policy of appointments in which civil servants who have contacts with the public are *required* (italics mine) to have an active command of Frisian or at least to be willing to attempt to acquire it.' A discussion followed on the imperative character of the motion. The wording was changed to: 'to develop a policy in which civil servants are *asked* (italics mine) to have an active command of Frisian . . . (etc.)' (Notulen 1978).

One of the most important elements of the interim report is the concept of a 'basic norm'. According to this, bilingualism in Friesland should mean that everybody can at least *understand* and *read* both languages. This norm is seen as a minimum requirement for any further development of Frisian in public administration. This is to counter an argument from the opposing camp that the use of Frisian by the government is prevented by a lack of even a passive knowledge of Frisian.

Developments in 1980

A design for a language law on the use of Frisian in public administration is being discussed in the provincial workgroup. It is based on the aforementioned principles of language equality, and contains a pattern for more-or-less planned development. Central to the act is that provincial government and all local municipal governments have to make what is called a 'policy-plan'. The use of Frisian and Dutch has to be on a basis of equality of rights and of status for both languages. The rest is left largely to the goodwill of local authorities. There are only two minimal requirements: (1) Frisian correspondence should be answered in Frisian; (2) spoken language at meetings should be recorded in writing in the language in which it was spoken. Added to this is a list of matters on which a policy has to be formulated for the language used on each occasion, e.g. agendas, public announcements, personnel advertisements, official proposals and formal decisions, decrees, circulars, place- and street-names.

This law may have the effect of forcing local councils to take a stand on the language issue. Many municipal councils have until now avoided this (De Vries 1980). But even in its very general form there is a real danger that councils will be satisfied with a minimum and not take any positive action. Another possible result of setting the minimum requirements relatively low may be a wide spectrum of policies differing from municipality to municipality. This may result in insecurity for the citizens. Already two municipalities have declared themselves prepared to attempt full implementation of the law. A language expert has been hired to assist them in the process of 'Frisianisation' of administrative affairs.

The province itself has already formulated a four-year plan, based on the policy intentions of 1978. But only a few of those intentions have been acted on. For example, the number of Frisian-language proposals sent from the Central Board to the General Council has not risen in the last few years. In 1968, the figure was 2 out of 95. The highest so far reached has been 6 out of 103, in 1976. In 1979, it was 3 out of 94.

The aim of the four-year plan is to Frisianise administrative affairs extensively. The most conspicuous action in 1980 in this regard was that the provincial government from 1 January began to issue all its job-announcements in the regional newspapers in Frisian. This policy aroused some protests from some law-court clerks, but their effort to have the policy overruled by the Secretary of the Interior was unsuccessful. In a letter dated 9 July 1980 the Secretary answered the charge of discrimination and making job-opportunities unequal through the use of Frisian by stating that an active or passive proficiency in the Frisian language can justifiably be included among job-requirements. His reaction shows that something may have been changing on the national level, because he informed the claimants that in a fairly short time a national commission would look into the matter of Frisian in administrative affairs. It may be hoped that this new commission will take a more realistic standpoint than the one of ten years ago. It ought to see the need for more and further-reaching affirmative action and less voluntarism in order to ensure that the language survives in the long run.

Another important event in 1980 was the founding in August of a language bureau by the Fryske Akademy, a bureau for language development and assistance. Until now that work was done on a small scale in ad-hoc commissions or by individuals. The bureau is one of the results of the 1978 interim report. Its initial task is to focus on the terminology of administrative affairs.

As a final point, the spelling reform that became effective from 1 January 1980 should be mentioned. It has been implemented without much trouble now, but for many years previously there had been intense disagreements over spelling.

Conclusion

Frisian no longer has the strong position it once had. Its position, like that of other minority languages, has been affected by factors operating in most if not all societies of the western world. Let me roughly summarise them:

(1) *mass-media*, which have influenced the patterns of everyday behaviour of large parts of the population. On average an inhabitant of Friesland watches Dutch television for about two hours each day.

(2) *mass-bureaucracy*, which has registered everybody in a thousand

ways. The number of forms each citizen has to fill out each year still seems to increase. All these forms are in Dutch in Friesland, as are accompanying announcements and instructions.

(3) *mass-education*, with an increase in the average educational level of the population; but also often with the effect that the standard dominant language of the school system is better known in many domains than the mother-tongue.

(4) *mass-production*, in the de-personalised work circumstances of (inter-)nationally oriented companies. Those companies usually take with them Dutch management and experts.

(5) *mass-transportation*, which has made a greater mobility of people possible, has contributed to the suburbanisation of the countryside. It has made it possible for a greater number of temporary or retiring immigrants to come to economically less attractive areas, without losing all contact with family, friends and neighbourhood. It is a condition for the phenomenon of the weekend-house of the (upper) middle classes. Finally, the expansion of mass-transportation, especially private cars, has gradually made a mass tourism possible.

These factors are in general not to the advantage of a minority language. They have encroached upon an existing social, cultural and economic structure in which languages like Frisian had flourished for centuries. In the last few decades there have been signs of a more favourable political climate. But that alone is of course not enough. Chances for survival will increase when the socio-economic base becomes more 'friendly' towards small groups, with fewer de-personalised relationships. Whether optimism or pessimism is justified is very uncertain. It should be clear that Frisian will be alive for at least another generation. The question is whether provincial policies to support Frisian can be successful. But it is to be hoped that there will not come a day when all inhabitants of the province of Friesland can read and understand Frisian, while only a very small minority actually speaks and writes it.

References
De Vries, H. (1980) Frysk as taal fan de legere oerheid, *Leeuwarder Courant* (4 articles).
Gorter, D. (1979) Een Friese taalkwestie?, in *Toegepaste Taalwetenschap in Artikelen 6* (ed. J. F. Matter) (with English summaries). Amsterdam: Anéla.
Interim Report (1978) Wurkgroep Frysk yn it officiele ferkear, Ljouwert.
Notulen (1978) Notulen en verslag der handelingen van de vergadering van provinciale staten van Friesland van 15 november 1978.
Report (1970) Commissie Friese Taalpolitiek, met aanhangsels, Den Haag, Staatsdrukkerij.

1989: A Decade of Progress?

Re-reading the synopsis of developments in language planning in Friesland almost a decade later makes one aware of the fact that language planning is

17. The Recent Situation of the Ferring Language,
the North-Frisian Language of
the Islands Föhr and Amrum

Anyone who wants to understand the relation of the Ferring language to the other Frisian dialects and the other Nordic and Germanic languages should be aware of one basic fact of geology. The two islands on which the Ferring language is spoken are – together with the islands of Heligoland and Sylt – the only remains of the big land-mass which until early neolithic times covered the southern part of the North Sea between the Frisian coast and Britain. The many other West-, East-, and North-Frisian islands, as well as the main part of the Frisian mainland, have either been reclaimed from the sea by dykes or are still being shaped and transformed by sand dunes; and therefore they are relatively new. The fact that these two old islands, called the Geest Islands, have been continuously inhabited, and indeed densely populated, since the early Stone Age or the end of the last Ice Age, may be why the Ferring language has some archaic structures and words which do not occur in the other Frisian languages, pointing to a pre-Germanic origin.

If I have to place the Ferring language among its neighbours, there can be no doubt that its closest relative is the English language. I have not made a statistical study of the relative frequency of words in our language but I think that by far the majority of all Ferring words are either identical or very closely related to old Anglic words, and that the rest are identical or closely related to Scandinavian words. This basic structure of our language has in modern times been profoundly influenced from two sides. From the fifteenth to the early nineteenth century the influence of Dutch was very strong. It has given us a great number of Dutch words, especially in the field of shipping and commerce. From the eighteenth century until now the German language – in earlier times Low German and after the last war High German – has been rapidly changing our language. German not only causes the replacement of old Frisian words by more German-like words, but also influences the whole structure of the language by changing traditional grammatical structures to German structures. Thus the *th*-sound has disappeared from our language in recent decades or during the last century just because this sound does not occur in German and is not taught in German schools. Another example can be the dual number, which we have in our language beside the singular and plural. The dual is practically disappearing because it does not occur in any of the languages the children learn in school.

The close relationship of Ferring to English is not only based on the similarity of the stock of words, but also on the similarity of the patterns of the languages. Thus our language – like the English language – uses more verbs than substantives, whereas German does just the opposite: the Germans prefer distinction by substantives and not by verbs. To give an example of the richness of our language in this respect, I can mention that a little Ferring poem uses more than ninety different verbs for 'go'. Thus more than ninety different ways of going can be expressed by different verbs in the Ferring language. I could give other examples of the astonishing richness and distinctiveness of this little language. I do not know how many Ferring words have been collected by the North-Frisian Institute at the University of Kiel, but my guess is that the number of words registered is somewhere between two and three hundred thousand. Thus it is indeed a very rich and very expressive language. This is still more astounding as it has practically no real literature. We have no old Frisian texts in North-Frisland, as the East- and West-Frisians have in their old lawbooks from early medieval times. The first written and printed texts in the Ferring language date from the end of the eighteenth and the beginning of the nineteenth century. Even today there exists only a very little and locally limited literature. An early review of all existing printed material was produced by Otto Bremer (1888), and a more recent one by Nils Arhammar (1964; 1975).

History

I cannot examine here the history of our islands – I will mention only that both islands belonged to the Kingdom of Denmark until 1865, when they were conquered by the Prussians and the Austrians; and later in 1871 became a part of the German empire. The Western part of Föhr and the whole of Amrum never belonged to Schleswig or South Jutland, over which the Danes and Germans have fought so many wars. Amrum and the Western part of Föhr belonged to Northern Jutland. The long political integration with the Danish realm, which incorporated parts of Sweden, all of Norway, Iceland, and the Faroe Islands, may be the explanation for the fact that a great number of different Scandinavian words are used in the Ferring language.

Statistics

I mentioned earlier that almost four thousand people today speak the Ferring language. This is based on a very reliable statistical investigation carried out by Nils Århammar in 1976. It showed that on the islands, which now have around nine to ten thousand inhabitants and in summer time an additional thirty to forty thousand German tourists, today around two thousand people, or twenty per cent, still speak Ferring. A similar number of Ferring-speakers live in the United States: half of them in New York, the rest in Petaluma in California, in Santa Rosa County north of San Francisco. We are quite proud of the fact that in the winter of 1979–80 a course in the Ferring language was given in New York to the second and third generation of Ferring immigrants, and that this course will continue to be held. To the figure of four thousand people should perhaps be added a further one or two thousand who can understand the language, though they speak it imperfectly.

Altogether there are now living in the U.S.A. five to six thousand people of Ferring descent who regard themselves as Ferrings; but only two thousand of them still speak and understand Ferring. For them the second language is English. For the two thousand people living on Föhr and Amrum, the second language now is in almost all cases High German, although it was Low German or Saxon before the War for the majority of the people. Only a few people have Dutch, Danish or other Scandinavian languages as the second language. The complicated language situation on Föhr has recently been treated by N. Århammar (1975).

The Official or Second Language and the Minority Language

As more and more defenders of minority languages are beginning to understand, the problem of the official or second language may be as important or more important for the survival of the minority language than the care for this language itself. In this respect the Ferring language is a good example. It is indeed probable that our use of different second languages, nowadays English and German and to a somewhat lesser extent Danish, may be one of the reasons for the survival of Ferring. Equally important, perhaps, is the historic fact of the repeated shifting of the second language among the Ferring people. In medieval times it was Latin for the educated people and Low German for others, as everywhere in Northern Europe. From 1500 onward, for almost three centuries, it was Dutch; and from 1800 until now, German, and English, and to a lesser extent Scandinavian. The experiences we have had with these different second languages permit one conclusion: the choice of the second language is important. A small linguistic and ethnic group like ours should do everything in its power to maintain the freedom of choice. We are therefore in favour of the Danish schools in North-Frisland. And we all should work for a compulsory and early training in English for all our children, and even outside the schools promote the use of English. These two languages have in our experience supported the maintenance of the Ferring language; whereas Dutch and German, especially Low German, have changed its very structure and individual nature.

Our history teaches us that we have to be bilingual or still better plurilingual. Greene (present volume, p.2) quotes O'Rahilly's dictum that if all speakers of a minority language are bilingual the language is bound to die. I think the Ferring language shows that this is not always the case, at least not for a small language. What are now the chances of survival? In several ways it is astounding that the Ferring language has survived until our time. It is spoken by very few people, who furthermore have never been geographically isolated but in fact have been more mobile than most other people. They have always been seafarers and merchants in many parts of the world. Even for the Frisians themselves the survival of their language has been an astonishing fact. Each generation believed that they were the last who would speak Frisian. Five hundred years ago, a North-Frisian historian from the Southern part of the country was already saying that, though the Frisian language was still in existence, in a hundred years nobody would speak Frisian any more. In 1880 Professor Bremer, the first scientist who seriously studied Ferring, wrote that in a hundred years the language would be extinct. Yet it is still living today in many ways, more strongly than half a century ago – and the number of people speaking it has not decreased. In fact, in several villages it has definitely increased. The reason for the increase is probably the decline of the Low German language, which even in the Netherlands has always been the main competitor with Frisian and the main cause of its retreat in Groningen in the Netherlands as well as in East-Frisland and North-Frisland.

It is difficult to give a full explanation for this power of survival. One reason may be that on their islands the Ferring people still live in a largely closed community with very old and strict customs, which still today – to some extent – are maintained. Furthermore, our people are using the language to build a wall around their island. The defence of the language is a compensation for the lack of political independence, which they have not had, even as a political goal, in modern times. The fact that the language is spoken on an island is not as important as one might believe. There are many other Frisian islands where the language has disappeared, e.g. on the East-Frisian island of Wangerooge the last speaker died at the beginning of this century. Of course we often speak enviously about the lucky inhabitants of the Faroe Islands, and wish that our islands might be placed somewhere in the Atlantic, as remote from the continent as they are. These islands, like Iceland, represent for us an ideal in their successful revival of their old languages. We would like to follow, but are well aware that we will never succeed as well as they have done.

Thus isolation as such has played little or no part in the survival of the Ferring language. The community feeling, however, certainly is a main factor for survival. Let me illustrate this with one single Ferring word. The word *wet* means in Dutch the law, in Swedish it means commonsense, in Ferring it means something in between: an old custom which cannot be broken without consequences for the transgressor. Although these old, rigid customs are becoming fewer, they still exist. There seems indeed to be a tendency among the young people on our island to maintain them, even to strengthen them. Among our young people, the use of the Ferring language has thus become a symbol of belonging to the community and a means of distancing themselves from the immigrants and the German tourists who annually flood our islands.

Our economic history, too, has played a role in preserving the Ferring language. For centuries a young sailor in Dutch, German, Danish or British harbours could be pretty sure to find a good job, if he spoke Ferring. There was always a ship with a Ferring captain who would take him.

Another positive factor has been that the island during the last century has again and again had a few men and women who have undertaken work for the preservation of the language.

Although we have now seemingly reached a level of stabilisation of our language, the outlook for the further future is dark. All the factors which endanger all minority languages anywhere are of course also acting on our island. Let me here mention only the rapid decrease in the number of farmers, the social pressures which virtually force anyone with a higher education or professional training to leave the island, and the overwhelming impact of the German mass media – only a few of the many negative factors. Therefore we cannot just sit down and be satisfied with the situation as it is. We have to think of ways of counterbalancing these dangers.

What can we do?
For a small language like ours I think there is only one chance of survival for several generations ahead, and that is to give the language a new function. It may be impossible to find a new function for such a small linguistic and ethnic group. But allow me to play a little with an idea which to most defenders of minority languages may sound heretical. I could think of our language turning into a secret language. In fact for many of our people it always has been a secret language; and especially among the older people there has always been a quite strong resistance against printing and writing the Ferring language, because they said it would enable other people to learn to understand our language – something that we should not support but on the contrary try to prevent.

What I am aiming at is what Professor Greene touched upon (present volume, p.8) when he said that for the survival or revival of a minority language a network is not enough: it requires a society. I fully agree with him. The Ferring language has survived – against all odds – most probably because we had such a society. This little island society is now in a state of decomposition, but it is not yet totally destroyed. This means that if we want to save our language we will have to save or restore the Ferring island society.

In modern history people who have fought to save their language have generally had as a political goal a national, sovereign state, based on their language and their national identity. We are too small a people to have such an ambition; and furthermore, such a political goal is counter to all Frisian tradition and history.

Professor Greene mentioned another motivation which could be strong enough to revive a dying language: religion. He was of course thinking of the revival of the Hebrew language. I will not say that this would be totally imposssible for the Frisians as a group. There have been some tendencies in this direction in our history, such as the Mennonites and the Quakers, which I will not treat here. There is, however, a third motivation which Professor Greene mentioned briefly, and which may be more realistic for just such a small nation as ours, namely *economics*.

Let me give you one example of our economic history. In the early sixteenth century our people had been living well from the herring fishing around Heligoland. In 1520 the herring suddenly disappeared, and some years of severe economic depression followed. But then one man had an idea. His name was Ricardus Petri or Richard Petersen, and he was a minister. He began to teach the young boys on the island the craft of navigation. The admittance to this first school of navigation was free, but each boy had to sign a promise, that he too would give free navigation courses, after he had retired from the sea. Our island was thus able to offer the new Dutch overseas companies a great number of well-trained sailors and officers, mainly for whaling in the Arctic and for the Far East shipping. This gave us almost three centuries of economic independence and relatively good living. It also meant that speaking Ferring was an advantage. An immigrant had to learn it, if he wanted to be accepted as a member of this closed seafaring community. Can we find similar solutions now? I think we can. It should not be by starting new industries on an island, but, in the tradition of Ricardus Petri, in starting very specialised schools, making our young people expert in some particular economic area which is not important or interesting enough for bigger countries. It could, for example, be something in a limited field of commerce or banking. Such a specialist training could be combined with the Ferring language. Here the function of a secret language could perhaps be an advantage.

Professor Haugen (present volume, p.114) coined a new term, the 'market value' of a language. I would like to accept this term, but to add that there are big markets and small markets, markets for oil and airlines, but also markets for rare flowers or for rare hormones, where a few hundred grams can cover the world's demands.

In modern society, where belonging to a little group has become attractive again, this may be a way to keep together our people in different parts of the world and to tie them to their home island; but then of course the function of the secret language would require a far stronger solidarity between the speakers than we now have: a solidarity which could be political, economic, religious, or something else. When the British economist Schumacher a few years ago published his famous book *Small is beautiful* he certainly was not thinking of languages. But perhaps it is also true for a language.

Why Should we Maintain a Small Language?
One may ask if – in our time – it is right to work for the survival or revival of a

small language like Ferring. I think it is, not only for the social reasons I have given earlier but also from a more general point of view. I believe that cultural growth and linguistic growth are both based on differentiation. The maintenance and development of a small language with highly specialised functions may be useful not only for the few people who speak it but also for other languages and of course for different fields of science.

That history and linguistics are among the fields that may benefit from our language work will be easily accepted. But I can also give an example to demonstrate that an old language also preserves knowledge, that in fact it can have an effect on a modern science like my own. My field of science is endocrinology, hormone research. In this research my work has always been limited to one single hormone-producing gland: the pituitary gland, the mediator between the brain and the body. In all modern European languages this gland has a Latin or Greek name, in English the word 'pituitary' or in German *hypofysis*. But in the Ferring language it has an old established name, namely *brajnknoop* or 'brain button'. The explanation for this is probably that the Ferring people, during their centuries as whalers around Greenland, noticed this gland, which in whales is the size of an orange. Since in man or in domesticated animals it is only the size of a pea, it is not noticed by farmers or by butchers of pigs, sheep and cattle. Now the Ferring language not only has the word for the pituitary gland, but is also has a proverb about it which certainly has been used since the great whaling period. It sounds like this: *Hi wiar so areg, at ham a brajnknoop baarst*, which means 'he was so angry that his pituitary burst'. The whalers, we can assume, had noticed that a whale which had fought a long and hard fight with the harpooners, showed bleedings in the *brajnknoop*. When the Canadian endocrinologist Selye thirty years ago published his stress theory and thus invented the word stress, he confirmed by experimental research what this Ferring proverb had been saying for centuries – namely, that danger may cause damage to the pituitary. One could probably find more examples to show that saving an old language can also mean saving old knowledge; knowledge that would otherwise be lost.

But more important than all this, is what Professor Haugen called the ecology of languages. As we now have learned that the loss of one species on our globe may be an irrevocable loss to other species including man, so we have to learn that the loss of a small language is likewise a loss to all of us.

References
Århammar, Nils (1964) Die Amringer Literatur, in *Amrum-Geschichte und Gestalt einer Insel*. Itzehoe: Verlag Hansen & Hansen.
— (1975) *Die Sprachen der Insel Föhr*, Anm.10.S.34-6. Wyk/Föhr: Museumsverein Insel Föhr.
Bremer, Otto (1888) Einleitung zu einer Amringisch-Föhringischen Sprachlehre, in *Jahrbuch des Vereins für Niederdeutsche Sprachforschung*, Vol. 13. Leipzig: Norden.
Wurdenbuk för Feer an Oomram. Frisian Dictionary for Föhr and Amrum. Verlag Jens Quedens, Amrum, 1986.

DIETRICH STRAUSS

18. Aspects of German as
a Minority Language in Western Europe

Since with about 92 million speakers German ranks second after Russian in Europe (Haarmann 1975, p.253), it may at first sight seem surprising that it can also be a minority language. And yet German exists as a minority language in at least ten European countries.

I intend to take a closer look at the ethnopolitical and sociolinguistic conditions under which German exists in four member states of the European Community: Belgium, Denmark, France and Italy. It is hoped that the phenomenon of a major language existing under the conditions of a minority language – a phenomenon not so very common – will cast some new light on other problems. I intend to demonstrate the differences found in the four countries, and to discuss the extent and importance of these differences, in order to arrive at a sort of paradigm of conditions under which minority languages can exist. Attention will be paid, on the one hand, to the constitutional sides of the question and the attitudes of the respective central governments, to the influence of the educational systems and the mass media; and, on the other hand, to the actual extent to which German is used, and to the linguistic spheres and social groups and strata in which it is used.

My tables show basic linguistic data, the constitutional conditions, the rôle of ecclesiastical services, the scope of the media, and historical factors of importance. They then set forth the present sociolinguistic situation and give an estimate of the present trends in the number of speakers of German in the respective regions. These are all general surveys, since there are no comprehensive and detailed investigations of recent date that cover all aspects in the four regions.

The importance of the historical background to any given ethnopolitical and sociolinguistic grouping cannot possibly be overrated. Otherwise the contrasting developments that have taken place in Alsace-Lorraine and South Tyrol could not be explained at all. Indeed this historical aspect deserves much more space than can be allowed here. As most of the data given in the tables is of an almost self-explanatory nature, these will not be

Figure 18.1. Germanic idioms in Central Europe. Hatching shows regions with German-speaking populations in Belgium, Denmark, France and Italy.

discussed at any great length. Only those that seem to defy reasonable interpretation will have to be looked at somewhat more closely.

The object of this survey of data is to produce characterisations of the four regions which not only demonstrate the unique nature of the conditions under which German exists as a minority language, but provide a comprehensive explanation for these conditions. Why is it, for example, that the German-speaking South Tyrolese, whose socio-economic situation is comparatively satisfactory, are opposed to the state into which they are incorporated, but that the German-speaking population in Alsace-Lorraine, irrespective of their present socio-economic lot (and in Lorraine it certainly

190

could be better both in comparison with other regions in France and with West Germany) adhere so staunchly to France?

To begin with Alsace-Lorraine, many factors contribute to the present ethnopolitical consciousness of its population.

(1) It has to be remembered that in France as early as 1539 an ordinance of King Francis I declared French (i.e. the *langue d'oïl*) to be the only official language of the realm: all official or juridical matters 'soient prononcez, enregistrez et délivrez aux parties en langaige maternel françois et non autrement' (Gossen 1957, p.436). True, this was primarily directed against the *langue d'oc* in the South; but in due course it was likewise used against other idioms of the country. So, to some degree the French linguistic domination began as soon as Alsace-Lorraine passed to France in the second half of the seventeenth century.

(2) The French Revolution gave additional weight to the endeavours of the government to enforce unitary linguistic standards on every citizen, because this was now seen as a consequence of the political aim of *égalité*. At the same time, the other languages spoken in France were denounced as 'un reste de barbarie des siècles passés', and their complete disappearance was held to be wholly desirable (Sérant 1965, p.30). Though the population of Alsace-Lorraine remained for some time rather reluctant to accept the revolutionary ideas, after 1815, when revolutionary radicalism was no longer menacing, the liberal elements of those ideas were adopted by continuously increasing numbers of people in Alsace-Lorraine – who also became more and more willing to accept the linguistic consequence of the idea of *égalité* in centralised France: the use of French as the one national language of all citizens.

(3) The situation became more unfavourable for German in the early nineteenth century, when – rather belatedly by comparison with most of Europe – German national sentiments took hold of larger sections of the population of Germany. This new feeling did not reach the people of Alsace-Lorraine, since they already lived outside the German borders.

(4) When the new Prussian-dominated German Reich compelled the French to hand over Alsace-Lorraine in 1871, the introduction of a régime of Prussian discipline and effectiveness did so much to strengthen liberal sentiments in Alsace-Lorraine, sentiments that now began to turn strongly against Germany, that in 1918 the French troops were hailed as liberators. In 1944, even more intensely, the same thing happened once again.

It is these four historical factors that almost exclusively determine the present ethnopolitical consciousness of the population of Alsace-Lorraine: an ethnopolitical consciousness which is decidedly French. If it were not for these weighty reasons, one phenomenon, probably unique in Western Europe's more recent ethnolinguistic history, would remain totally inexplicable. Alsace-Lorraine is a region that from the beginning of German history contributed abundantly to German culture: one immediately thinks of such examples as the medieval poet Gottfried of Strasbourg, of Strasbourg as a home of German humanism (after Mainz the oldest centre of printing, and birthplace of an early translation of the Bible), of Strasbourg's advanced form of municipal self-government before Louis xiv, and of the outstanding reputation of Strasbourg University everywhere in German-speaking countries until its closure by the revolutionary government in Paris (to be re-opened almost a century later). Nonetheless, the people of this region completely changed their national loyalties and sentiments, accepting, as a consequence of this change, a sociolinguistic situation in which the continued use not only of High German, but even of the regional German idioms, is critically endangered.

The movement of the 'autonomists', who between the two World Wars tried to secure a certain amount of constitutionally legalised self-government for Alsace-Lorraine, did not achieve anything.

After the Second World War the activities of the René Schickele Circle, and more recently those of the group whose protagonist is André Weckmann, have been endeavouring to maintain German as one of the spoken idioms of the region, either in its High German form, or in its Alsatian and Lorrainese dialects. The existence of other autochthonous ethnolinguistic minorities in the same state may, provided that these become politically active, prove advantageous for any such minority. In France the Basques, the Bretons and the Occitanians have since the nineteenth century (a longer period than the German-speakers of Alsace-Lorraine) been trying with at least partial success to improve the situations of their languages and secure them a place alongside French. In the late 1950s they founded the *Conseil national de Défence des Langues et Cultures régionales* (Haarmann 1972, p.333). Representatives of Alsace-Lorraine were not present then. There are, however, indications that the activities of these minorities – and of late those of the Italian-speaking Corsicans – function as stimuli in Alsace-Lorraine.

In South Tyrol, developments took in almost every respect an opposite course. Before the 'land' of Tyrol passed into the hands of the Hapsburgs, it had evolved sociopolitical conditions that were, by medieval standards, progressive – almost democratic. A certain number of peasants were entitled to sit in the Tyrolese Diet – a comparatively rare phenomenon in the constitutional history of medieval Europe (Frisia, Iceland, Scandinavia and Switzerland providing other examples); the peasants were allowed to carry weapons, and were on the other hand obliged to participate in the defence of the 'land' whenever danger from outside arose. When in 1363 the Hapsburgs took over political power in Tyrol, they were prudent enough not to change the sociopolitical arrangements there to any substantial degree.

Consequently a strong feeling of loyalty to the House of Hapsburg developed, coexisting from then on with the inherited consciousness of forming a comparatively freely organised society. This loyalty was not seriously endangered even by the unifying reforms of Empress Maria Theresa and her son, Emperor Joseph ii. For a long time the Tyrolese continued to enjoy the privilege of not being obliged to perform any sort of military service that was not directly connected with defending Tyrol. This, however, they did valiantly on their own and the House of Hapsburg's behalf whenever need arose. Therefore it was an extreme shock for them (though not without precedent: during the Napoleonic Wars Austria had, from 1805 to 1815, been forced to surrender the whole of Tyrol) when in 1919 part of their territory, South Tyrol, had to be handed over to Italy. The aftermath of this shock is visible to this day: the resolute rejection by the South Tyrolese of everything that is considered to be Italian.

This aversion did not even noticeably diminish when after 1972 the ethnopolitical and sociolinguistic conditions in South Tyrol improved considerably, reinstituting German as one of the two languages of the region: indeed, virtually securing it first place in many fields, as it has proved difficult for Italians to acquire a standard of German that qualifies them for official jobs, whereas it seems comparatively easy for the Tyrolese to reach an equivalent standard of Italian, German being the more difficult language to learn.

The fact that the South Tyrolese, themselves a small minority within the Italian state, act as the protectors of an even smaller minority in the same region, the Rhaeto-Romanic group of the Ladins, surely serves to increase their self-assurance. The political interests of the Ladins are not defended by a separate political party, but by the *Südtiroler Volkspartei* (South Tyrolese People's Party), which vigorously interferes whenever legitimate positions of the Ladins are infringed by Italians or the Italian State. The South Tyrolese thus provide an example of a minority protecting another minority that is not only much smaller, but moreover of different ethnic origin and of different sociocultural traditions and ways of life – an example probably unique in Western Europe, and certainly remarkable. (As the loyalties of the Frisians in South Schleswig are only partly Danish, the relation of the Danish and Frisian minorities in South Schleswig is comparable only in part to the situation in South Tyrol.)

However, in the light of the constitutional safeguards that have been granted for their ethnic existence, in the light of what has been achieved for the use of German in so many fields, and in the light of the social climate prevailing in the region, the strong, almost rigid anti-Italian attitude of the Tyrolese must necessarily surprise the less informed. And indeed it would be impossible to account for it, if it were not for Tyrol's history, which, vividly living on in the minds of the great majority of the South Tyrolese, explains the urgent desire to preserve the Tyrolese ethnic identity – a desire so intense that fears are recurrently expressed of a threatening *Verelsässerung*, i.e. of a development of the ethnopolitical and sociolinguistic conditions in a direction leading to what is reality in Alsace-Lorraine.

There are other German-speaking areas in Italy, some bordering on Switzerland, others in Venezia. Their total number of German-speakers certainly amounts to less than 10,000, though reliable figures are not available. These speakers of German have preserved very archaic forms of their language: one region, that of the *siben kameun* (*sette comuni*/seven communities), has kept alive a form of German that was once probably influenced by Langobardian, a High German dialect which itself died out long ago (Schweizer 1948). All these forms of German are of great interest to the comparative linguist. The speakers of German in these areas enjoy no form of official recognition as ethnic or linguistic minorities, though in the case of the *siben kameun* one can discern a mild interest in the preservation of the ancient German idiom among local Italian authorities.

I now consider the historical background for the speakers of German in Belgium: (1) The region of Arlon was annexed to Belgium in 1839, only nine years after that state had come into being. Subsequently a strong feeling of loyalty to Belgium developed among the German-speaking population in that region. Strong pro-German sentiments never appeared, probably owing in part to the geographical fact that Luxembourg is situated between the Arlon people and Germany. (2) The region of Eupen and St Vith was incorporated into Belgium after World War I in consequence of a dubious referendum-like procedure. Naturally, the German-speaking population of that area had reservations about their new state. (3) The recent constitutional settlement of the long and bitter language dispute between Flemings and Walloons generated, as a sort of by-product, cultural autonomy for the German-speaking region of Eupen and St Vith; so that German was promoted to one of the three official languages of Belgium, functioning as such, however, only in that area (not in the 'Old Belgian' region of Arlon).

The coexistence of two German-speaking groups in Belgium, of which one enjoys scarcely any of the rights of a minority but accepts almost with indifference, for reasons of traditional loyalty to Belgium, a linguistic position greatly endangered by their Walloon compatriots, while the other has been granted an extensive amount of self-government in cultural and linguistic matters and is self-assured as to the use of German, has no doubt removed much intolerance and, as a consequence, many of the anxieties of the latter group; producing in East Belgium a comparatively liberal ethno-political climate.

The situation of the speakers of German in Denmark differs yet again in its nature and complexity. (1) Holstein and Schleswig were to remain *ewich tosamende ungedelt* (forever together undivided) according to the avowal of King Christian I of Denmark in 1460, after he had inherited these two dukedoms. Since Holstein was originally a German-speaking territory, whereas Schleswig was mainly inhabited by Danes and Frisians, that ancient union of the dukedoms bore within itself the reason for the language struggles of the nineteenth and twentieth centuries. (2) The influx of Germans of all trades ever since the Middle Ages, a phenomenon not uncommon in all Scandinavian countries, was especially intense in Schleswig, so that the language border was steadily shifted further north. That tendency was, for the last time, intensified when Prussia acquired Schleswig in 1864–6 as a consequence of victories over first Denmark and then Austria. (3) In 1919 a referendum was held, the result of which led to the partition of Schleswig, its northern part being reattached to Denmark. Though this referendum took place under more or less fair conditions, it initially, as might have been expected, caused new bitterness on both sides, until in the fifties the ethnolinguistic questions of that border country began to be seen in a wider perspective.

On both sides of the border a new consciousness began to develop among the respective majority and minority populations: the consciousness of being, all of them, legitimate inhabitants of the same country. This consciousness was intensified by the fact that the Frisians, the smallest minority in the region, have never unanimously decided in favour of giving support to either of the two larger ethnic groups; and it has drawn additional strength from the fact that both the Danish and the German minorities enjoy uninhibited access to the cultural and financial aids provided by both Denmark and West Germany for their minorities. Indeed it is certainly unique in Europe, perhaps in the world, that representatives of complementary minorities on both sides of a border now and then meet to discuss their ethnopolitical problems and questions of common interest. Thus, the Danish-German border country has become a region characterised by both serious attempts to secure the continuing existence of its minorities and a remarkably liberal attitude of mutual respect for the positions of Danes, Frisians and Germans.

	Belgium	Denmark	France	Italy
regions concerned	East Belgium (= regions of Arlon, Eupen, St Vith)	Northern Schleswig	Alsace-Lorraine (= Depts Bas-Rhin, Haut-Rhin, Moselle)	South Tyrol (= Province of Bozen/Bolzano)
numbers of speakers of German	c.110,000	c.23,000	c.1,200,000	c.235,000
language border easily discernible for the non-sociolinguist	yes, in Eupen and St Vith; no, in the region of Arlon	no	no	yes
dialects spoken in the regions and their linguistic distance from Standard High German	Ripuarian – considerable; Moselle-Franconian – considerable	Low Saxon (≈ Low German) – extreme; but prevailing form is Standard High German, spoken with a N. German accent	Moselle-Franconian and Rheno-Franconian, mainly Dept Moselle – considerable; Low Alemannic, mainly Depts Bas-Rhin and Haut-Rhin – extreme	South Bavarian influenced by High Alemannic – extreme
complementary minorities on other side of border of states	no	yes, c.50,000 Danes (and c.10,000 North Frisians)	no	no
co-existing minorities in the same region	no	no (North Frisians in former centuries)	no	Ladins, c.12,500 (a Rhaeto-Romanic group)
autochthonous co-existing minorities in the same state	no	no (Denmark without the Faroe Islands and Greenland)	Basques, Bretons, Catalans, Flemings, Italians, Occitanians	Albanians, Catalans (spoken in Alghero/Sardinia), French, Friulians (a Rhaeto-Romanic group), Germans in other regions of Northern Italy, Greeks, Sardinians, Serbo-Croatians, Slovenes

Linguistic Data

		guages of the state (though operative as such only in the region of Eupen and St Vith)	as language of a minority	guages in the above specified region
The Constitution	German as teaching language in schools	yes	yes	yes
	German as language of jurisdiction	yes (virtually restricted to the cantonal jurisdiction in the above specified region)	no, but German allowed as language of civil parties or accused person(s)	yes (restricted to the provincial jurisdiction in the above specified region)
	German as language in the armed forces	yes (in a smaller East Belgian unit of the army)	no	no
	German as language in broadcasting programmes	yes, on a proportional basis	very rare, and only in dialect programmes	yes, on a proportional basis; special arrangements with German and Austrian TV stations
	central government helping to maintain German as one of the acknowledged languages of the region	yes	yes	yes
The Church	German Christian names allowed	yes	yes	yes
	German in ecclesiastical services	yes	yes, but larger number of services delivered in French	yes

		Belgium	Denmark	France	Italy
The Press	German daily papers	yes	yes	no, but some papers containing German sections	yes
	German periodicals (mostly of local or parochial character)	yes	yes	yes	yes
	dialect publications of all kinds	yes	yes	yes, increasing in numbers	yes
Historical Data	literary and cultural traditions that have originated in the region and are of momentum for speakers of German living elsewhere	not of remarkable momentum	not of remarkable momentum	of outstanding momentum	of momentum
	end of German (or Austrian) sovereignty in the region	1918/1920 (1940-44 again part of Germany)	1920 (Danish sovereignty till 1864)	second half of 17th century, e.g. Strasbourg 1681 (1871-1918 & 1940-44)	1919 (1943-45 German administration)

		(German in all linguistic spheres, French only in official speech) in the region of Eupen and St Vith; diglossia (French in all linguistic spheres, German only in colloquial and intimate speech) in the region of Arlon	[...] linguistic spheres, German only in colloquial and intimate speech)	linguistic spheres, German only in colloquial and intimate speech)	linguistic spheres, Italian only in official speech)
Sociolinguistic Factors	degree of adherence to German in different social groups	no marked difference	no marked difference	stronger in rural areas, in the first two decades after World War II stronger in lower income groups	no marked difference
	prevailing comprehension of nationality	mainly coinciding with citizenship, comprehended ethnically by a minority	comprehended ethnically	coinciding with citizenship	comprehended ethnically. i.e. German (or Austrian)
	the socio-economic atmosphere (labour relations etc.) as compared to other regions of the state	comparatively good	good	comparatively good in Alsace (= Le jardin de la France), disturbances in Lorraine	comparatively good (since 1971; Southern Tyrol = Italy's Switzerland)
	majority of population satisfied with present political settlement of questions concerning nationality	yes	yes	yes	no
The Present Trend	numbers of speakers of German stable, decreasing or increasing	stable	stable	decreasing	stable

The figures are taken mainly from Haarman 1975, though Straka 1970 and Blaschke 1980 were also consulted.

References

Alcock, A. E. (1970) *The history of the South Tyrol question*. London.

Alleman, F. R. (1962) Die Elsässer – Eine Minorität, die keine sein will. *Der Monat 15*.

Balmer, E. (1949) *Die Walser in Piemont*. Bern.

Beer, W. R. (1977) The social class of ethnic activists in contemporary France, in *Ethnic conflict in the western world* (ed. M. J. Esman). Ithaca.

Blaschke, J. (ed.) (1980) *Handbuch der westeuropäischen Regional-bewegungen*. Frankfurt am Main.

Brandt, O. (1976) *Geschichte Schleswig-Holsteins*. Kiel.

Czikann-Zichy, M. (1960) *Turmoil in South Tyrol*. New York.

Ferrandi, M. (1955) *L'Alto Adige nella storia*. Bolzano/Bozen.

Finck, A. (1977) *Nachrichten aus dem Elsaß. Deutschsprachige Literatur in Frankreich*. Hildesheim, New York.

Gossen, C. Th. (1957) Die Einheit der französischen Schriftsprache im 15. und 16. Jahrhundert. *Zeitschrift für Romanische Philologie 73*.

Haarmann, H. (1972) Die Sprachen Frankreichs – Soziologische und politische Aspekte ihrer Entwicklung, in *Festschrift Wilhelm Giese, Beiträge zur Romanistik und allgemeinen Sprach-wissenschaft* (eds H. Haarmann and M. Studemund). Hamburg.

— (1975) *Soziologie und Politik der Sprachen Europas*. München.

Heuss, T. (1950) *Die deutsche Nationalidee im Wandel der Geschichte*. Stuttgart.

Huter, F. (1965) *Südtirol, eine Frage des europäischen Gewissens*. München.

Jensen, J. (1961) *Nordfriesland in den geistigen und politischen Strömungen des 19. Jahrhunderts (1797-1864)*. Neumünster.

Kloss, H. (1969) *Grundfragen der Ethnopolitik im 20. Jahrhundert* (=*Ethnos* vol. 7). Wien and Stuttgart.

Magnago, S. (1974) The situation of the German and Ladin linguistic minorities in South Tyrol. *Europa Ethnica 31*.

Maugué, P. (1970) *Le particularisme alsacien 1918-1967*. Paris.

René Schickele Kreis (eds) (1968) *Notre avenir est bilingue – Zweisprachig: Unsere Zukunft*. Strasbourg.

Reuss, R. (1925) *Histoire d'Alsace*. Paris.

Rusinow, D. I. (1969) *Italy's Austrian Heritage 1919-1946*. Oxford.

Schillings, H. (1965) Die deutsche Volksgruppe in Belgien. *Europa Ethnica 22*.

Schweizer, B. (1948) Die Herkunft der Zimbern, in *Die Nachbarn, Jahrbuch für vergleichende Volkskunde*, vol. 1.

Sérant, P. (1965) *La France des minorités*. Paris.

Straka, M. (ed.) (1970) *Handbuch der europäischen Volksgruppen* (=*Ethnos* vol. 8). Wien and Stuttgart.

Verdoodt, A. (1968) *Zweisprachige Nachbarn. Die deutschen Hochsprach- und Mundartgruppen in Ost-Belgien, dem Elsaß, Ost-Lothringen und Luxemburg* (=*Ethnos* vol. 6). Wien and Stuttgart.

Voltelini, H. v. (1919) *Die Deutschen und die Ladiner in Tirol*. Wien.

Wambaugh, S. (1933) *Plebiscites since the World War*. Washington.

Wurzer, B. (1969) *Die deutschen Sprachinseln in Oberitalien*. Bolzano/Bozen.

19. Triglossia in Luxemburg

Triglossia – or, if we consider the situation from the point of view of the spoken language, even tetraglossia – in Luxemburg goes back to a certain group of historical, ethnical and social factors which happened to come together for the first time almost 2,000 years ago. The language which may now be considered as that of the Luxemburgers was first spoken in what was to become Luxemburg, when around the year 300 the first Franks settled in the fertile valleys of the central part of the country, a region now called 'The Good Land'. Yet even in those days it was not the only language spoken in this region. Trilingualism is a legacy of the past which the Luxemburger has to bear to this day. Even in the first centuries A.D. the people there had to struggle with several languages, for there were at least three strata of population: the Celtic Treveri, whose numbers kept decreasing and whose language must have died out by the fifth century; the Germanic 'settlers' (Rhine-Franks) who came in ever-increasing numbers and spoke Germanic; and a limited number of Romans. Latin was the language used by the authorities. The language that the 'settlers' of the third century brought to Luxemburg was, three centuries later, subject to the active influence of Gallo-Roman speech habits. The traditional dualism of the inhabitants of Luxemburg, torn between the attraction of the Germanic east and the Romanic west, can be traced back to these early centuries. According to the theory of the 'Salian Circuit' elaborated by Robert Bruch (1953), it was the Salian Franks who were responsible for the very early impact of a western-ised culture and Gallo-Roman speech habits on a population whose ethnic substance was Germanic. As early as the fourth century A.D. they set forth from the lower Rhine – history knows them as 'North Sea Franks' or 'Francs maritimes' – to conquer Toxandria, the region of Antwerp. Eventually they reached the Loire and the Bassin de Paris. Following a route already used by Stone Age people, a route skirting the Ardennes and the Plateau de Briey, they marched eastwards again. Led by Clovis, the Merovingians conquered the region which Robert Bruch was later to call the Bay of Luxemburg

(Luxemburger Bucht), one of the poles of an axis formed by the rivers Moselle and Lahn. It was along this route that the Salian Franks brought with them a civilisation which, though basically Germanic, had however changed considerably through contact with the Gallo-Romans: a civilisation and a language which definitely influenced those of the ancestors of the present-day Luxemburgers.

It is also to this westernised civilisation introduced by the Salian Franks that the cultural dualism of the inhabitants of Luxemburg can be traced back. It explains the restlessness of the Luxemburger – hesitant and wavering between the attraction of the West and the East, of Germany and France. It also explains why the Luxemburgers resent being considered German. When in 1941 the Nazis tried to force the Luxemburgers to acknowledge German as their mother tongue, an overwhelming majority refused to do so in spite of the open threats, even though unaware of the historical development of their language. As I have pointed out, bilingualism (or trilingualism, or even tetralingualism) are part of a legacy of the past which the Luxemburger has had to bear throughout his history; he could not rid himself of this burden without giving up his own identity.

In 963 Sigfried, Count of the Ardennes, founded the county of Luxemburg in that region of the old Carolingian empire which is divided by the language frontier into two halves, these being the so-called 'Germania' and 'Romania'. The country whose foundations he laid comprised territory belonging to Higher and Lower Lorraine, with the language frontier running right through it, so that one part of the later Duchy spoke a Germanic language and the other part a Romance one. And ever since, no matter what happened, the country has remained bilingual; and when in the fourteenth century the authorities divided the country into a *quartier wallon* and a *quartier allemand*, that is, into a Walloon (French-speaking) and a German (German-speaking) district, the administrative services merely recognised the actual linguistic situation as it existed. Cut off from the rest of the German-speaking people in the east by geographical (the mountainous regions of the Ardennes, High Venn, Eifel, the narrow valley of the upper part of the Moselle), administrative, economic and cultural frontiers, the German district of the Duchy became a linguistic island, a relict area in which the language preserved old speech habits and words that had dropped out of use elsewhere; but an area that also was wide open to the influence of the West.

The strange thing is that the influence of French civilisation and literature dates from the time when the Dukes of Luxemburg became Emperors of the Holy Roman Empire. For while Charles IV carried German culture far into the East (he founded the University of Prague), it was his brother Wenceslaw I, Count of Luxemburg (1351–83), the son of Beatrix de Bourbon and the husband of Jeanne de Brabant, who invited the French chronicler Jean Froissart, and the French poet Eustache Deschamps, to stay at his court. He himself wrote French poems and promoted the spread of French civilisation.

The charters he granted to the towns of the German district were written in French. When the dynasty of Luxemburg lost its importance and its interest in the Duchy, the country became first a pawn and then a province in the hands of foreign masters – Burgundians, Spaniards, Frenchmen and Austrians – for nearly four hundred years. The council of the province responsible for the administration of the old Duchy during the Spanish and Austrian periods used French for most of its official correspondence with the authorities in Brussels, Madrid, Paris and Vienna, but German when corresponding with the German-speaking district. Yet practically all official decrees were published in French and then translated into German. The first news-sheet published in Luxemburg in 1704 – *Le Cabinet des Princes d'Europe* – printed French articles only, and thus could be read only by the nobility and the members of the upper class.

The country was forced to undergo three partitions; and the results were striking from the linguistic point of view. In 1669 such German-speaking regions as Thionville (Diedenhofen) in Lorraine and Rodemach-Sierck were annexed by Louis xiv. In 1815 the Prussians seized the German-speaking parts east of the Moselle, the Sure and the Our. The county of Bouillon in which Walloon French is spoken remained part of what was now the *Grand* Duchy of Luxemburg till 1839; and around 1815 the region in which Luxemburgish is spoken accounted for one third of the territory of the Grand Duchy. It is interesting to note that in this period King William ii of Holland, as King and Grand Duke the legitimate ruler of Luxemburg, actually promoted the French language in that part of the Grand Duchy in order to put a linguistic and cultural barrier between Prussia and German-speaking Luxemburg. In 1839 the country underwent its third dismemberment as a result of the decrees of the Treaty of London (twenty-four Articles) and the French-speaking region of Arlon became part of Belgium.

The linguistic situation of the Grand Duchy is now profoundly different. In the new Grand Duchy there live only people who speak Luxemburgish; but although there is nobody left whose mother tongue is French, French and German remain the official languages used by the authorities and administrative services. But the mother tongue, Luxemburgish, is beginning to play a more important part in every domain. The dates 1848, 1896, 1912 and 1941 are all important milestones along the way taken by Luxemburgish. Since the Romantic revival in the early days of the nineteenth century, poets and politicians, writers and representatives have been promoting the use of Luxemburgish in Parliament and literature, and the growing national consciousness of the Luxemburgers has been encouraging these pioneers.

Significantly, 1848 was the year when two representatives, Carl Matthias André and Norbert Metz, a lawyer and an industrial manager, first used Luxemburgish in Parliament. In 1896 on 10 November Caspar Matthias Spoo was the first deputy to make his maiden speech in Luxemburgish; yet in spite of his passionate plea for the native tongue, the members voted against the use of Luxemburgish in the Chamber of Deputies. In 1912, thanks to the same dogged perseverance by C. M. Spoo, the study of Luxemburgish became compulsory in elementary schools, and Nicholas Welter, another prominent statesman, scholar and writer, provided the first official spelling- and textbook: *Das Luxemburgische und sein Schrifttum* (Luxemburgish and its Literature).

In 1941, on the occasion of a census which 'Gauleiter' Gustav Simon, head of the Nazi *Zivilverwaltung* (Civil Affairs), had organised with the obvious aim of giving a look of legitimacy to the brutal annexation of Luxemburg, all Luxemburgers to a man, and in the teeth of the Nazis, proclaimed that they were Luxemburgers, not Germans, and that their native tongue was Luxemburgish and not German. After the Liberation in 1944, Luxemburgish became a compulsory subject in the lower forms of the secondary schools, and Luxemburgish prose and poetry came to occupy the place they deserve.

These dates show the ground that has been covered since 1829, the year when Anthony Meyers, Professor of Mathematics at the University of Liege, became the first Luxemburger to publish a small book of verses in Luxemburgish. To understand the situation and the status of Luxemburgish in these early years of the nineteenth century, it must be borne in mind that it was only in 1839 that Luxemburg officially regained its independence and that the national consciousness of the Luxemburgers developed slowly in the course of the nineteenth century. Even so, the more patriotic they became, the less willing they were to accept German and French in their songs, their poetry, their plays. Social and political developments also played their parts. The influence of French decreased with the gradual disappearance of the former 'notables': that is, wealthy persons of distinction and great political influence, whose education and way of life made their sympathies turn towards France rather than towards Germany. The instruments of communication among the lower social classes, whose political and social influence is growing, are High German and Luxemburgish. It is not by chance that the pioneers of socialism in Luxemburg, such as the physician Michel Welter or Caspar Matthias Spoo, were also resolute champions of Luxemburgish. After the Second World War the German language suffered a serious setback: without, however, any noticeable gains being made by French. In the patriotic fervour of the immediate post-war years, Luxemburgish gained strength as a vehicle of patriotic feelings, yet the situation gradually returned to normal. So much then for the historical evolution of triglossia in Luxemburg.

Let us now try to sketch out in a brief, condensed survey the current situation and the way the three languages function as means of oral and written communication among the Luxemburgers and in their contacts with foreigners. If we consider only and exclusively oral communication between natives, the Luxemburgers are, except in some special situations such as public speeches and lectures, sermons and homilies, religious services and school-lessons, strictly monolingual, if we do not consider the code-switching from the regional dialect into the *koinè* (see below, p.205). But although monolingual when he speaks to his compatriots, the Luxemburger is bilingual and even trilingual in a restricted number of specific situations of oral communication with Luxemburgers, which have just been mentioned, and in the matter of written communication. This co-ordinate trilingualism, acquired in distinct and separate social contexts, is the result of the bilingual school-system in Luxemburg, which itself is due to the geographical, cultural and historical situation of the Grand Duchy.

The institution of a compulsory primary school-system, which was initially for seven years and is now for nine years, makes a minimum of language-skills in French (covering the basic range of topics) and a far larger competence in German available to every Luxemburger. Higher skills in French and also in German depend on the educational and cultural level of the individual learner, which means that there is a certain correlation between social status and language skill.

But the description we have just given needs further differentiation, which is possible if we introduce the term *diglossia* as distinct from *bilingualism*. We understand *diglossia* in its broadest signification, meaning a community where different registers or varieties of speech, or even two different linguistic systems which need not necessarily have a genealogical link, are used according to strictly defined circumstances. We shall use the term *bilingualism* as Joshua Fishman does, meaning the faculty of the members of a speech-community to express what they feel and think equally well in both linguistic systems or varieties of speech functioning in the community. If we speak of *triglossia* or *trilingualism* the same applies to a community where three languages or speech-varieties are spoken. Thus we have four possibilities of communication:

(1) Diglossia + bilingualism.

(2) Bilingualism – diglossia.

(3) Diglossia – bilingualism.

(4) Neither diglossia nor bilingualism.

The situation in Luxemburg may be described as diglossia + bilingualism.

But this typological construct too needs further specification concerning the use of French and German. Skill in French differs with the educational level, as we have seen, and when we speak of diglossia (triglossia) + bilingualism (trilingualism) in Luxemburg the expression 'to speak a language' must be taken in its minimal extension as 'the faculty of expressing in single sentences the basic range of topics'. Concerning German, the situation in Luxemburg differs from that in Germany in so far as in the field of oral communication the place that spoken Standard German occupies in Germany is taken by the *koinè*, the super-regional (mainly phonological) standard version of Luxemburgish. Thus, native Luxemburgers coming from different regions of the Grand Duchy, where (above all phonetically, but also morphologically, syntactically, lexically and semantically) strongly differing sub-dialects are spoken, do not switch over to spoken Standard German, as would be the case in Germany, but to Standard Luxemburgish.

Our typological scheme makes a further differentiation possible if we introduce the Auburger-Kloss concepts of (a) official language (*Amtssprache*) – (1) of the State, (2) in the State; (b) national language (*Nationalsprache*); (c) working language (*Arbeitssprache, lingua franca*). The status of these languages can be (1) dominant; (2) co-dominant; (3) indominant.

If we consider that since 1848 every Constitution of the Grand Duchy of Luxemburg has stipulated the principle of the equality of status of German and French as official languages; and if we take further for granted that, though the Constitution of 1948 does not mention this principle any more for obvious reasons – German as one of Luxemburg's official languages only four years after the Nazi terror had come to an end was unthinkable! – the equality of both French and German as well as the liberty of choice are nevertheless understood (the regulations warranting this free choice within the Administration and its contacts with the public go back to the Grand-Ducal Decrees of 1830, 1831 and 1834), we are entitled to define plurilingualism in Luxemburg as a triglossia, where French and German are co-dominant 'official languages' of the State, whereas Lëtzeburgesch constitutes a non-dominant national language. But it must be emphasised that all that has been said up till now concerns only written communication. In the field of oral communication, Lëtzeburgesch is co-dominant.

A very controversial subject is whether Lëtzeburgesch should be considered as a dialect or a language. Though Lëtzeburgesch cannot be compared to major or world languages like English, French, Spanish, Russian, etc., the domains where it is used and the way it functions speak against labelling it as a dialect. Considering all this Lëtzeburgesch is what L. Auburger and H. Kloss call an *Ausbausprache*, i.e. a language that is not yet fully developed and perhaps never will be.

Details of how this Luxemburgish triglossia or even tetraglossia – for the majority of the native speakers speak a local sub-dialect and also the *koinè* – works in the manifold situations of verbal communication can be found in my book *Sprachen in Luxemburg* (1980). I shall limit myself to a few salient points here. The Luxemburgers speak Lëtzeburgesch and only Lëtzeburgesch when amongst themselves; provided that they are not in court, in church, in school, or delivering an official speech or a learned lecture. And even in these situations Lëtzeburgesch is gaining ground.

Though Lëtzeburgesch is used more frequently as an instrument of communication among Luxemburgers than it was twenty or even ten years ago, the Luxemburger still prefers to write German or French in his communications with compatriots. The upper classes and intellectuals prefer to use French (or even Lëtzeburgesch for their private notes of a very intimate nature), whereas the lower classes stick to German. They practically never use Lëtzeburgesch for their private correspondence. Lëtzeburgesch is not easy to read and actually to set it down in writing demands an intellectual effort easily avoided by sticking to the more familiar word- and sentence-patterns of High German. Although High (Standard) German remains the foremost vehicle of written verbal communication outside the official, administrative and cultural domains, Lëtzeburgesch is making progress. This is due to a certain number of factors such as the Luxemburger's unshakeable faith in his national identity, the growing interest in dialects and minority languages brought about by the building up of what might be called a world-wide ecological conscience, and, last but not least, by a growing number of Luxemburgish intellectuals who stand up against a form of lingustic and francophile snobbery that debased the Luxemburger's own mother tongue into being an idiom perhaps just good enough to speak to servants, dogs and horses.

If on the one hand Luxemburgish is one of the strongest pillars of the Luxemburger's national identity, on the other hand only lunatics would ever think of giving Luxemburgish the status of sole official language in the Grand Duchy of Luxemburg. Living in a tiny country between two dominant civilisations, the Luxemburger has to learn German and French besides Luxemburgish. This does not mean he should despise his mother tongue. On the contrary, if the Luxemburgers have managed to survive as an independent nation to this day, this historical miracle is due, among a lot of lucky circumstances, to the very strong national feeling just mentioned which has been building up since the nineteenth century, Lëtzeburgesch and its literature being one of its foremost media and supports. In other words the Luxemburger's mother tongue is at one and the same time the chief supporting structure and expression of this national feeling.

References
Braunshausen, N. (1935) *La question linguistique dans le Grand-Duché de Luxembourg.* Luxemburg.
Bruch, R. (1953) *Grundlegung einer Geschichte des Luxemburgischen.* Luxemburg.
Hoffmann, F. (1965, 1967) *Geschichte der Luxemburger Mundartdichtung.* Bd. 1: Luxemburg 1965, Bd. 2: Luxemburg 1967.
— (1974) *Standort Luxemburg.* Luxemburg.
— (1980) *Sprachen in Luxemburg.* Luxemburg and Wiesbaden.
Ries, N. (1911) *Le dualisme linguistique et psychologique du peuple luxembourgeois.* Luxemburg: Diekirch.
— (1920) *Psychologie du peuple luxembourgeois.* Luxemburg: Diekirch.

1989: A last step in the promotion of Luxemburgish was done by a law of February 1984 which establishes Luxemburgish as the national and third official language of the Luxemburgers.

Hoffman, Fernand (1987) Lëtzebbuergesch, Mundart und Nationalsprache. Sprachenpolitische und sprachsoziologische Überlegungen zum luxemburgischen Triglossie-Problem und zum Sprachengesetz von 1984, in *Probleme von Grenzregionen.* Das Beispiel SAAR-LOR-LUX-Raum, Saarbrücken, S.49-67.
— (1988) Luxemburg, in *Sociolinguistics. An International Handbook of the Science of Language in Society,* Second Volume. Berlin, New York, pp.1334-40.

20. Bilingualism and
Language Shift in Sardinia

The descriptions of Sardinian bilingualism which have so far appeared have been concerned primarily with the structural aspect of contact and mutual interference between the Italian and the Sardinian language systems. There is scarcely any evidence about the social determinants and the behavioural usage of Sardinian bilingualism. It is the purpose of this chapter to analyse more thoroughly the special patterns of bilingual usage and proficiency in a rural Sardinian area on the basis of empirical data. This will enable us to obtain exact information about a current language shift in favour of Italian, and to state precisely the degree to which this acculturation process has been completed.

The Sardinian language, which less than thirty years ago was still considered to be the native tongue of the Sardinians, whereas Italian was regarded as a foreign language (Rindler Schjerve 1980a, b), has been reduced to the status of a subordinate Italian dialect. Especially in urban areas it is used by a diminishing number of speakers, and even in its function as a home language it is being increasingly replaced by Italian. According to recent estimates (Cossu 1978) Sardinian is spoken by approximately 1,200,000 people on the island and about 700,000 Sardinians who have emigrated to the continent or to some other country. These estimates show that fifty per cent of the island's population speak Sardinian as an active language, ninety per cent understand it, and ten per cent – mostly members of the Ligurian and Catalan minorities – do not understand it.

Sardinian does not have a standard-language variety in terms of a codified norm, even though there are grammars and dictionaries as well as a literary tradition. There is no spoken variety which comprises all dialectal areas, and can thus act as an interdialectal lingua franca. The term Sardinian thus refers to different dialects which can be divided into two principal koinès: Logudorese and Campidanese. Apart from those, there are the subdialectal areas of Barbaricino, Gallurese and Sassarese.

Politically and sociologically, Sardinian has the status of an Italian dialect (cf. Salvi 1973, Murra Corriga 1977). From a linguistic point of view, it is defined as an autonomous Romance language (cf. Wagner 1950, Sanna 1957, Pittau 1975). Following Kloss's terminology (Kloss 1952), it may be referred to as an *Abstandsprache* which has recently shown a certain tendency to become an *Ausbausprache*. The language of education is Italian. Except in the urban centres the importance of Italian for everyday communication is rather limited, but it frequently serves to bridge interdialectal barriers.

Since Italian has increasingly come to assume the function of primary linguistic socialisation even in rural areas during the last few years, the otherwise stable domains of usage of Sardinian and Italian overlap. This phenomenon could be an indication of a language shift.

The present investigation is the result of a recently conducted pilot-study of the habitual language usage of two different speech communities in a rural area in Northern Sardinia. The data were obtained using techniques of interview and participant observation (cf. Friedrichs 1973). Since we have previously not had reliable data about the language attitudes in Sardinia as far as the rural area is concerned, we prepared a questionnaire on the basis of our own preliminary studies (Rindler Schjerve 1980a, b) and secondary material. This questionnaire then helped us to decide on our interview-questions. In preparing the contents of the interview schedule we used two standardised questionnaires on the linguistic attitudes of two bilingual ethnic minorities (cf. Dressler-Leodolter 1973, Gal 1979). We concentrated the topics on language attitudes and usage in certain domains of social interaction such as religion, work, shopping, school, neighbourhood, kinship, friends, mass media and officialdom. Here we used the sociolinguistic concept of domain developed by Fishman (1964, 1969). The questions of our interviews referred to the use of Italian, of Sardinian, and of both in the various domains. The evaluation of the material thus obtained, which was conducted by W. Weisz of the Interfakultäres Rechenzentrum, University of Vienna, was done by establishing four sex-specific age groups (I: 15–25, II: 26–50, III; 51–69, IV: 70–85). The age limits were determined in the course of our investigation, during which we found out that there existed four different language-attitude patterns in our subjects correlating with the established age groups.

The target groups of our investigation were two dialectally and sociologically different linguistic communities. By comparing an industrialised area with an area having a firmly established traditional structure, we hoped to obtain a preliminary cross-section of the linguistic situation in rural Sardinia.

The first place we investigated was a community near Sassari called Ottava. There we studied nineteen households consisting of ninety subjects. The selection of this sample resulted from the composition of an elementary-school class; the access to the respondents' homes was gained with the help of the local teacher. Ottava proved to be promising for our purposes, since it came into being as a community only twenty years ago, as a result of a large

influx of people from other parts of the country caused by extensive industrialisation of the area. Fourteen of the respondent families had come to
Ottava from other dialectal areas of Sardinia. The subjects thus were mostly
immigrants, even though in terms of age, economic status and recent arrival
they represented a fairly homogeneous lower-income group with most of
them working in the local industry.

Ottava is situated in northwestern Logudoro, in an area which must be
defined, however, as the catchment area of Sassarese due to the industrialisation of the whole region. Besides a Logudorese variety, Sassarese is the
main vehicle of communication. Immigrants from other dialect areas are
forced either to acquire some knowledge of the lexically and phonetically
different Sassarese or to make themselves understood in the supra-regional
Italian language. Our domain-based questioning proved to be useful, as it
enabled us to obtain information about the functional distribution of Italian
and Sardinian which partly contradicted our expectations.

The situation in the bilingual setting of Bonorva, the second place that we
investigated, seems to be different. Disregarding a small-scale exodus of the
younger generation, Bonorva's demographic and social structure is fairly
stable. Situated in the heart of Logudoro and characterised by Sardinian
cultural tradition, this town justly claims to be the Siena of Sardinia. We
soon discovered that working with questionnaires was not conducive to
achieving our aims, since we encountered widespread functional monolingualism. To obtain exact information about the actual language attitudes of
the Bonorvese, we had no choice but to collect data during a four-week stay
by participant observation. Our study concentrated on those linguistic interactions in which we could observe code-switching. The sample we were able
to investigate comprised about three hundred people, and our data refer to
daily contact in the household of a large family of three generations: their
neighbourhood, their friends and their relations with the outside world. The
particular speech community in which we conducted our research was a
lower-income neighbourhood of mostly peasants and shepherds.

We based our investigation on the assumption that Sardinian is used to a
decreasing extent in rural areas, since

1. The traditional setting in rural areas is changing due to migration
phenomena, urbanisation and industrialisation, and acculturation promoted
by the mass media and the school system. The linguistic effect of this
development is a trend to using a language associated with 'modern life' and
higher standards of living, namely Italian.

2. This results in generation-specific communication needs reflected in
different usages in different age groups, i.e. a tendency towards Italian
particularly in the younger generation.

3. Consequently the primary socialisation in the family is increasingly
done in Italian, with Sardinian losing its importance as the home language, a
reason for which the formerly stable domain-separation of usage seems
likely to disappear.

We have already pointed out that Ottava is a community consisting mostly of immigrants. Since Sardinian includes some relatively autonomous dialectal varieties, which occasionally show interdialectal barriers, it is surprising to find that Italian is not always used as a mediator language. We have material which shows that in the case of interdialectal barriers of communication people are more likely to acquire some knowledge of the local dialect than to use Italian. Our question concerning the necessity of Italian as a supraregional variety received a negative answer from fifty-six per cent of our respondents.

If we now study the data regarding the functional distribution of Italian and Sardinian in the various domains previously listed, we may conclude that there is a certain amount of diglossia, because there exists a more-or-less-marked separation between Italian as a 'High' variety and Sardinian as a 'Low' – especially in domains where speech contexts are characterised by a certain formality, e.g. city hall, police stations, registrars' offices, etc. Nonetheless, the most important variable we were able to single out in our material is the age of the speaker. Thus, with a total of eighty per cent for Italian in dealing with public authorities, we obtained the following values:

Public authorities: Italian: total 80 per cent

Group I	100.0 per cent
II	66.7
III	83.3
IV	33.3

In the domains 'doctor' and 'church' we discovered a similar generation-specific disparity in use, with forty-eight per cent of all the subjects indicating Italian as the language in which they communicate with the priest, and thirty-eight per cent saying that Italian was the language they used with the doctor:

Priest: Italian: total 48 per cent		Doctor: Italian: total 38 per cent	
Group I	71.4 per cent	Group I	50.0 per cent
II	50.0	II	37.0
III	16.0	III	33.3
IV	16.0	IV	16.7

We thus see that the domains which regulate social intergroup contacts at a more institutional level are not absolutely dominated by Italian. People do speak Sardinian with persons such as the priest, the doctor, the lawyer, the mayor and the policeman – but, of course, only if these people are personally known to the speaker.

On the other hand, all information we have concerning habitual language choice in post-offices, the chemist's, hospitals and on public transport was in favour of Italian (e.g. seventy-six per cent in hospitals, forty-eight per cent at the chemist's, ninety per cent in the post-office).

At a less formal intragroup level, language usage patterns are different: sixty-one per cent of the males indicate that they talk Sardinian at their place of work, while two-thirds claim to use Italian at trade-union meetings – above all, when addressing an official audience and when trying to eliminate interdialectal barriers of communication. As far as Sardinian usage at work is concerned, we have to note that our subjects belonged to low and medium categories of the industrial career-hierarchy.

In this context, we encountered the first significant sex-specific differences. In the case of the working women – found almost exclusively in the low ranks – there was a strong tendency towards Italian. Only 3.1 per cent admitted to using Sardinian at their place of work. Generally our questioning showed that men – independent of their age – have a language awareness of Sardinian that is largely determined by ideological factors and that they are less inclined to change their language behaviour from domain to domain than women, who, in general, tend to adapt their form of linguistic interaction to that of their interlocutor.

We have ascertained age- and sex-determined tendencies in the linguistic behaviour of our subjects at all levels of social interaction; but we must add that age-determined differences are more significant in females than in males. This fact was especially evident in households with respondents belonging to four generations. An eighty-year-old grandmother was illiterate and monolingually Sardinian, the fifty-five-year-old mother, due to insufficient education, had a rather limited proficiency in Italian, the thirty-year-old daughter, having been to school for eight years, spoke Italian well, though not perfectly, and used it when talking to her children, while she used Sardinian with her husband. Her reason for using Italian with her children is to avoid their being discriminated against in school; this, of course, resulted in the twelve-year-old schoolboy's having only a limited command of Sardinian and speaking a rather monostylistic and often Sardicised Italian. According to the results of our evaluation, thirty-eight per cent of the total number of persons interviewed speak Italian with their children, with the following values for each group:

With children: Italian: total 38 per cent		With children: Italian and Sardinian: total 18 per cent	
Group I	21 per cent	Group II	25 per cent
II	50	III	50
III	0		
IV	0		

Eighteen per cent use both languages, whereas fifty per cent of the members of Group III talk Sardinian with their children.

The data referring to the language used between spouses are: a total of eleven per cent use Italian, sixty-eight per cent Sardinian and fourteen per cent use both languages.

Spouses: Sardinian: total 68 per cent	
Group II	75 per cent
III	100
IV	100

The numbers of persons using Italian for educating their children to prevent the latter from being discriminated against in school are illustrative, as well:

Group I   21.4 per cent
   II   79.0
   III   50.0

In this context, the data regarding the functional distribution when interacting with the grandparents seem of interest, too:

Grandparents: Italian: 4 per cent
Sardinian: 94 per cent   both languages: 2 per cent
Group I   85.7 per cent
   II   95.8
   III   100.0

The following figures show the degree of proficiency of the total number of the subjects:

Italian: perfect:		Good, but not perfect
total 8 per cent		total 74 per cent
Group I	14.3 per cent	85.7 per cent
II	8.3	75.0
III	0	66.7
IV	0	50.0
Italian: not good:		No Italian:
total 14 per cent		total 4 per cent
I	0 per cent	0 per cent
II	16.7	0
III	33.3	0
IV	16.7	33.3

Interestingly, we found that there is a tendency among young people between fifteen and twenty towards using Sardinian actively again, even though their deplorably low proficiency in Sardinian frequently causes their parents to ask them to use Italian instead. This linguistic behaviour is likely to be due to their leaving school and also to intergroup forces which, on account of the political implication of the Sardinian issue, favour the use of Sardinian. The extent to which this casts doubt on our impression that Italian is becoming the language of primary socialisation cannot be determined as yet.

These figures show that Sardinian holds central importance, especially in the fields of unofficial interaction. The same is true of neighbourhood relationships and shopping situations. In shopping, intimacy plays an important part. At the market or in the grocery store Sardinian is spoken by sixty-eight per cent. At the grocery store in the nearby town only thirty per cent speak Sardinian and thirty-eight per cent use both Italian and Sardinian. In supermarkets one either does not speak at all or speaks Italian.

We may conclude, therefore, that in the Ottava linguistic community there is a surprising tendency to language maintenance, which, on the whole, is characteristic not only of the older generation, but also of the young generation in the low and medium income brackets.

Turning to the Bonorva study, as already mentioned, we discovered a widespread functional monolingualism. However, it has to be pointed out that we also encountered a diglossic usage of Italian and Sardinian, insofar as there is a fairly stable distribution of both languages in certain domains. Religion, school education and culture are exclusively Italian. The functional distribution in the domains of public administration is less clear-cut, since the dominance of Italian in this field is less, to a surprising degree, than one would normally assume. In those cases where we were able to record Italian usage – such instances were rare – linguistic interaction was characterised by the fact that differences in status in the role-relationship of the interlocutors were reflected in the civil servant's using Italian. Interestingly enough, in most cases we observed that in conversation between the civil servant and the interlocutor two codes were involved: the visitor spoke Sardinian and the official Italian. Code-switching only took place when the conversation became more personal; if the institutionalised authority did not make any personal contacts possible, the conversation was in Italian.

Thus a higher-ranking civil servant uses Italian when speaking to his secretary and she answers in Sardinian; the telephone rings and the secretary talks Italian, although the conversation shows that she knows her interlocutor personally and that he is a local.

Significantly, both subsystems of complementary social values are also expressed in the topically regulated language choice, where the use of Italian in an otherwise Sardinian conversation always indicates personal detachment vis-à-vis the object or the authority of the institution connected to the object. For example, on one occasion a family was talking about a cousin against whom they had instituted legal proceedings because of some piece of land. When the speaker described the court-room situation he switched to Italian.

The son of the family is eighteen years old and insists on doing his military service immediately. His mother answers in Italian that he will have to wait till he is called up.

Women talk about their experiences in hospitals, and as soon as their conversation starts dealing with the qualities of a doctor they talk Italian, but then continue their conversation in Sardinian.

The language-maintenance tendencies which we discovered in the Bonorvese community at the institutional level seem to indicate that ideological and cultural values are reflected in usage and choice of language, and that these values differ from those of an urbanised and industrialised language community. According to the material we have gathered, there is no evidence that the local speech-form in Bonorva is deprecated or derided; on the contrary, we found a language awareness which has been produced by the cultural tradition and position of Bonorva, and which has assumed the position of an ideology through the discussions of Sardinian autonomy of the last few decades. We repeatedly observed that faulty grammatical structures in the Sardinian speech of the young Bonorvese were rigorously corrected by the speakers of the older generation.

Now, if we take a look at intergroup language habits, we will find a widespread functional monolingualism which occasionally shows a trend towards bilingualism without diglossia. These bilingual speech habits were observed in the interaction of speakers with babies and small children, whose language acquisition was still in its beginnings and with whom they talked Italian, while at the same time addressing children of two and three years in Sardinian. This phenomenon could be explained by the fact that here prosodic factors play a certain role in the choice of language. Our investigations on language attitudes include a number of instances in which many native speakers of Sardinian with excellent proficiency in Italian felt inhibited when speaking Italian because they were forced to modify speed and volume. At this point, the question arises whether there is a connection between language choice and interaction-induced modification of behaviour in a bilingual setting; if there is, the language choice in such instances could be explained and understood.

Once more we want to point out that our material concerning intergroup language habits of the Bonorvese speech community consists mainly of observations made in the lower-income group. A more extensive study that would permit relevant information about the linguistic behaviour of other social groups has not been conducted so far.

In conclusion, we can say that in both the areas that we have investigated there exists bilingualism with diglossia. Our study, however, shows clearly that one cannot speak of a serious decline in the use of Sardinian in rural areas: on the contrary, we encountered a marked tendency towards language maintenance shared also by the younger generation, at least as regards the lower income brackets. One cannot, however, show conclusively whether it is a stable bilingualism, since no exact assessment has as yet been made of the influence of the Italian primary socialisation that has been active during the last ten to fifteen years. One can say, however, that owing to the influence of Italian on the Sardinian home-domain there have been changes in the socio-cultural setting, which, at the linguistic level, manifest themselves in a shift of usage and which will eventually be seen in language habits outside the family.

References
Alziator, F. (1954) *Storia della letteratura di Sardegna.*
    Cagliari: La Zattera.
Calvet, L. J. (1978) *Die Sprachfresser. Ein Versuch über Linguistik und
    Kolonialismus.* Berlin: Das Arsenal.
Carta Raspi, R. (1974) *Storia della Sardegna.* Milano: Mursia.
Casula, F. C. (1978) *Breve storia della scrittura in Sardegna.*
    Cagliari: EDES.
Cicourel, A. V. (1974) *Methode und Messung in der Soziologie.*
    Frankfurt: Suhrkamp.

Cossu, A. (1978) Cultura e identità, in *Segones Jornades del CIEMEN de Cuixà*, 16-22 d'agost de 1977. Publications de l'abadia de Montserrat 1978.

Dettori, A. (1976) Industrializzazione e situazione linguistica in Sardegna. Inchiesta pilota in un'industria di Macomer, *Archivio sardo del movimento operaio contadino e autonomistico 6/7*, 147-59.

Dressler, W. and Leodolter, R. (1973) Sprachbewahrung und Sprachtod in der Bretagne. Eine soziologische Voruntersuchung zum Status des Bretonischen in Tregor, *Wiener Linguistische Gazette 3*, 45-58.

Ferguson, C. (1964) Diglossia, in *Language in culture and society* (ed. D. Hymes), 429-37. New York: Harper and Row.

Fishman, J. A. (1964) Language maintenance and language shift as fields of inquiry, *Linguistics 9*, 32-70.

— (1971) Societal bilingualism: stable and transitional, in *Bilingualism in the Barrio* (eds J. Fishman *et al.*), 539-55. Indiana: Indiana University and Mouton.

— (ed.) (1972) *Readings in the sociology of language.* The Hague and Paris: Mouton.

— (1975) *Soziologie der Sprache.* München: Hueber.

Friedrichs, J. (1973) *Methoden empirischer Sozialforschung.* Reinbek bei Hamburg: Rowohlt.

Gal, S. (1979) *Language shift. Social determinants of linguistic change in bilingual Austria.* New York, San Francisco and London: Academic Press.

Gumperz, J. J. (1962) Types of linguistic communities, *Anthropological Linguistics 4*, 28-40.

Haugen, E. (1966) Dialect, language, nation, *American Anthropologist 68* (4), 922-35.

Hymes, D. H. (1962) The ethnography of speaking, in *Anthropology and human behavior* (eds T. Gladwin and W. C. Sturtevant), 13-53. Washington, D.C.: Anthropology Society of Washington.

Kloss, H. (1952) *Die Entwicklung neuer germanischer Kultursprachen von 1800-1950.* München: Pohl.

Kremnitz, G. (Hrsg.) (1979) *Sprachen im Konflikt. Theorie und Praxis der katalanischen Soziolinguisten.* Tübingen: Gunter Narr.

Lavinio, C. (1975) *L'insegnamento dell'italiano. Un'inchiesta campione in una scuola media sarda.* Cagliari: EDES.

Melis, G. (1979) Dal sardismo al neosardismo: crisi autonomistica e mitologia locale, *Il Mulino 3*, 418-40.

Mercurio Gregorini, R. (1975) L'italiano e il sardo nelle scuole elementari, *Archivio sardo del movimento operaio contadino e autonomistico 4-5*, 160-8.

Murra Corriga, G. (ed.) (1977) *Etnia, lingua, cultura. Un dibattito aperto in Sardegna.* Cagliari: EDES.

Pittau, M. (1975) *Problemi di lingua sarda.* Sassari: Dessì.

Rindler Schjerve, R. (1980a) Zur aktuellen Konfliksituation des Sardischen als Minoritätensprache, in *Sprachkontakt und Sprachkonflikt* (ed. H. P. Nelde), ZDL Beihefte, 32, 201-8.

— (1980b, in press) Zweisprachigkeit in Sardinien: Ihre kultur- und schulpolitischen Auswirkungen, in *Sprachen in Kontakt*, Sammelband des 3. Internationalen Kolloquium, Gießen, Grossen-Linden: Hoffmann.

Salvi, S. (1973) *Le nazioni proibite.* Firenze: Vallecchi.

Sanna, A. (1957) *Introduzione agli studi di linguistica sarda.* Cagliari: Valdes.

— (1976) La situazione linguistica e sociolinguistica della Sardegna, *Archivio sardo del movimento operaio contadino e autonomistico 6/7*, 127-38.

Spano, G. (1840) *Ortografia sarda nazionale ossia grammatica della lingua logudorese paragonata all'italiano*. Cagliari: Edizioni Anastatiche.

Wagner, M. L. (1932) Die sardische Sprache in ihrem Verhältnis zur sardischen Kultur, *Volkstum und Kultur der Romanen* v, 21-49.

— (1943) La questione del posto da assegnare al gallurese e al sassarese, *Cultura Neolatina* iii, 243-67.

— (1950) *La lingua sarda. Storia spirito e forma*. Bern: Francke.

Weinreich, U. (1976) *Sprachen in Kontakt. Ergebnisse und Probleme der Zweisprachigkeitsforschung. Mit einem Nachwort von A. de Vincenz*. München: Beck.

21. British Sign Language

It is particularly appropriate in a book on minority languages to include one chapter on a language which, though used by over thirty thousand people in Britain, is almost unknown to the majority of the population. We briefly introduce the community of users of this language, and the language itself, British Sign Language (BSL). We will describe what is known of BSL in recent history and some common myths about the language, going on to a discussion of the membership of the BSL community and varieties of signing.

Deaf people communicate in a language foreign to most of the population, despite the fact that they are neither an immigrant group nor living in geographical isolation from the rest of the population. They form one of the least-understood minorities in our community: about thirty thousand people in the United Kingdom, whose serious or profound hearing loss began at birth or before they developed language.

Any discussion of the history of British Sign Language is intimately bound up with the education of the deaf. Educators have chosen to emphasise the integration of deaf people into society by suppressing their language, and teaching speech exclusively. However, BSL has proved resistant to the pressures on its deaf users. Even with the punishment of children for signing in school, such as holding their arms immobile at their sides, making them sit on their hands, or putting paper bags over their heads, the predominant oral method of education has not succeeded in eradicating it.

Very little is known of the early history of BSL, although there are references to sign languages in the middle ages; but one can assume that wherever groups of deaf people have been in contact, sign languages have been established. While it may be assumed that deaf families have always signed, the role of schools for the deaf in bringing together groups of deaf children must not be underestimated, since only five per cent of deaf children have deaf parents. Certainly, with the founding of the first schools for the deaf in Britain in the eighteenth century, BSL was firmly established among deaf children who did not have deaf parents. By the 1820s signs were being used-as the communication medium in the education of the deaf throughout Western Europe and America (Hippisley Tuckfield 1839, Dickens 1865, Scott 1870, Lane 1976). By the end of the nineteenth century, however, the doctrine of oralism had spread, and schools were gradually converted to the belief that signing was degenerate and inadequate as a form of communication, and that only speech should be provided to a deaf child. Parents of deaf children were told that they must not learn or use signs and gestures with their children, as the learning of BSL would inhibit the development of spoken language. There are, of course, many valid reasons for wanting to integrate deaf people into hearing society through speech: ninety-five per cent of the parents of deaf people are not deaf; their aspirations for their children include their integration into hearing society; the native language of teachers of the deaf is English; and deaf people who prefer to use sign languages have often been labelled as 'not very bright' or 'of low verbal ability'.

Others working with the deaf, even those who use BSL professionally, such as social workers or clergy, as well as teachers, may have negative attitudes towards BSL. The belief is expressed that hearing people must try to improve deaf people's signing, eliminating 'vulgarities' and 'correcting errors'. Some have suggested that deaf people have only tentatively adopted signing, that it is chaotic and idiosyncratic, and that it could easily be replaced. Despite the influence of such attitudes and the pressure of the dominant hearing culture, BSL has survived.

But what is BSL? Is it really a language? What are its unique features? A number of myths have grown up about British Sign Language and other sign languages, and one way to shed light on the nature of sign languages is to discuss these myths.

Myth 1. There is One Universal Sign Language
Some people have suggested that sign language is universal, easy to learn and can be used by people anywhere with ease of understanding. However, this is not the case. Deaf people of one country use different sign languages from deaf people of another country (Battison and Jordan 1976, Jordan and Battison 1976, Moody 1979). For example, American Sign Language (ASL) and BSL differ from each other much more than American and British English, and are, in fact, mutually unintelligible. Figure 21.1 shows how the 'same' sign may have different meanings in ASL and BSL, and figure 21.2 shows how the same meaning is conveyed by different signs in each language. (Sign glosses are conventionally represented in upper-case letters.) It is really not surprising that this should be the case. Deaf people do not generally move from one country to another; many countries ban deaf people as immigrants. Those sign languages which are similar have in most cases been influenced by educationalists who have trained in other countries and brought back signs to schools in their home countries. In the case of, for example, Australian Sign Language, which is closely related to BSL, both the

ASL SALT
BSL FATHER

Figure 21.1. Same form, different meanings.

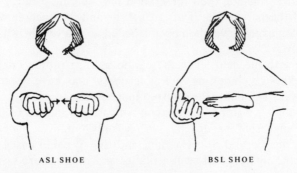

ASL SHOE   BSL SHOE

Figure 21.2. Different forms, same meaning.

influence of educators and a single, large family with hereditary deafness, have been responsible. Some American and British signs appear to be cognates, but not enough is known of the history of either language to explain this adequately.

Myth 2. Sign Language is Derived from Visual Pictures

While many signs seem to support this claim, other signs seem to bear little or no visual relationship to their referents. The issue of the iconicity of signs is rather complex. We have already seen that the same meaning may be expressed by different signs in different sign languages. This may occur because the signs, although iconic, represent different features or properties of the referent. While some signs may have iconic elements, such as in figure 21.3a, speakers of the language may not necessarily know the source of the iconicity. A child learning the sign MILK may never have seen a cow being milked by hand, and the German army no longer wears helmets with spikes. This in no way impairs or assists the learning of new vocabulary. In addition, iconic origins are often imputed to signs where none is known, or where the known origin of the sign is iconic, but different. The BSL sign WOMAN (figure 21.4a) is sometimes etymologised as deriving from 'a woman's cheek being soft', while others say that it derives from the bonnet strings of the eighteenth century. The American sign CRACKER is etymologised as deriving

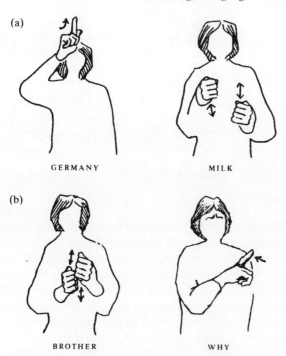

Figure 21.3. (a) Iconicity of signs, (b) non-iconicity of signs

from the British sign BISCUIT (figure 21.4b), the origin of which is explained as deriving from the way the Scots break hard biscuits with their elbows. A large number of signs, however, do seem to represent their referents iconically. This feature of sign languages is usually held to be in contrast with the form of words in spoken languages, where there is an arbitrary relationship between symbol and referent. The words in spoken languages which are non-arbitrary, such as onomatopoeic words, or those involving sound symbolism, are regarded as peripheral. As sign languages represent iconically referents that can be described with a visual image, so spoken languages represent 'iconically' objects that can be described with a sound image. As more objects can be represented with a picture than with a sound, the contrast between spoken and sign languages may be one of degree rather than of kind.

Myth 3. Signs are Only Gestures

While it is recognised that spoken languages have phonologies consisting of a limited number of sounds which differ from language to language, and a limited number of combinations of these sounds, the claim has been made that sign languages consist of unlimited numbers of gestures which are infinitely variable. If this were true, sign languages would be very unlike spoken languages. Spoken languages consist of a limited number of con-

221

WOMAN   BSL BISCUIT   ASL CRACKER

Figure 21.4. Etymology of signs.

stituent sounds, combining in a limited number of ways one after the other to form a word. Sign languages also contain a limited inventory of constituents; but these are location, handshape, movement, and orientation, and instead of occurring successively like the phonemes of a language, they occur simultaneously. Each sign, therefore, consists of a simultaneous bundle of these four elements or parameters. The number of each of these parameters is limited, just as the number of phonemes in a spoken language and the way in which they combine is limited. Additional constraints prohibit, for example, signs where the two hands move independently, constraints which do not operate in gesture or mime. Figure 21.5 shows pairs of BSL signs, each of which differs in one parameter from the other, and thus form minimal pairs. These small but significant contrasts enable the language to use a small number of elements to form a great many signs.

Myth 4. Sign Language is Just Parasitic on English
Many hearing people learn the manual alphabet as children – in the Boy Scouts or Girl Guides – and often think that BSL is just the fingerspelling of words from English or other spoken languages. We have seen already that signs may not be at all like English words, but a number of points should be made about the manual alphabet in its own right. First, there is more than one manual alphabet. Apart from Great Britain and countries such as Australia and New Zealand, most manual alphabets are one-handed, and there are several different one-handed alphabets, such as the Irish, American, French and Swedish. Most deaf people know and use fingerspelling, and it can serve a number of roles. Fingerspelling can be used for proper names, place names and technical vocabulary for which signs do not exist. Signs derived from fingerspelling may also be used, often so accommodated and modified in their borrowing that they are unrecognisable as having originated in fingerspelled words. Signers may use both fingerspelled forms and signs for the same referent, depending upon context and audience. Most signs, however, are neither derived from, nor are one-to-one translations of, English words. For example, signs like SMELL–COOKING and NOT–LIKE

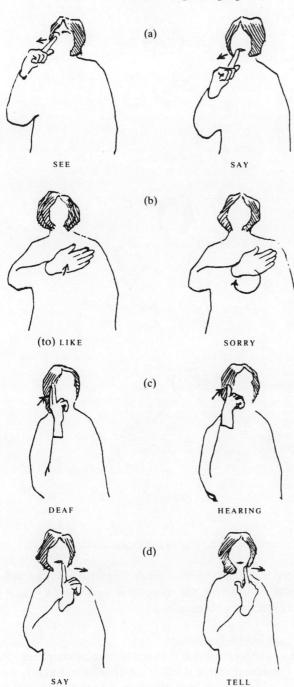

Figure 21.5. Minimal pairs: (a) location,
(b) movement, (c) handshape, (d) orientation

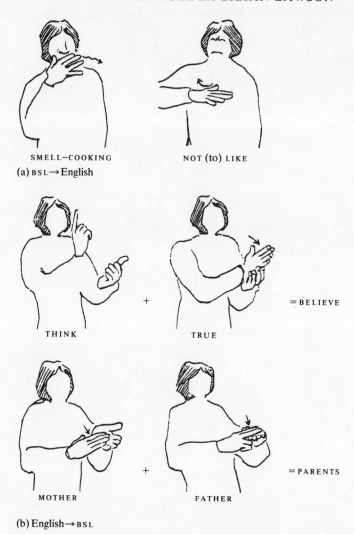

SMELL–COOKING   NOT (to) LIKE

(a) BSL → English

THINK   +   TRUE   = BELIEVE

MOTHER   +   FATHER   = PARENTS

(b) English → BSL

Figure 21.6. Non-equivalence of BSL–English and English–BSL translations.

can only be translated by English phrases, while English words like 'believe' and 'parents' have as equivalents the compound signs THINK–TRUE and MOTHER–FATHER respectively (Figure 21.6).

Myth 5. Sign Language has no Grammar

The notion that BSL is ungrammatical is based on two assumptions: First, the rather confused assumption that if BSL is a derivative of English, then it must be structured just like English, and therefore, where it is unlike English it has no grammar. The second assumption is that sign languages must be structured just like spoken languages, even if not like English. BSL is an

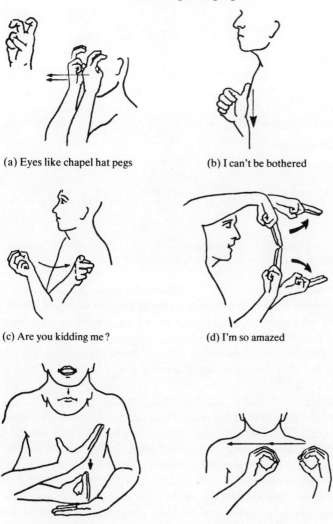

(a) Eyes like chapel hat pegs

(b) I can't be bothered

(c) Are you kidding me?

(d) I'm so amazed

(e) It should have happened
but it didn't

(f) Nothing for a long time

Figure 21.7. Complex signs and idioms.

independent language, however, with its own grammar, and this is the grammar of a visual-manual language, sharply different from the grammar of an auditory-articulatory language. A number of the most interesting and different features of BSL grammar will be dealt with at length below.

Complex Signs

'Complex signs' may be considered to be the equivalent of English idioms in the sense that complex signs, like English idioms, are not easily understood

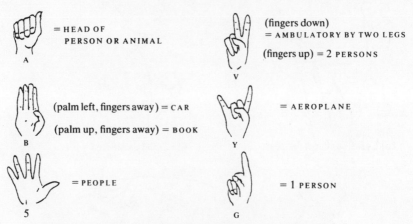

= HEAD OF
PERSON OR ANIMAL

A

(fingers down)
= AMBULATORY BY TWO LEGS

(fingers up) = 2 PERSONS

V

(palm left, fingers away) = CAR

(palm up, fingers away) = BOOK

B

= AEROPLANE

Y

= PEOPLE

5

= 1 PERSON

G

Figure 21.8. Classifiers. Labels of handshape such as A, B, 5, refer to notation system: see Kyle, Woll and Carter 1979 for details.

by people who are not members of the deaf community. It is usually not possible to translate complex signs into simple English words or glosses; it is often found necessary to use phrases or whole sentences to explain the meaning of complex signs. Like idioms, complex signs may be 'forms of expression peculiar to language or person' (definition from the *Oxford English Dictionary*). Complex signs may be also compared to 'colloquialisms', because like colloquialisms, these signs are usually found in informal settings and are not found in such formal settings as conferences and meetings. Complex signs, in the past, were (and still are by some) considered to be 'vulgar signs', 'home-made signs', 'childish signs', and 'deaf–dumb signs' by some deaf people who are very verbal, and also by teachers of the deaf and social workers of the deaf. Reasons for such opinions are that complex signs are not always understood by hearing people; that complex signs are used by fluent BSL users who were, in the past, usually dumb as well as deaf, and were regarded by teachers of the deaf (incorrectly) as 'naive and low verbal persons'; and that mouth movements found with complex signs are usually unrelated to English spoken words and are therefore not acceptable. Only since research into BSL began in the late nineteen seventies, are people now looking in a different way at complex signs, realising their important role in BSL. Figure 21.7 gives several examples of complex signs. These complex signs frequently incorporate other essential features of face and body movements, such as specific mouth movements, eye movements, and blowing out or sucking in of the cheeks. The mouth movements, in particular, are typically unrelated to spoken English words.

Classifiers

'Classifiers' of BSL are in many ways similar to classifiers of American Sign Language, and so it is quite appropriate here to quote Wilbur's definition of

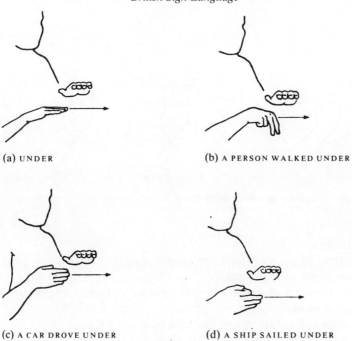

(a) UNDER

(b) A PERSON WALKED UNDER

(c) A CAR DROVE UNDER

(d) A SHIP SAILED UNDER

Figure 21.9. Classifier incorporation.

classifiers: 'Classifiers (the term attributed to Frishberg 1975) are a form of pronoun in ASL that seem to be defined primarily by the handshape. They are substituted into a sentence when potential violations of signing space occur. . . . They also occur in place of a noun when that noun cannot phonologically blend into the verb' (Wilbur 1979, p.57). A partial list of BSL classifiers is given in Figure 21.8. The occurrence of classifiers is morpho-phonologically governed. When these classifiers occur, they may serve as dummy pronominal elements which in certain environments can be replaced by other lexical items (Wilbur 1979, p.58). For example, UNDER in citation form is made with the flat hand palm down, below the left hand, palm down. To indicate 'the person walked under it', the right handshape in UNDER would be replaced with the BY-LEGS classifier. In the sentence 'the car drove under it', the right handshape is replaced with the BY-CAR classifier. Similarly, in the sentence 'the ship sailed under it', the right handshape is replaced by the BY-BOAT classifier (figure 21.9). What has changed in these examples is the information about what noun class is under consideration. The motion and location of the classifier defines the subject and object of the verb (Kegl 1979). Classifiers thus serve to focus on certain qualities or features of their noun referents in very precise ways. For example, a classifier might identify a class of objects that is one-dimensional, two-dimensional, or three-dimensional, flexible or rigid, of prominent curved exterior, long or round.

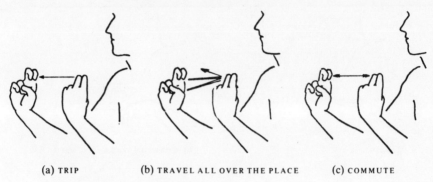

(a) TRIP   (b) TRAVEL ALL OVER THE PLACE   (c) COMMUTE

Figure 21.10. Base form and modulation.

Modulation

'Modulation' of signs involves inflectional changes of signs from their citation forms. Such changes include

Reduplication of a sign, where the motion of hand(s) may be repeated
once or more.

Change of location during the articulation of a sign.

Change of duration of articulation of signs.

The example TRIP may help to illustrate the notion of modulation. The
citation form of TRIP is made with a left bent v handshape placed behind the
right bent v handshape which moves forward (away from the signer) (figure
21.10). COMMUTING is a modulation of TRIP: the modulated sign involves
repetition of movement of the right hand several times (figure 21.10).
TRAVEL ALL OVER THE PLACE is also a modulation of TRIP: the modulated
sign involves changes of direction of articulation or movement of the right
hand, which starts by moving to the left of the signing space, returns to the
left hand, moves forward, and finally returns to the left hand and moves to
the right of the signing space (figure 21.10).

Membership of the Deaf Community

The features of BSL discussed above are found in the language of both native
and non-native signers who have been accepted as members of the deaf
community by other members. Native signers are those who are deaf children of deaf parents, acquiring BSL as their first language, and English at a
later age. Other native signers include deaf children of hearing parents,
deafened at a very early age, or those who are born deaf, that is, prelingually
deaf. These latter two groups of native signers acquire BSL before they learn
or master the English language, either from their peers with deaf parents or
from other deaf children who have already undergone this process of encul-
turation (figure 21.11). The group of non-native signers includes children
deafened after their acquisition of English, that is post-lingually deaf, and
also those who were deafened pre-lingually, but for one reason or another,

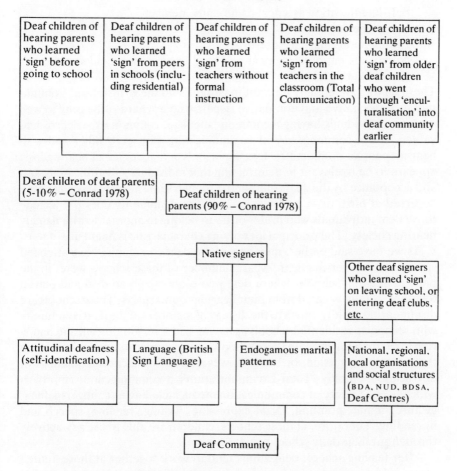

Figure 21.11. Membership of the deaf community and ethnic characteristics.

do not acquire BSL until a much later age. This may be for a number of reasons: they may have been educated orally at a school where BSL was not permitted, or have been educated privately where there were no other deaf children from whom to learn and with whom to communicate in BSL, or have been educated at a school for normally-hearing children, and met no fluent users of BSL. Non-native signers often meet other deaf people during later school years or early adult years when they join a local deaf club or meet people who introduce them to other deaf young people. Although non-native signers can gain relative fluency in BSL they may still fail to master the use of BSL as well as the native signer.

Four main factors have been identified as being responsible for membership of the American Deaf Community (Croneberg 1976, Markowicz 1979, Woodward 1975, 1978):

Self-identification as a deaf community member.

Language use.

Endogamous marital patterns.

Numerous national regional and local organisations and social structures (figure 21.11).

These factors are equally relevant in Britain, and the British Deaf Community includes native and non-native signers who are hard-of-hearing as well as deaf, individuals having a common language, common experiences and values, and a common way of communicating with each other and with hearing people. Audiometric loss, a person's actual degree of hearing loss, appears to be irrelevant in determining that individual's identification with and acceptance by the deaf community, though some hearing loss must have occurred at birth or at a very early age. The community does not include those deaf individuals who prefer or try to belong to another world, namely hearing society. The principal identifying characteristic is fluent use of BSL.

As we have said earlier, members of the deaf community have attended special schools for the deaf. A large number of these schools were, in the past, residential schools, where deaf pupils ate, slept, studied and played together, totally isolated from their hearing counterparts. These schools are disappearing rapidly, much to the dismay of members of the deaf community who recognise residential schools as having had a very important and happy role in their young lives. In these schools, children used BSL actively either in the classroom, outside, or both. However, a slowly increasing number of day schools employ 'Total Communication', a communication approach which uses a variety of communication media including BSL, fingerspelling, gesture, mime, pointing, facial expressing, writing, reading, speech and lipreading. Therefore, at these schools, children are able to use BSL actively throughout their daily school hours.

After leaving school, deaf adults tend to work together at those limited places which already employ a number of deaf adults. Most of the adult deaf – over ninety per cent – marry within the deaf community. Happy and long successful marriages are far more common among deaf couples than among mixed deaf-hearing couples (Markowicz, personal communication). Throughout their school and adult years, the deaf are also drawn together by numerous sporting opportunities which are organised at the national, regional, and local levels as well as at international level in the quadrennial Deaf World Games. The deaf are also drawn together by school reunions (Old Pupils' Associations have large and active memberships), and by social activities such as those arranged by local deaf clubs. The result is that the deaf have formed a cohesive and supportive community. The majority of deaf people have two hearing parents. As the parents use a language which the deaf child cannot hear and consequently cannot use with any fluency, communication with family members is often very limited (Deuchar, 1981). It is at school among peers that most close social relationships are developed.

At the heart of every community is its language. This language embodies

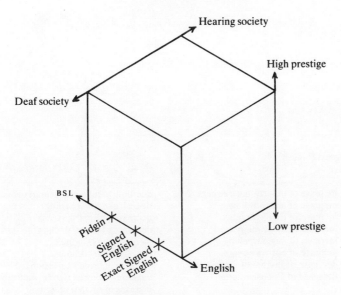

Figure 21.12. BSL–English continuum.

the thoughts and experiences of its users, and they, in turn, learn about their culture or heritage and share in it together through BSL. Self-identification as deaf is therefore crucial in determining membership of the deaf community, and this attitudinal deafness can always be paralleled by appropriate language use.

BSL Varieties

Native and non-native signers have access to a number of varieties of BSL when communicating with each other at home, club, informal meetings, parties and other informal settings, as well as when communicating with hearing signers who have no native knowledge of BSL and in situations where evidence of a good command of English is expected.

A number of sign language researchers have suggested the existence of a diglossic community among the deaf (Stokoe 1969, Deuchar 1977), with English at one end and BSL at the other. While BSL and English are very dissimilar, signers who are bilingual, with a good command of English as well as BSL, may use sign varieties which mix features of both: for example, using English syntax and fingerspelling many English function words, while omitting most English tense and number markers. Thus their communication may contain some features of both languages, and this may be represented with a diglossic continuum, shown as multidimensional (following Stokoe 1979). Figure 21.12 shows that the BSL–English continuum may be associated with differing judgments of prestige, depending upon the social identity of the speaker. The language variety described above may be called Signed English, containing as it does features of both languages. This variety

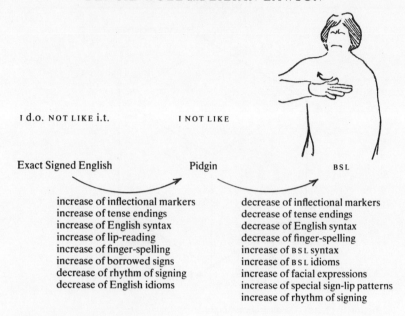

I d.o. NOT LIKE i.t.   I NOT LIKE

Exact Signed English	Pidgin	BSL

increase of inflectional markers
increase of tense endings
increase of English syntax
increase of lip-reading
increase of finger-spelling
increase of borrowed signs
decrease of rhythm of signing
decrease of English idioms

decrease of inflectional markers
decrease of tense endings
decrease of English syntax
decrease of finger-spelling
increase of BSL syntax
increase of BSL idioms
increase of facial expressions
increase of special sign-lip patterns
increase of rhythm of signing

Figure 21.13. Sign varieties.

can be placed in about the middle of the English-to-BSL continuum.

Signers, including hearing signers who are teachers of the deaf, who wish to teach deaf children English through a visual-manual medium, use a language variety which may be called 'Exactly Signed English'. This language variety is placed much closer to the English end of the continuum, because it contains many more English language features than BSL features. As much as possible, inflectional markers which include specially created signs for tense endings, plurality, definite articles, the copula, and possessives are used. Utterances are signed in English word order. Fingerspelling is used a great deal where there are no specially created signs or borrowed signs for specific English words.

Other language varieties may be placed closer to the BSL end of the continuum. One such variety is a Pidgin of BSL and Signed English (Fischer 1978). Pidgin utterances may be in BSL syntax but with less use of complex signs and modulation than in BSL. Figure 21.13 illustrates how one utterance would appear in the varieties discussed above. The attempt to include features of spoken language in signing has pronounced effects. Lip speaking may become prominent. The use of English inflectional markers and finger-spelling to a great extent may cause the signer to lose many important non-manual features and distort BSL syntax.

Not all deaf individuals are fully competent in English, although each member of the deaf community has a range of language varieties available to him. Many of these varieties are not on an English–BSL continuum but involve formal–informal distinctions wholly within BSL such as forming informal one-handed signs with two hands in formal settings (Deuchar 1981).

It has often been suggested that English-like varieties of signing are more proper and correct for usage in situations such as church services, lectures, deaf club meetings, etc., and that BSL is not suitable for communication with hearing people, even those who know it, or for use in the education of the deaf. Deaf people state that those other deaf people who have competence only in non-English varieties are not as bright as those with good command of English-like varieties. However, deaf people appear to produce these statements for the benefit of the 'hearing public', since on matched-guise tests of signers using different varieties of signing, the BSL signer was rated more positively than the 'English' variety signer (Llewellyn-Jones *et al.* 1979). It is perhaps surprising that deaf people's expressed opinions differ from their covert attitudes. Trudgill (1972) provides a precedent in his finding that non-standard speech may be highly valued in a manner not usually expressed.

Deaf people speak passionately of the beauty of signing, and cherish it as part of their birthright as deaf people. Despite the suppression of BSL, and of its speakers, this linguistic minority has continued using their language until now. BSL is worthy of our respect, research and support.

Acknowledgement
This research is supported by grants from the DHSS 'Sign Language Learning and Use', and from the SED 'Tense and Aspect in BSL'.

References
Battison, R. and Jordan, I. K. (1976) Cross-Cultural Communication with Foreign Signers: Fact and Fancy, *Sign Language Studies 10*, 53-68.
Brennan, M. (1978) Communication, paper presented at the Strathclyde Regional Inservice Course on Deaf Education.
Conrad, R. (1979) *The Deaf School Child*. London: Harper & Row.
Croneberg, C. (1976) The Linguistic Community, in *A Dictionary of American Sign Language* (W. C. Stokoe, D. Casterline and C. Croneberg). Silver Spring: Linstok Press.
Deuchar, M. (1977) Sign language diglossia in a British deaf community, *Sign Language Studies 17*, 347-56.
— (1981) Variation in British Sign Language, in *Perspectives on British Sign Language* (eds B. Woll, J. G. Kyle and M. Deuchar). London: Croom Helm.
Dickens, C. (1865) Dr. Marigold's Prescription. Reprinted in *Christmas Books, Tales, and Sketches*. Garden City: Nelson Doubleday.
Fischer, S. D. (1978) Sign Language and Creoles. Chapter 13 of *Understanding Language through Sign Language Research* (ed. P. Siple). Academic Press.
Frischberg, N. (1975) Arbitrariness and iconicity: historical change in American Sign Language, *Language 51*, 696-719.
Hippisley Tuckfield, Mrs (1839) *Education for the People*. London: Taylor & Walton.
Jordan, I. K. and Battison, R. (1976) A Referential Communication Experiment with Foreign Sign Languages, *Sign Language Studies 10*, 69-78.

Kegl, J. (1979) Further Breaking Down the ASL Verb. Paper presented at the NATO Advanced Institute on Sign Language, Copenhagen.

Kyle, J. G., Woll, B. and Carter, M. (1979) *Coding British Sign Language*. University of Bristol, School of Education Research Unit.

Lane, H. (1976) *The Wild Boy of Aveyron*. Cambridge, Mass.: Harvard University Press.

Lawson, L. (in press) The Role of Sign in the Structure of the Deaf Community, in *Perspectives on British Sign Language* (eds B. Woll, J. G. Kyle and M. Deuchar). London: Croom Helm.

Llewellyn-Jones, P., Kyle, J. G. and Woll, B. (1979) Sign Language Communication. Paper presented at the International Conference on the Social Psychology of Language, Bristol.

Markowicz, H. (1979) Sign languages and the maintenance of the deaf community. Paper presented at the NATO Symposium on Sign Language Research, Copenhagen.

Moody, W. (1979) La Communication Internationale chez les Sourds, *Reéducation Orthophonique 17*, 213-23.

Scott, W. R. (1870) *The Deaf and Dumb*. London: Bell and Daldy.

Stokoe, W. C. (1969) Sign Language Diglossia, *Studies in Linguistics 21*, 27-41.

— (1979) Diglossia Revisited and Bilingualism Related. Unpublished paper.

Trudgill, P. (1972) Sex, Covert Prestige and Linguistic Change in the Urban British English of Norwich, *Language in Society 1*, 179-96.

Wilbur, R. B. (1979) *American Sign Language and Sign Systems*. Maryland: University Park Press.

Woodward, J. (1975) How you gonna get to heaven if you can't talk with Jesus?: the Educational Establishment versus the Deaf Community. Paper presented at the Annual Meeting of the Society for Applied Anthropology, Amsterdam.

1989: A number of developments have occurred which relate to a changing role and status for the BSL. It is now shown regularly on television, both through interpretation and on magazine programmes. Schools for the deaf have largely changed over to Total Communication and even this is being superseded by a bilingual approach, which presents deaf children with English and BSL as two separate languages, rather than using Sign Pidgin English. As a consequence, BSL is gaining in prestige among both the hearing and deaf.

Research on BSL has continued, with recent studies including BSL acquisition; variation and historical change in BSL; descriptive grammars; and a BSL–English dictionary. The teaching of BSL has also become widespread, with courses offered through adult education institutes and universities.

Brennan, M., Colville, M. and Lawson, L. (1984) *Words in Hand: a structural analysis of the signs of British Sign Language*. Edinburgh: Moray House Publications.

Deuchar, M. (1984) *British Sign Language*. London: Routledge and Kegan Paul.

Kyle, J. G. (1987) *Sign and School*. Clevedon: Multilingual Matters.

— and Woll, B. (1985) *Sign Language: the study of deaf people and their language*. Cambridge: Cambridge University Press.

Woll, B., Kyle, J. G. and Deuchar, M. (eds) (1981) *Perspectives on British Sign Language and Deafness*. London: Croom Helm.

J.M.Y.SIMPSON

22. The Challenge of Minority Languages

Minority languages offer challenges of various kinds. To the second-language learner they present problems additional to – and different from – those encountered in acquiring the more commonly taught 'majority languages'. Minority languages also offer a challenge of a political nature, even in the most innocuous sense of the word: a minority language presents to every individual inhabitant of the area in which it is spoken the problem of deciding where he or she stands with regard to it and such a decision may have practical consequences. But there is a third kind of challenge, those which minority languages present to the general linguist. These are the subject of the present paper.

The general linguist, according to the so-called 'father of linguistics', Ferdinand de Saussure (1916), has a threefold task. To paraphrase his words: the linguist will describe individual languages, postulate their history and show their relationships to other languages; he will look for universals of language, not only static phenomena common to all tongues, but also dynamic forces that change languages; and he will decide what the boundaries of linguistics are going to be.

The first of these tasks, description, has been carried out in terms of system, a homogeneous framework. This framework has been seen to be in three parts, dealing respectively with sound-system, grammar and meaning. For any language, that is, we are presented with a system of vowels and consonants used in various combinations that are somehow enumerated; further, we have a grammatical system of elements that are also combined to give a predictable range of possibilities: morphological variations and syntactic frameworks. (I omit the consideration of meaning.) Moreover the theoretical linguist is vitally concerned, perhaps over-anxious, to construct theoretical frameworks according to which he may describe such systems.

So much for the linguist. What is a minority language? It seems safe to say that it exhibits the following characteristics.

(a) It is not the language of all areas of activity indulged in by its speakers:

235

for example, it may be excluded from administration or education, being confined to home, religious life or literature.

(b) It may live in the shadow of a culturally dominant language, dominant because of political, educational, social or religious factors.

(c) It may be at risk from opponents dedicated to its extirpation (and these may even include native speakers).

(d) It may lack areas of vocabulary found in other languages that cover the same general culture. Indeed its vocabulary may be influenced by that of the dominant language to the extent of accepting borrowings where native terms exist.

(e) Bilingualism is a characteristic of its speakers.

(f) There may not be a recognised norm for communication in the minority language; that is to say, there may be no 'standard language'.

(g) Because the language may lack areas of vocabulary, or because its speakers do not recognise a standard, or because they are completely bilingual, there may be reluctance on the part of native-speakers to speak the language to learners or even to those from different dialect areas of the minority language; thus it becomes felt as the marker of an increasingly smaller in-group.

(h) Opponents of a minority language may gleefully exaggerate the deficiency of vocabulary, the absence of a recognised norm, the reluctance to speak the language to outsiders – this to demonstrate that the language is in some sense 'inferior'.

(i) The cause of minority languages may be taken up by proponents (groups or individuals) who are not native speakers; sometimes these may be of doubtful rationality and/or of extremist tendencies – in both cases there is consequent unhelpful publicity in the majority-language media.

(j) Efforts to promote minority languages may include language-planning or language-purification (though this is not confined to minority languages, witness French, German, Icelandic and Hebrew).

(k) Problems arise in education: what is the official attitude to the minority language? should it be ignored or actively suppressed? should it itself be taught as a subject? should it be the medium of instruction for some subjects or even for all?

(l) Historical factors may be relevant. The language may not always have been a minority one and it may therefore have possessed at least written norms that it now lacks. Hence a modern writer may incorporate usages from an earlier written language that are no longer found in any spoken variety. (Again this is not confined to minority languages; modern literary Arabic does the same.)

These are characteristics that, at least partially, may be held in common by minority languages. For the rest, they may be strikingly heterogeneous. They can belong to any language-group: Celtic, Germanic, Romance, Slavonic from the Indo-European family; Finno-Ugrian and Basque from non-Indo-European phyla. The number of speakers is not the deciding factor:

Icelandic with some 200,000 speakers is not a minority language in our sense; Welsh and Breton, each with something like twice that number, are. There may have been widespread religious movements among the speakers with strikingly different results: revivifying the language, as in the case of Welsh non-conformism, or undermining it, as in the case of the Scottish Reformation and the Scots language. Some languages may have a centuries-old tradition of writing, like Irish; others, like Faroese, may only comparatively recently have been committed to script. A minority language may in fact be an official one, like Romansch, or even *the* official one, like Irish. Finally, whether or not a language is a minority one has nothing to do with the language, but everything to do with the situation in which it finds itself: Danish is the threatening language for Faroese but is itself a minority language in Germany, German in turn is a minority language in Italy, while Italian is a minority language in France and Yugoslavia.

Now these and similar facts are crucially important for the language in its natural context, and thus should surely appear in any description of the language. Admittedly they may well be alluded to, as a preamble or as an interesting afterthought, but they are not given theoretical recognition by linguists as being part of linguistic description. I contend that such theoretical recognition ought to be accorded. A description which confines itself to sound-system and grammar is arid, and so too is the theoretical linguistics which supplies the descriptive categories involved. What Einar Haugen (1972) has called 'the ecology of language' ought not to be an optional extra, but an integral part of linguistic description: who speaks the language, where and in what circumstances. That is one kind of challenge presented by minority languages to the general linguist.

Linguists on occasion use languages to test their already formulated hypotheses or speculations about language. Some European minority languages may be interesting in this respect, insofar as they provide examples of phenomena that one has otherwise to look for much further afield. Scots Gaelic is of great interest to the phonetician because of a whole complex of exotic phonetic features; the syntactician finds that Basque and the Celtic languages as a group present phenomena to be found nowhere else in Europe. But this is not necessarily so. A minority language need not exhibit any features different from those of neighbouring majority ones: Scots, for example, has little to offer the phonetician or syntactician who knows English, and I would venture that the same holds true of Catalan vis-à-vis Castilian. For a microlinguist, there is not necessarily much of interest at all in minority languages, at least as far as his descriptive framework minus 'ecology of language' is concerned.

A curious claim sometimes advanced for minority languages is that they are 'old'. Both Scots Gaelic and Welsh are often described as 'ancient tongues'; indeed in *The Radio Times* dated 6–12 September 1980 a reader's letter attempts to prove which is the *more* ancient of these two (and it also contrives to describe Basque as a 'relic from the Stone Age'). If such descriptions have any meaning, either it is that a previous form of the language in question was first written down at an earlier date than others with which it is being compared, or else it represents an alleged earlier state in historical development, the preservation of archaic features. And Professor Haugen reminds us that such archaicism was explicitly advanced to promote the case for Icelandic. But of course one has to *select* the archaic features; all languages are in a state of change and while a particular language may show an allegedly primitive state from one point of view, from another it may be quite modern. Icelandic may be morphologically 'ancient', but in terms of its phonetics it is strikingly innovatory. But in any event it is quite unclear what 'oldness' in either of our two interpretations has to do with the value of a language. One would hope that it would be superfluous to point this out; unfortunately the idea keeps cropping up as a kind of guarantee of respectability.

Yet there is at least one further way in which minority languages present a challenge to the general linguist. We are generally conditioned to think of languages as being rigidly compartmentalised. We have language-names to make the point: 'German' is different from 'Dutch'. Various educational systems teach institutionalised 'German' or 'Dutch' norms and we can buy teaching-grammars of 'German' or 'Dutch'. But we all know that it is possible to take a trip down the Rhine from a Swiss German area to a Dutch area without encountering any sharp linguistic break; yet both Swiss German and Dutch are mutually incomprehensible, though it is probably safe to say that the inhabitants of any one town can understand without difficulty those of the next town upstream and the next town downstream. In reality, instead of two monolithic linguistic areas we find one large linguistic area composed of related varieties in which not everyone can understand everyone else.

This situation can arise in the case of a single majority language, such as English. This occupies a world-wide geographical area with great variation, even at the level of sounds. A speaker from the Southern States of the USA and a speaker from Bangladesh may be mutually unintelligible, though both claim to talk English. When to differences of pronunciation we add differences of vocabulary and of grammar, as in dialects of various sorts, then the complexity is enormous. This reality is masked in the case of majority languages by the existence of standards. And so we find studies which purport to be studies 'of English', but in fact are studies of a particular standard. One thinks of *The pronunciation of English* by Daniel Jones (1909) and *The sound-pattern of English* by Chomsky and Halle (1968): they are not talking about the same thing.

Minority languages often do not have a standard and so the linguist is obliged to take explicit account of regional varietes. In this case we find studies of such things as the Gaelic of Leurbost (Oftedal 1956), the Breton of the Ile de Groix (Ternes 1970), the phonemic analysis of the Gaelic of Applecross (Ternes 1973: although that particular study goes under the name of *The phonemic analysis of Scottish Gaelic*, the author takes as his material data from a very restricted geographical area). The linguistic study of minority languages forces us to look at a phenomenon that is typical of perhaps every language-area.

There is another reason for the monolithic description of languages: the tenet, alluded to in the third paragraph of this chapter, that language could be described in terms of a system, that language indeed *was* a system. This is explicitly stated in the work of de Saussure: he envisaged the system of a language as being as inflexible as the rules of chess. And the idea reappears in the work of Bloomfield, of Chomsky and of various European followers of de Saussure, most extremely in the 'axiomatic functionalism' of J. W. F. Mulder and S. J. G. Hervey, expounded in their *The strategy of linguistics* (1980). This depends on axioms, definitions and set theory, but it has as a premiss the notion that language is a rigid system. Such an attitude is facilitated by dealing with a standard and calling it 'the language'.

We might argue that this is useful as a descriptive fiction and indeed it may be necessary in order to achieve any description at all. It could be held to be an example of Vaihinger's *als ob* ('as if') philosophy (1911): we behave *as if* this were the case and proceed to the appropriate description, as a first stage. We may then commit the 'antithetic error' by introducing another fiction to correct the first, by saying in effect 'But of course speakers depart from this rigid system in such and such directions in the following circumstances'. I do not disagree with this viewpoint; such a two-stage procedure may be necessary. But I do disagree with a point of view that regards the first description of a rigid system as being an account of 'the language', a view that we find in Chomsky (1965: 3: 'A grammar of a language purports to be the description of the ideal speaker–hearer's intrinsic competence') and at the other end of the linguistic spectrum in axiomatic functionalism. To identify the first descriptive approximation with 'the language' is untenable as a model of language. It may well be that we cannot at the moment think of a better way to describe languages than in two stages, but that is not to say that the first stage is 'truth'. Unfortunately some never get beyond this first stage. I suggest that they would not be tempted to regard a language as monolithic if they knew a minority language.

In a different, non-geographical, sense the heterogeneity of a natural language was emphasised as early as 1911 by the great Czech linguist Vilém Mathesius in a lecture whose title is translated as 'On the potentiality of the phenomena of language' where he points to an oscillation or fluctuation (the 'potentiality' of his title) in natural languages. So what I am arguing for is theoretical recognition of something that is well known. Such oscillation is the fact that, to put it crudely, the same words in the same environment will not always be pronounced in the same way; for example, the absolute length of vowels and consonants may vary. One particular kind of oscillation is relevant here.

De Saussure made a sharp distinction between the synchronic axis of language and the diachronic. The synchronic allegedly describes the condition of the language at one moment of time: in English the relationship between *foot* and *feet* is synchronic, a relationship of 'singular' versus 'plural' on an axis of simultaneity. The diachronic axis is historical: along it we can study the adventures of an element of the language through time, for example, the relationship between *foot* and its postulated Proto-Germanic ancestor, **fôt*. It was a salutary distinction to make at the beginning of this century, for previously there had sometimes been a certain confusion between describing what a particular situation was and describing how it came about. Henceforward one would describe two systems and show how elements of the earlier system became elements of the later.

Again this two-stage procedure is handy, but it is a fiction nonetheless, and we must not claim that this fiction directly reflects people's language behaviour. The claim has sometimes seemed to be made that it does. Thus at the end of last century, just before de Saussure produced his terminology, the group of philologists known as the Neogrammarians claimed that sound-changes took place inexorably and gradually, and would affect all 'sensitive' sounds. Recently in the USA William S.-Y. Wang (1976) and his associates have maintained that a sound-change can affect individual words suddenly and, by a series of similar such alterations can gradually, perhaps over a long period, spread over a whole vocabulary.

But it would seem that what happens is more complicated: there is no reason why some individual speakers should not oscillate between an old pronunciation and a new. To some extent there is evidence for this, in the already mentioned *The phonemic analysis of Scottish Gaelic* by Elmar Ternes. Ternes notes a 'phonemically sudden' sound-change of a voiced dental nasal /n/ becoming a voiced palatalised dental nasal /n'/, spreading from north to south across the Applecross peninsula and affecting more and more forms. It would appear that the sound-change does not however occur irreversibly, for the author quotes a phonemic transcription of a text from one speaker in which the word *sneachd* 'snow' appears in three consecutive sentences, the first time with the (neutral) nasal, the second time with the palatalised and the third time with the neutral again.

The same phenomenon of new forms spreading out and with increasingly fewer examples on the periphery of the appropriate area has been noted for Welsh by Ceinwen Thomas (1975–6). It would be interesting to discover whether speakers here oscillate between old and new forms and, if so, to what extent. One could form the hypothesis that it might be possible to detect in one speaker the occurrence of a particular sound-change. This suggests the actual counting of variant forms of the same word in a real-life text, an undoubtedly time-consuming task and one that would require the solution of several practical problems. Such an approach would accord with a tendency, detectable once more in linguistics, to base studies on corpuses of various kinds, that is, collections of what speakers or writers have actually produced, rather than what the linguist thinks *could* be said or written, witness the Brown Corpus of American English and the Lancaster Corpus of British English. But my suggestion would require the statistical observation of phonetic detail.

I have proposed three respects in which the study of minority languages can present a challenge to common assumptions in linguistics: it emphasises the importance of the 'ecology' of language; it emphasises the falsity of a monolithic system common to a speech-community; and it emphasises the artificiality of a synchronic/diachronic distinction. For the study of minority languages has to do more with speakers than with systems or standards, and languages after all are spoken by individuals.

References

Chen, M. Y. and Wang, W. S.-Y. (1975) Sound change: actuation and implementation, *Language 15*, 255-81.

Chomsky, Noam (1965) *Aspects of the theory of syntax*. Cambridge, Mass.

Chomsky, Noam and Halle, Morris (1968) *The sound-pattern of English*. New York.

Haugen, Einar (1972) *The ecology of language*, 325-37. Stanford.

Jones, Daniel (1909) *The pronunciation of English*, 4th ed. (1958). Cambridge.

Mathesius, Vilém (1964) On the potentiality of the phenomena of language (1911), trans. and repr. in ed. Josef Vachek: *A Prague school reader in linguistics*, 1-32. Bloomington.

Mulder, J. W. F. and Hervey, S. J. G. (1980) *The strategy of linguistics*. Edinburgh.

Oftedal, Magne (1956) *The Gaelic of Leurbost, Isle of Lewis*. Oslo.

Saussure, Ferdinand de (1916) *Cours de linguistique générale*, 5th ed. (1962), pp.20 and 120. Paris.

Ternes, Elmar (1970) *Grammaire structurale du Breton de l'Ile de Groix*. Heidelberg.

— (1973) *The phonemic analysis of Scottish Gaelic: based on the dialect of Applecross, Ross-shire*, p.150. Hamburg.

Thomas, Ceinwen H. (1975-6) Some phonological features of dialects in south-east Wales, *Studia Celtica* x-xi, 345-66, in particular 360ff.

Vaihinger. H. (1911) *Die Philosophie des 'Als Ob'*. Berlin.

Wang, William S.-Y. (1976) Language change, *Annals of the New York Academy of Sciences 280*, 61-72.

Contributors to this Volume

Adam J. Aitken, Editor of the *Dictionary of the Older Scottish Tongue*, University of Edinburgh.

John E. Ambrose, Department of Geography and Sociology, North Staffordshire Polytechnic.

Antonia Feitsma, Professor, Studierichting Fries, Vrije Universiteit, Amsterdam.

Desmond Fennell, Department of History, University College, Galway.

Durk Gorter, Fryske Akademy, Leeuwarden.

† David Greene, Director, School of Celtic Studies, Dublin Institute for Advanced Studies.

Einar Haugen, V. S. Thomas Professor of Scandinavian and Linguistics, emeritus, Harvard University, Cambridge, Massachusetts.

Fernand Hoffmann, Professor, Centre Universitaire, Luxembourg.

Bedwyr Lewis Jones, Professor of Welsh Language and Literature, University College of North Wales, Bangor.

Alf Isak Keskitalo, Sámi Instituhtta, Guovdageaidnu Kautokeino, Norway.

Lilian Lawson, Sign Language Research Project, Moray House College of Education, Edinburgh.

J. Derrick McClure, Department of English, University of Aberdeen.

Magne Oftedal, Professor of Celtic Languages, University of Oslo.

Frederik Paulsen, Chairman of the North Frisian Institute, Bredsted, Netherlands.

Jóhan Hendrik W. Poulsen, Fróðskaparsetur Føroya, Tórshavn, Faroe Islands.

J. I. Prattis, Department of Sociology and Anthropology, Carleton University, Ottawa.

Mikael Reuter, Byrån för Svenska Språket, Helsingfors, Finland.

Rosita Rindler Schjerve, Institut für Romanistik, University of Vienna.

J. M. Y. Simpson, Department of Linguistics and Phonetics, University of Glasgow.

Bent Søndergaard, Pädagogische Hochschule, Flensburg, W. Germany.

Dietrich Strauss, Institut für England- und Amerikastudien, University of Frankfurt-Main.

Derick Thomson, Professor of Celtic, University of Glasgow.

Colin H. Williams, Department of Geography and Sociology, North Staffordshire Polytechnic.

Bencie Woll, Research Unit, School of Education, University of Bristol.

Other Papers
Read at the Conference

The problem of minority languages: Canadian and European contrasts.
ALAN B. ANDERSON, University of Saskatchewan.
A quantitative approach to language shift in the light of
decennial censuses in Wales, 1891-1971.
LLUIS V. ARACIL, University of Barcelona.
Languages and school in Catalunya.
JOAQUIN ARNAU, University of Barcelona.
Creolese and Sranan: an ethnolinguistic study of
two minority languages in Europe.
PETRONELLA BREINBURG, University of Keele.
An elusive territorial component in the attempt to
accommodate a minority language population in Canada.
DON CARTWRIGHT, University of Western Ontario.
The secret languages of the Scottish tinkers.
R. DAVID CLEMENT, University of Edinburgh.
Social and demographic factors affecting the prevalence
of Swedish-Finnish bilingualism in Finland, 1950.
JOHN DE VRIES, Carleton University, Ottawa.
Communicative and symbolic aspects of the Sámi language in Sweden.
ELINA HELANDER, University of Umeå.
Vernacular re-structuring in twentieth-century Scottish speech.
JOHN M. KIRK, University of Sheffield.
The use of and attitudes towards Irish among the young, middle and
old age-groups in the parish of Ballyvourney, County Cork.
TONY LUNNY, Queen's University, Belfast.
The status of Scots.
CAROLINE MACAFEE, University of Glasgow.
Some functions of Gaelic-English switching in
buying and selling transactions.
DONALD MACAULAY, University of Aberdeen.
Code-switching as a discourse mode: some preliminary
evidence from bilingual communities in Britain.
MARILYN MARTIN-JONES, University of London.
Problems of multilingualism in Eastern Belgium.
PETER H. NELDE, University of Brussels.
Some influences on Donegal Irish.
CATHAIR Ó DOCHARTAIGH, University of Aberdeen.
Scotland as a linguistic area.
SUZANNE ROMAINE, University of Birmingham, and
NANCY DORIAN, Bryn Mawr College, Pennsylvania.

243

Language choice and alteration in bilingual families.
MIGUEL SIGUÁN, University of Barcelona.
Ethnicity in Friesland between definition and reality.
P. H. VAN DER PLANK, Rijksuniversiteit Groningen, Leeuwarden.
On the choice between two standard languages in Norway.
KJELL VENÅS, University of Oslo.
On the treatment of English loan-words in
a Gaelic dialect, with some Irish comparisons.
SEOSAMH WATSON, University College, Dublin.
The past and present position of Gaelic in Scotland:
a framework for analysis.
CHARLES W. J. WITHERS, University of Cambridge.

Index

Aasen, Ivar, 110, 123-5
Abercrombie, David, 74
Agricola, Mikael, 103
Aitken, A. J., vii-xii, 72-90
Alaska, 111
Allardt, Erik, 134, 136
Alsace-Lorraine, 190 ; German speakers of
    Alsace-Lorraine, 189-200 ; effects of
    French Revolution on, 191 ; during
    German Reich, 191 ; Strasbourg, 191-2 ;
    Alsatian and Lorrainese dialects, 192
Ambrose, J. E. (see also Williams, Colin H.),
    53-71
America (see also United States) : Finnish
    emigration, 131
American Deaf Community, 229-30
American Indians, 111
American Sign Language, 219-21, 226-7,
An Comunn Gaidhealach, 17
André, Carl Matthias, 203
Andrew of Wyntoun, 94
Anglo-Saxon, 105
Angus, David, 77
Århammar, Nils, 183-4
Arabic, 235
Association for Scottish Literary Studies,
    Language Committee, Council, xi ;
    International Conference of 1975 on
    Medieval Language and Literature, xii
Auburger, L., 206
Australian Sign Language, 219-20
Austria, 193, 195

Bangor, 3
Basque, 192, 235-6
Belgium, 189, 203 ; German speakers in, 194 ;
    Flemings and Walloons, 194 ; Arlon,
    Eupen, St Vith regions, 194 ; East
    Belgium, 194
Bergroth, Hugo, 107

Bergsland, Knut, 155
Bible : translations, 103, 155, 167
Bibliography for Scottish Linguistic Studies,
    79
bilingualism, 1, 4-8, 48-50, 114-15, 166, 178,
    205, 231, 235 ; bilingual education, 6, 13,
    29 ; Gaelic Bilingual Project, 13 ; bilin-
    gual policy in Western Isles Region, 19,
    29-30 ; bilingual Welsh-English, 40-71 ;
    'official bilingualism', 107, 130-7 ; u.s.
    Bilingual Act of 1968, 112 ; in Finland,
    107, 130-7 ; in Southern Schleswig, 141-2 ;
    in Friesland, 177-9, 184 ; in Luxemburg,
    202, 205 ; in Sardinia, 208-17
Binchy, D. A., 3
Bloomfield, Leonard, 238
Bokmål (see also Riksmål), 101, 109-10,
    120-1, 123-4, 126-8 ; social status, 125 ;
    radical, 126 ; moderate, 126 ; in schools,
    126 ; used by writers, 126 ; in govern-
    ment, 126, 128-9 ; people, 123
Boswell, James, 83
Bowen and Carter, 44-5, 62
Bremer, Otto, 183, 185
Breton, 1, 3, 236-7
British Deaf Community, 230
British Sign Language, viii-ix, 218-233 ;
    complex signs, 225-6 ; classifiers, 226-7 ;
    modulation, 228 ; varieties of, 231-2
Brittany, 8
Brougham, Lord, 76
Brown Corpus of American English, 240
Bruch, Robert, 201
Buchan, John, 85
Burns, Robert, 72, 77, 83, 93

Caernarfon, 3
Canada, 11, 131 ; language problems, viii ;
    Language Bill, 16
Cardiganshire, 5

245